Vedic Culture

Vedic Culture

The Difference It Can
Make In Your Life

Edited by

Stephen Knapp

iUniverse, Inc.
New York Lincoln Shanghai

Vedic Culture
The Difference It Can Make In Your Life

Copyright © 2005 by Stephen Knapp

iUniverse books may be ordered through booksellers or by contacting:

iUniverse
2021 Pine Lake Road, Suite 100
Lincoln, NE 68512
www.iuniverse.com
1-800-Authors (1-800-288-4677)

This book has been produced by the Vedic Friends Association whose goal is to help others understand, practice and promote the Universal Truths found in the Vedic Dharma.

ISBN-13: 978-0-595-37120-4 (pbk)
ISBN-13: 978-0-595-81519-7 (ebk)
ISBN-10: 0-595-37120-5 (pbk)
ISBN-10: 0-595-81519-7 (ebk)

Printed in the United States of America

This book is dedicated to all
Who are ready and willing
To look at the Eastern Paths
For the material and spiritual means of
Fulfillment and self-realization.

Blessings

I am very pleased to know that a book of articles on different topics by learned authors unfolding the depth and profundity of the Vedic Culture is being brought out under the title "Vedic Culture: The Difference It can Make in Your Life".

This is a valuable contribution by the members of the Vedic Friends Association, USA. The editor of the book, Mr. Stephen Knapp, has a deep appreciation of and commitment to the Vedic View and Way of Life. I thank him and other authors for giving us this revealing book.

Swami Dayananda Sarasvati

 Swami Dayananda Sarasvati is a sannyasi of the Adi Shankara and Veda Vyasa tradition and founder of the Arsha Vidya centers in the USA, Canada, Australia and India. He is highly regarded as an outstanding scholar and teacher in the line of the traditional teachers of Vedanta. He has taught in India for the past thirty-five years, and since 1976 has lectured extensively in the West. Since 1968, he has served as an executive administrator, director and trustee of several religious, educational and cultural organizations.

Contents

Part Two: The Vedic Arts & Sciences

Foreword

The *Vedas* are the oldest documented spiritual teachings of humanity, with their roots going back over five thousand years in ancient India. They are the best preserved record of our spiritual ancestors—the famous ancient sages and seers of many traditions—dwarfing in size the few ancient teachings that have managed to survive elsewhere in the world. The many thousands of pages of Vedic texts have not only been preserved but are still chanted and used in Vedic rituals and meditation practices that millions of people follow on a daily basis.

The *Vedas* formed the foundation for the great civilization of India, which has dominated Asia spiritually and produced many important religious and spiritual movements within Hindu, Buddhist, Jain and Sikh traditions. While not all these traditions simply follow the *Vedas*, they all share an orientation towards dharma, a recognition of the law of karma and rebirth, and the practices of yoga, mantra and meditation as the basis of the spiritual life. Most importantly, they all share a pluralistic view of truth—that though truth is One and undivided, there are many paths and approaches to it, ultimately as many as there are individuals—which pluralism is the hallmark of Vedic thought.

Yet we should not limit our understanding of Vedic culture to ancient Vedic texts, however important these can be. Even ancient Vedic texts proclaim that 'the *Vedas* are infinite'. Vedic texts are just the starting point for the development of Vedic knowledge, which is a living tradition of spiritual realization and communion with the infinite that is relevant to everyone and that exists more as an inner than as an outer reality.

The Vedic tradition is not so much a collection of books or set codified teachings as it is a certain way of life, a way of natural and conscious living, yoga and meditation that is passed on from individual to individual. This transmission does not occur merely through reading books, nor can it be understood from the outside. Much of it occurs from a direct contact with living Vedic teachers, who provide us a living example and practical guidance in how to use and adapt these teachings. Another important aspect of it, which usually arises from this contact but can start prior to it, is our own practice of Vedic teachings, which may be mantra, meditation, vegetarianism or the promotion of non-violence that puts us in the greater stream of Vedic culture. Living a Vedic life, following Vedic values, and participating in a Vedic community are important aspects of really learning what the Vedic tradition is all about.

The Vedic tradition has managed to sustain and transform itself over the many millennia, enduring wars, cataclysms, and cultural changes of every type. Probably no other ancient tradition has demonstrated such endurance and adaptability. This is owing to both its firm foundation in universal truth and its capacity to renew itself in every generation.

Most notably the Vedic tradition has gone global in modern times, with Vedic teachings in various forms now occurring in all lands and countries. This new global Vedic renaissance is one of the most dynamic spiritual currents throughout the world, flowering in many diverse names and forms. It is bound to grow further as humanity searches for meaning in life beyond the limitations of both scientific materialism and religious dogma.

THE CONSCIOUS UNIVERSE

To appreciate the Vedic tradition, we must first understand the Vedic view of the universe, which can be rather different than what we are taught in the western world. The Vedic view of the universe is of One Being, Consciousness and Bliss yet expressing itself through innumerable names, forms, worlds and creatures. It is not a simple scientific or theological view of the universe, such as most of us are acquainted with, though it can accept aspects of these on certain levels.

This cosmic being is the Atman or Purusha, the universal Self of Vedic thought. An understanding of this Purusha principle is essential to appreciating the Vedic approach to life. We must learn to work with and embrace all of life as an unfoldment of the same Self and being that is our own true nature. This is the Vedic way of growth that links the human being and the world of nature to the deeper consciousness and energy behind both.

We live in a user friendly conscious universe. Consciousness pervades everything from the rocks on Earth to the most distant reaches of space beyond the stars. This consciousness may not be embodied to the same degree in every creature but it remains as the substratum of all existence even in the inanimate world. The world of nature is the body of this greater awareness that is the spirit or Self behind it. And all of this is part of who we really are beyond the veils of our bodies and minds.

Our real quest as human beings is to discover that universal being within and around us, to learn our place in the cosmic order and to do our work for the unfoldment or evolution of consciousness in the world. The current pursuit of outer power and fulfillment that dominates our present civilization is at best a step in this greater quest, at worst a terrible deviation.

This conscious universe is our inner friend and guide, not an alien force or God apart from us. Divine powers and principles—the Gods and Goddesses or *Devatas* of Vedic thought—exist everywhere to help us. The forces of the five great elements of earth, water, fire, air and ether, for example, are not just material constructions. Behind each is a divine or conscious power that we can commune with in order to better work with the great forces of life. Vedic knowledge teaches us how to work with these powers of the conscious universe from the biological forces in our bodies, to the psychological forces in our minds, to the spiritual energies of the soul but as linked to all the energies of the cosmos, which are part of one greater being.

THE TRUE MEANING OF CULTURE

In portraying the Vedic tradition, perhaps this term culture is the best word that we can use. Culture implies a broad field of knowledge and creativity that provides much room for various groups and individuals, like different plants, to extract nourishment and grow according to their capacities. Yet Vedic culture is not limited to an intellectual or social culture, such as the term often implies, but centers on a spiritual culture, a culture for the development of our higher Self.

Vedic culture is a universal culture that seeks to embrace the greater living universe. It is not a mere human-centered culture that seeks human welfare at the cost of the happiness of other creatures. It is not just a culture of the human brain and intellect and its historical development but one that is rooted in the cosmic mind and in the eternal truth. The Vedic has a holistic view that includes not only all aspects of human culture but looks at the entire universe as a culture of consciousness.

We could first of all call Vedic culture as 'the culture of dharma'. The Vedic view rests upon a recognition of certain natural and universal laws behind the universe called dharmas. In this regard each thing has its appropriate nature or dharma.

Vedic culture recognizes the values of all dharmas. In the human realm, there is not only the dharma of the individual but that of the family, community, nation and society. There is a dharma or way of life for the child, the youth, the parent, the grandparent, the male and the female. There is a dharma of the yogi, priest, poet, businessman, soldier and artist. Vedic culture is about recognizing and honoring all these dharmas, honoring all the different capacities not only of human beings but of other creatures.

We could also call Vedic culture the 'greater culture of yoga'. Vedic culture takes a yogic—that is an awareness-promoting and integrative approach—to all aspects of life including art, music, science, medicine, history, philosophy and religion.

In the West we are used to thinking in rather restrictive categories of religion, philosophy, art and science. Vedic culture contains aspects of all of these and yet cannot be reduced to any one of them. For it, art can also be yoga or a spiritual path. Even business can be karma yoga. Philosophy or even medicine can be poetry. And everything can and should be a form of worship or honoring the wonderful sacred universe in which we live.

Much of Vedic culture is a 'self-culture'. It encourages self-empowerment, self-growth, self-healing and, ultimately, Self-realization. It provides the aware and receptive individual with many tools of self-unfoldment, aiding in the access of our higher human and spiritual potentials of awareness, creativity, vitality and perception. Yet Vedic culture is not a self-culture in the limiting sense of the word self. It does not promote self-indulgence or self-promotion. The Vedic view of self is of the conscious being within the person, not the limiting ego. It is a culture of the united self, not the seperative self. It helps us appreciate the needs of others and the needs of our greater environment, bringing us to true compassion as well.

This Vedic idea of culture reflects its own world view, its own sense of the purpose of humanity, and its own prescriptions for our greater well being both as individuals and as a species. These can be different from or challenging to our current views of history, humanity and progress. But such a more universe and consciousness-centered view of life can provide a good alternative and a necessary view to help us move into a planetary age in which we must look beyond the limitations of our own species to the greater needs of life as a whole.

VEDIC TEACHINGS AND THE WEST

Vedic teachings have come to the West in many forms, not as an overt effort to convert people to a belief or to spread a particular ideology, but as a sharing of spiritual and healing practices in many forms. Millions of people in the West today follow teachings and perform practices that have their origins in the Vedic tradition and its view of dharma.

Most obvious is Yoga, which many people not only follow as an exercise system but have also embraced as a philosophy and a way of life. Vedantic philosophy, Ayurvedic medicine, Vedic astrology (Jyotish), Vastu Shastra (directional science and architecture), Hindu music and dance and the Sanskrit language itself are other aspects of this vast tradition which has many sides and levels to its teaching and embraces all the arts and sciences in a higher vision. People are recognizing that the Vedic practices are universal teachings that can benefit everyone, such as the term *Sanatana Dharma* or the 'Universal Dharma', the original name for the Vedic tradition indicates.

Many people follow Yoga gurus from India whose teachings go back to different branches of Hindu and Vedic thought. Such movements as TM (Transcendental Meditation), ISKCON (International Society for Krishna Consciousness), Ramakrishna-Vedanta and SRF (Self-realization Fellowship) have become quite large, with followers numbering into the hundreds of thousands, with extensive centers and schools of their own.

Gurus and Swamis from India, both male and female, ever since the time of Swami Vivekananda over a hundred years ago, have made their place in western culture and counterculture. Such well known names of gurus who have lived and taught in the West include Paramahansa Yogananda, Satchidananda, Ammachi, Prabhupada, Maharishi Mahesh Yogi and Swami Rama to mention but a few. And many other great gurus from India have significant followings in the West, though they have never visited this country. These include Mahatma Gandhi, Rabindranath Tagore, Ramana Maharshi, Sri Aurobindo, Anandamayi Ma, Sai Baba, Nityananda and Neem Karoli Baba.

Sanskrit and yogic terms like guru, pandit, mantra and yoga have entered into general usage into the English language, while more specific terms like Kundalini, chakras, shakti and prana, are common throughout spiritual thought and alternative medicine in the West.

Vedic thought through the *Bhagavad Gita, Upanishads*, Vedanta and the *Vedas* has influenced many great western writers and thinkers including Voltaire of France, Goethe and Schopenhauer of Germany, and Emerson and Thoreau of the United States. Much of New Age thought in the West, with its acceptance of karma and rebirth and its quest for the higher Self, reflects a Vedic view of life.

Vedic thought has had its impact on western religions as well, with Vedic ideas and insights occurring in Christian mystics, Sufis and Jewish Kabbalists. Also, some scholars have argued that Jesus was trained in India under Yoga masters from the Vedic tradition because of certain indications in his teachings.

The Vedic culture is also the world's oldest native tradition, reflecting the indigenous people and culture of the Indian subcontinent. It has much in common with other ancient indigenous ways whether the traditions of pre-Christian Europe like the Greek, Roman and Celt, the teachings of ancient Egypt, Babylonia and Persia, Chinese Taoism, Japanese Shinto, or the practices of Native Americans, Native Africans or the Pacific Islanders.

Yet many people who follow Vedic teachings or similar traditions are not aware of the full scope of the Vedic tradition or all the Vedic arts and sciences. Nor do they necessarily understand the Vedic philosophy behind these apparently different pursuits. The following book can help remedy this.

THIS BOOK

The following book, *Vedic Culture: The Difference It Can Make In Your Life*, is meant to provide a new view on Vedic Dharma from those inside the tradition, particularly from westerners who have made their home and found their true identity in a Vedic vocation. Such first hand and personal accounts are hard to find and seldom clearly articulated in available books today. Academic studies of the Vedic tradition are usually done from the outside, from people who do not have a first hand experience, and who often come from a world view which prevents them from really understanding the Vedic approach. They do not take you into the Vedic life but view it with their own colored glasses at a distance.

This book presents statements from a broad array of individuals active in Vedic culture. It consists of different chapters by notable individuals in their respective fields, each one of which has imbibed the true spirit of Vedic Dharma and put it to work in their own particular life. Such living expressions of Vedic knowledge help us adapt it today to the circumstances of our own lives. These individuals are pioneers and prototypes for Vedic careers for the future and for the types of insights that a Vedic renaissance is likely to foster.

Yet the purpose of the book is not simply to extol the value of Vedic culture, it aims at showing its relevance for everyone today, including for those who may not have previously considered it to be important. Vedic culture presents a remarkable array of teachings and practices that have value for all of us because they address the critical issues of life from how to eat and breathe, to how to think and feel, to how to be healthy, happy and responsible citizens of the entire world. Taking these teachings up is a matter of more conscious living, not of simply following some ritual or dogma. They only require that one is willing to look deeper into one's own nature and into the nature of the universe as a whole.

Please look into these Vedic systems that so many talented writers have presented with such personal insight. See if this knowledge can work for you, not in the mere outer sense of affording more personal happiness, but in the inner sense of giving you more spiritual fulfillment in life, greater self-knowledge and self-awareness. The Vedic prescription is always practical, reflecting the wisdom of life, not mere concepts, and can help you in many ways, including how to deal with the many karmas that all of us have to deal with.

This book also presents the approach of a remarkable new organization, the Vedic Friends Association (VFA), whose main purpose is to promote this true Vedic culture in the modern world. VFA is not limited to any particular guru or sect, nor does it focus on only one branch of Vedic learning. It offers a doorway to all the resources of Vedic knowledge for the benefit of all sincere seekers. The book's editor, Stephen Knapp, also the director of the VFA, has done a great job and service by organizing this project and bringing it out to the public.

Vedic Culture: The Difference It Can Make In Your Life can spearhead a new literature on Vedic Dharma and bring a new view of it to the world as a whole. There is certainly much that Vedic Dharma has to offer the world today, particularly in this time of planetary crisis in which we must recognize the greater conscious universe and can no longer take a species centered view of life.

May that wisdom of the *Vedas* come to you through these pages, not simply as a lofty philosophy, but as the profound life experience of these different writers who have so eloquently embodied it!

Dr. David Frawley (Pandit Vamadeva Shastri)
September, 2004

Introduction

Stephen Knapp

First I want to thank all the authors in this book for responding to my invitation to participate in this idea, to present a book that introduces some of the many avenues one can take for self-development that are offered in the Vedic culture. As I went through and arranged the articles of this book, I was especially touched by how people have entered into the research and practice of Vedic knowledge and its philosophy in their own way. Often it is a way that they especially needed at the time, and which changed their lives forever, leaving them more uplifted and happier than before.

I feel that this book can help people understand how Vedic culture has assisted society in the past and also how it can help us now in the present. After all, it is both practical and applicable for everyone, regardless of one's background or cultural heritage. It is universal in nature. The writers in this book certainly show how Vedic culture is not a relic of the past, but is as relevant now as ever. It has so much to offer and covers every angle of existence, only a few of which are presented in this volume.

By investigating the knowledge and viewpoints that are related in this book we can certainly see that the practice and utilization of this Vedic knowledge can indeed assist us in many ways. And in regard to all the trouble we presently find in this world, maybe it is time to look at things through a different and deeper view to find the answers and directions that are so needed. The knowledge and understandings of this great Vedic culture may indeed be what will help us see through the fog of confusion that seems to envelope so much of the world.

What we find in Vedic culture are areas of study, progress and expression that are as relevant today for human advancement as they were hundreds or thousands of years ago. For example, Vāstu Shāstra, the Vedic counterpart of the Chinese Feng Shui, is an ancient art but gaining in popularity. Furthermore, Vedic mathematics is an ancient development that continues to play an important part in modern society.

Without the advancements in math that had been established by Vedic culture and passed along to others, such as the Greeks and Romans, we would not have many of the developments and inventions that we enjoy today. The Greek alphabet, for example, was a great hindrance to calculating. The Egyptians also did not have a numerical system suitable for large calculations. For the number 986 they had to use 23 symbols. Even after the Greeks, the Romans also were in want of a system of mathematical calculations. Only after they adopted the Indian system that was called Arabic numerals did they find what they needed.

The difference was that Vedic mathematics had developed the system of tens, hundreds, thousands, etc., and the basis of carrying the remainder of one column of numbers over to the next. This made for easy calculations of large numbers that was nearly impossible in other systems, as found with the Greeks, Romans, Egyptians and even Chinese. The Vedic system had also invented the zero, which has been called one of the greatest developments in the history of mathematics.

The numeral script from India is said to have evolved from the Brahmi numerals. This spread to Arabia through traders and merchants, and from there up into Europe and elsewhere. It became known as the Arabic numerals, yet the Arabians had called them "Indian figures" (*Al-Arqan-Al-Hindu*) and the system of math was known as *hindisat*, or the Indian art.

Vedic culture already had an established mathematical system that had been recorded in the *Shulba Sutras*. These are known to date back to the 8th century BC. The name *Shulba Sutras* meant "codes of rope". This was because such calculations were used for measuring precise distances for altars and temple structures by using lengths of rope.

The *Shulba Sutras* were actually a portion of a larger text on mathematics known as the *Kalpa Sutras*. These and the Vedic mathematicians were recognized for their developments in arithmetic and algebra. Indians were the first to use letters of the alphabet to represent unknowns. But they were especially known for what they could do in geometry. In fact, geometrical instruments had been found in the Indus Valley dating back to 2500 BC. Furthermore, what became known as the Pythagorean theorem was already existing in the *Baudhayana*, the earliest of the *Shulba Sutras* before the 8th century BC. This was presented by Pythagoras around 540 BC after he discovered it in his travels to India. So this shows the advanced nature of the Vedic civilization.

After the *Shulba Sutras*, Vedic mathematics enjoyed further development in the field of Jyotish, Vedic astronomy, which used all forms of math. Indian mathematicians continued creating systems that were not known in Europe until much later in the Renaissance period. For example, Aryabhatta in the 6th century introduced sines and versed sines. He was followed by Brahmagupta (7th century), Mahavira (9th century) and Bhaskara (12th century). Mahavira made great strides in the use of fractions and figuring out how to divide one fraction by another. Bhaskara made progress in spherical trigonometry and principles of calculus before Newton by 500 years.

The Vedic system of math, as explained in the *sutras*, also reduced the number of steps in calculations to merely a few that otherwise required many steps by conventional methods. Thus, this ancient science is still worthy of study today.

Vedic art is another ancient development that still holds much appreciation in modern times. Art in the Vedic tradition was never a mere representation of an artist's imagination. It was always a vehicle to convey higher truths and principles, levels of reality that may exist beyond our sense perception. It was always used to bring us to a higher purpose of existence. In this way, it was always sacred and beheld the sacred. Still today it is used to allow others to enter into a transcendental experience. It may also present the devotional objects of our meditation.

Vedic paintings or symbols are unique in that they can deliver the same spiritual energy, vibration and insight that it represents. Through the meditation and devotional mood of the artist, the art becomes a manifestation of the higher reality. In other words, the painting or symbol becomes the doorway to the spiritual essence contained within. They are like windows into the spiritual world. Through that window we can have the experience of *darshan* of the Divine or divinities, God or His associates. Darshan is not merely seeing the Divine but it is also entering into the exchange of seeing and being seen by the Divine.

Thus the art, or the Deity, is beyond mundane principles or ingredients, such as paint, paper, stone or metal with which it may be made, but it becomes completely spiritual through which the Deity can reveal Himself or Herself. Thus, the truth of spiritual reality can pierce through the darkness of the material energy and enter our mind and illuminate our consciousness.

To convey higher realities in paintings and sculpture, everything has a meaning. The postures, gestures, colors, instruments or weapons, everything conveys a principle or purpose, which often must be explained to those who lack understanding. Thus, knowing the inner meaning of the painting increases its depth for those who can perceive it, which makes it worthy of further meditation and contemplation.

As with art, dance in India was not merely an expression of an artist's emotional mindset or imagination, but was meant to be an interpretation or conveyance of higher spiritual principles or pastimes of the Divine. In fact, in the Vedic pantheon Shiva is known as Nataraja, the king of dancers. Shiva's dance was also not without a more significant purpose. His dance was based on the rhythm of cosmic energy that pervades the universe, and the destruction of the illusory energy by which all souls are given the opportunity for release from the illusion to attain liberation, *moksha*.

In this way, traditional Indian dance is highly spiritual and often accompanies important religious rituals and holy days and festivals. Vedic dance goes back to prehistoric times. Bharata Muni wrote his *Natya Shastra*, science of drama and dance, over 2000 years ago. In it he explains that it was Lord Brahma, the secondary engineer of the universal creation, who brought dance (*natya*) and drama to the people of Earth millions of years ago, shortly after the Earth was created.

Now dance has evolved into a tradition involving various schools and styles but with strict discipline. It is not uncommon that Indian families will have their daughters spend at least several years or more in such study and practice. There is a precise method of postures, facial and hand gestures (*mudras*), and movements, along with footwork that must be learned and synchronized to the beat and music in order to convey specific meanings, moods and stories to the audience. Many temples, especially in South India, were known for maintaining large groups of dancers that performed at festivals and religious functions.

When the dance is performed according to the spiritual standards, which some view as similar to the practice of yoga, even the dancers can invoke a high degree of spirituality in their own consciousness and bring unity between their inner selves and God. Then the transcendental atmosphere can manifest and draw the Divine to appear in the performers on stage. Thus, the environment becomes transformed and the audience may also experience *darshan* of the Divine and experience an inspiring upliftment in their own consciousness. In this way, the dance is divine beauty in motion.

Various schools of dance include Bharata Natyam, Kathakali, Manipuri, Orissi, Kathak, Mohini Atam, Krishna Atam, Bhagavata Mela, etc. Thus, we may have many dances that convey stories from the *Ramayana* and *Mahabharata* or Krishna-lila from the *Bhagavata Purana*. Nowadays this ancient art of Indian dance is enjoying a wide audience and a prominent place on the international stage.

So, what is here in this book can serve as a well-rounded introduction to some of the many fields of study and awareness that the Vedic culture has dealt with. From here, a student can easily pick out the area in which they may benefit the most and continue their study of it through more advanced avenues. The authors herein are all very knowledgeable in their particular fields of Vedic study, and most have written their own books that go much deeper into various topics that can be of further assistance. Be sure to read the author bios in the back of the book. I hope this book can show the practicality, both materially and spiritually, of the knowledge and awareness that is discussed.

PART ONE

The Vedic Spiritual Paths

Vedic Culture:
The Last Bastion of Deep Spiritual Truth

Stephen Knapp

Even when I was a little boy I had an inclination for a spiritual quest, even though I was not so well aware of it at the time. I remember when I was about five years old, lying in bed on a Saturday morning when everything was quiet, the rest of the family was still sleeping, and I would wonder why I happened to get the body I had. Why was I born in this body, looking out from behind these eyes? Why did I get the parents that I did. Why wasn't I born in a different family, with a different body? What is it that determines such things? And where am I supposed to go and what am I supposed to do in this life?

Even at that age, one of my pet peeves was why we had to feed this body. Why did it need food? And then why did we need to take it to the bathroom later on? Why was it arranged like this? Why did we need to sleep? And why was the body so fragile that if it did not get a chance to breathe for a few minutes, it could die? All these things I wondered about, and even though I did not have the answers then, such questions would come up in my life from time to time. All these questions that I had reflected the fact that ever since I was young, I had never felt real comfortable being inside this material contraption called a body. It all seemed foreign and rather strange to me.

While growing up in the small town of Buchanan, Michigan, my mother especially made sure I went to Church and Sunday School. That gave me some elementary spiritual understanding, but it still did not answer the original questions I had about life. And the minister wasn't all that helpful either, even though he did what he could. The hard part came when I went for two years of confirmation classes when I had to memorize all these verses and priniciples. I was just supposed to believe in what they gave me, and then everything was supposed to turn out all right. Well, just believing in something was not enough for me. I wanted information, insight, and my own perception of things.

Life went on as usual for a small town existence. In many ways I was lucky for that. Nothing very special happened, and I was bored and without much direction. Then the Beatles came to America and everything started to change. I took up playing guitar, and really liked the bass guitar. So after my father bought me my first bass when I was 16, I could not stop playing it. Then my friend Mike, who went to my Sunday School, and his friend Tucker, had a musical band they had started and were looking for a bass player. So they got me to join the band.

The thing about playing music is that it opens channels of awareness and energy in your psyche that otherwise might not be activated. And that's what happened. I started hanging out with other musicians and hippies at the time who were all questioning life and the direction of a materialistic lifestyle, and were open to higher messages about the purpose of it. Naturally, there were other activities that were a part of that musician and hippie lifestyle, but it all lent toward experiences that opened us up to the Eastern philosophy and yoga that we may have ignored otherwise, which was also becoming increasingly popular among our generation.

Through my group of friends, I had met Rusty. We shared a curiosity about a lot of supernatural things and practiced Tarot together. I was also reading a lot of other topics at the time too, such as books on Egyptology, the I Ching, Tibetan Buddhism, Judaism, Theosophy, yoga, magic, witchcraft, the history of Christianity, and lots more. We would always get together and discuss the various books we had been reading. I could see I was putting together a puzzle of what the Truth really was, and things were getting clearer. I could see how everything was connected. Rusty had also met the Hare Krishna devotees on the streets of Toronto. He had the address where you could send for books, such as the Bhagavad-gita. So I sent away for it and once I read that I knew I had found the final piece of the puzzle that I needed to start completing the picture of the Truth. And after reading that I knew I had to get more books about Vedic philosophy. It came at just the right time. I was ready for it and I was hooked.

At the same time, what made things more difficult for my faith in Christianity was when I started doing my own independent research and learned about the bloody history of the Church. How they slaughtered so many so-called witches, heretics, or pagans throughout Europe, and then the Mayan and Inca people, or the Native Americans. Whoa! They never taught me any of this in Sunday School or Church. This was a whole new side to Christianity that I never knew about, and I became angry that I had been kept in the dark about this dark side of Christianity and only knew of the good side of the faith. This seemed to be, in many ways, far from reality. It made me wonder what other areas of Christianity I didn't know about.

At the time, I also met another friend, Ellie, who was a vegetarian. I also had been reading books that explained how a person on a genuine spiritual path should not kill animals simply to satisfy the tongue when other foods are available. So with her influence, plus the fact that I never liked eating meat anyway, I became a vegetarian. That was early 1972. My parents were not too happy about that, but being the hippie kind of person I was, I remained determined to do my own thing. And I have stayed a vegetarian ever since.

Shortly after that, I had two other friends, John and Jeff, who were going to move from our small hometown and go out west. John especially convinced me that it was time to leave for new horizons. I could do my music someplace else that may have more opportunities. So we packed up our vans, me with my guitars and books on Eastern philosophy, and out west we went. Therefore, as I've related, it was in this particular time of development that I met the friends that were most influential in helping direct me to be the person that I've become today. And I've told them if they don't like the way I turned out, they have got nobody to blame but themselves.

On our way out west, we first went to New Mexico and then up to Denver. John and Jeff had some friends there, and soon with their help we got settled into a house of our own. It wasn't long after our arrival that they mentioned that there was a Krishna temple in town. And in a day or two I had made contact with the local temple. I started to go regularly and learned temple etiquette and various ways of meditation, chanting, and prayers. I became quite familiar with the practice of bhakti-yoga, while at the same time I bought more books and also visited the local New Age bookstores for acquiring more books on the *Vedas* of India. I was still very attached to the idea of being a musician, and music had played a special part in our lives, but I was also spending a lot of time reading and studying.

I was never the kind of person to join anything. So it took a couple more years of traveling, playing in bands, living in various cities, until I finally decided that I had enough of that lifestyle and it was time to try living in an ashrama. Then in 1975 I returned to Denver to join the Krishna temple ashrama. Later I was initiated by Srila A. C. Bhaktivedanta Swami in 1976. Even then, I continued to travel and lived in a few different temples over the years. I kept up my yoga practice and the devotional principles, as well as my study and research until I reached a point where I had many of my own realizations and perceptions of spiritual reality. Then I also started writing my own books to try to simplify the Eastern philosophy and the spiritual knowledge for others. Through that avenue, things have gradually opened up, and I've reached many other people who have also been on the path of self-inquiry and spiritual knowledge.

Throughout all this time, I've also continued to study other religions and philosophies in a comparative manner, and have traveled all over India. I've now seen almost all of the major holy places of India, and numerous minor ones, and have met many spiritually oriented people and gurus. I have now reached the point wherein I can understand more clearly than ever the great advantages that the Vedic culture has to offer anyone, of any background, ethnic group, or religious affiliation, who is looking to deepen their spiritual understanding and perspectives.

So, why would I call Vedic culture the last bastion of deep spiritual truth? It does not take much to understand, at least after a little investigation, that the Vedic process of spiritual advancement promotes individual freedom of thought, complete liberty of inquiry, and the privilege of independent and personal development through one's own spiritual experiences. This degree of latitude for self-discovery is found in few other cultures or spiritual processes.

The fact is that the Vedic literature consists of the oldest and most complete spiritual scriptures available. It contains more in-depth knowledge of the identity of the spiritual being and its connection with the universe and God than most anything else. It provides more information about the spiritual domain, the characteristics of God and our relationship with the Supreme.

Furthermore, the spiritual principles in the Vedic system are universal truths, meaning they can be applied in any time or place in the universe, and for any culture. In fact, even a Christian, a Muslim, a Jew, or anyone can understand his or her own religion more deeply by investigating the Vedic spiritual knowledge.

The Vedic system expects the individual to make his or her own progress and not merely stay on the level of blind faith. The Vedic path does not rely on faith or beliefs alone, but offers the methodologies that a person can use to refine one's consciousness. Then he or she can personally perceive the higher levels of reality and spiritual truths of which the Vedic instructions speak. In fact, the many Vedic holy men are often those who have had various levels of success in experiencing aspects of spiritual reality, and then can relay that information and directions to others. This is also why portions of Vedic philosophy are expressions of one's spiritual experience, followed by instructions enabling others to reach that same experience in perceiving the Absolute Truth.

The Vedic process allows full freedom to investigate spiritual matters and for one to ask all the questions that may come to mind, without restrictions or the possibility of being called a doubting person or a blasphemer. The Vedic approach knows that the Absolute can be perceived in different ways, thus the Vedic system accommodates this and allows for the individual to pursue the level of Truth that he or she wants to perceive. The Vedic path also makes no restrictions on our right to use whatever resources we can to help ourselves understand our spiritual nature. This it is why Vedic followers can look at any religion and find truth in it.

The Vedic system also acknowledges that we all have a unique relationship with God, and that this does not depend on the approval of a church, an institution, or a cleric or priest. It is eternal. The Vedic process merely provides the means or methodologies by which we can awaken that relationship and the awareness of our spiritual identity. By this approach, we stimulate our own perception of spiritual reality rather than merely being forced to accept a dogma presented by some religious institution.

On the other hand, we see the conventional religions of the West. They are often monotheistic constructs that are based primarily on faith, beliefs, and fear. Their faith is often directed toward the idea that if you follow what your church authorities tell you, or what you read in your scripture, you will go to heaven and be "saved". Belief usually amounts to accepting something that is still beyond your experience. And fear in most religions is based on the idea that if you do not follow the tenants of your faith or church, or if you question it, you may find yourself being excommunicated and outcaste from your religion, or even told that you will go to hell. Thus, you will have no relationship or connection with God. Fear in this regard is also displayed as a fanatical defense of one's ideas, that everyone else but you and your clan are going to hell, and that you are the only ones who really know the truth. In this way, they allow for little freedom of thought or inquiry, or for the individual to seek out answers to questions that are not described in its scripture. Anything that is not included is labeled as either demonic or something that will lead one to hell.

One problem with the religions that primarily are based on belief and faith is that they can become an effective means of manipulating the masses who follow them. If you can convince people to believe that by doing something they can go to heaven, then you can get them to do almost anything. For example, Pope Urban II implied to the soldiers who were going out on the first crusade that if they died in the name of Christ, they would ascend to heaven and live in the association of God. Thus, they rode out to fearlessly and mercilessly conquer the "heathens" or non-believers, and were willing to die to reach heaven.

This is the same effect we see with the suicide bombers amongst the Palestinian youth or the insurgents in Iraq, that if they die in the name of Islam they will immediately go to the seventh level of heaven and take pleasure in wondrous gardens in the company of beautiful virgins. It is found that the more fantastic the heaven, the more hope and conviction will be seen in the followers.

Another problem with this is that the beliefs that are given to you to accept often change with time, or according to the needs of the church to keep a congregation. As explained in a recent issue of Newsweek magazine (August 12, 2002), the concept of heaven has changed with the ages. "Dante saw heaven as the universe, and Thomas Aquinas thought of it as a brilliant place, full of light and knowledge. In the 18th century, Emanuel Swedenborg imagined heaven as a tangible world, with public gardens and parks." Nowadays you can imagine heaven to be whatever you need it to be. This gives impetus for you to do whatever you feel you should do for your beliefs, and have it justified by your religion. However, in actuality, in the Bible, the Koran, or Torah, there is little in the way of specific information of where or what is heaven. And this leaves much for the imagination.

Another problem with religious processes that rely mostly on faith and belief is that peer pressure and the need for conformity and acceptance or approval stifles and restricts one's ability to develop or inquire to one's fullest. We often see children tolerated for their deep and thoughtful questions, while the adults fear to reveal their ignorance of the topics or will even stifle a child's inquisitiveness. So such religions act like self-policing institutions wherein individuals are not encouraged to develop their own spiritual realizations or ask too many questions. They are encouraged to leave it up to faith and the dictates of the institution. They are told that we are not meant to know certain things, and that faith alone in a particular savior or the power of the church is enough to take you to heaven. But if you lack faith or question it, or do not follow the dictates of the church or scripture, you will not go to heaven. Thus, you must look good in the eyes of the church authorities and your fellow members or there will be no room for you, and thus you will be sent to hell.

The second kind of fear is the fear that you may be wrong, or the church and its doctrines may be wrong, or there may be weaknesses in its philosophy. So people become defensive of their beliefs, sometimes defending it like life itself. Thus, they condemn and criticize those who are of other religions without trying to understand them. Sometimes you can see this amongst the sects in the same religion. We already see so many divisions within Christianity, as well as Islam and Judaism. And each one often feels they are the only ones that are true followers of Jesus or Mohammed, and all others are going to hell. So it can become extremely divisive even within the same faith.

In fact, some people of particular religions may feel it is their God-given mandate that when someone is a so-called non-believer, he should be converted and "saved" at whatever cost, and then deprived of any freedom to follow an alternative view. A person in another religion may brand "nonbelievers" as infidels, and thus feel it is his duty to convert, destroy or even kill such a person, and that doing so may even be a favor to God. In either case, they may use coercion, manipulation, or simply take advantage of poor and vulnerable people to bring them over to their faith. And in such cases, the people of these religions feel they are doing God's work, and that they are justified in what they do.

However, it is refreshing to see that you usually do not have this kind of divisiveness or criticism in the Vedic system. It is much more open and provides the individual the freedom to pursue the level of experience that he or she needs in this lifetime for his or her own development and still be a part of the Vedic process.

Religion, when used improperly or without the real essence of spiritual truth, can also be a way of confining and restricting people of a wider understanding of the universe and themselves. This is done through the use of fear, guilt, violence, and the oppression of anything that shows a different view than what is being indoctrinated into society. It has been the most militant of religions that has suppressed the ancient avenues of reaching higher levels of understanding our multidimensional or spiritual nature. Thus, by mere blind faith in whatever the church or priests are giving us, or allowing us to know, we are kept in a lower consciousness than what is really possible. In this way, higher realms of thought, wisdom, love, and knowledge are kept away from the masses. After all, knowledge is power, and your ignorance is my strength. To keep power over others, the church and monotheistic religions in general have systematically abolished a wide range of spiritual and esoteric knowledge that would, otherwise, give mankind the ultimate freedom. And because people who understand their true spiritual nature and the power that lies within themselves become impossible to manipulate, it is necessary to keep this knowledge hidden. So the idea would be to keep the truly spiritual knowledge concealed while creating and perpetuating a religion, or a standard of "science", that keeps people bound by the above mentioned factors: fear, guilt, violence, and intimidation. The implication is that to tread outside the accepted jurisdiction of knowledge or understanding, or outside the rules of the institution, will bring fear. This is fear of uncertainty or disapproval by the institution, or of going to hell, as previously mentioned. Questioning the present system, or doubting its effectiveness, or desiring more knowledge about God than the church provides, will bring guilt. In this way, some religious institutions have made such ancient sciences as astrology, yoga, meditation, or the deepest understandings of the soul, or other topics, to look evil or even absurd, and thus be dismissed, or preferably even outlawed. We need to understand and recognize this pattern, which has been used in varying degrees in numerous places in the world.

In this regard, reports have been given about how huge libraries and collections of ancient and esoteric books have been destroyed or were kept out of circulation from the public. This indicates the methodical removal of various levels of spiritual and metaphysical knowledge from society, while claiming that anything other than the established doctrine of the church is satanic, evil, and hell bound. The Christian Inquisition, for example, was a wonderful method of producing this effect. Even today we can see how some people are so influenced by this tyrannical tendency that they still are afraid of looking at anything other than what the Church condones. However, most of these people are totally unaware of the "pagan" heritage found in Christianity or Judaism, which makes it very similar to pre-Christian ways, but with a different name. It is practically the same medicine in a different bottle. To remove this understanding from public knowledge, it became necessary that whenever Christianity or other militant religions conquered a country or culture, the first thing that was done was to capture or destroy all of the ancient sacred texts. However, any organization that destroys the ancient knowledge and historical records of a civilization is never going to present the true history of the world, or the spiritual wisdom of any previous culture. Thus, the view of history is controlled and the population is kept in ignorance and under subtle restraint. And the people who are allowed to understand any of the truth are those of the elite or who are already in power.

By taking a look at the history of the conventional or western religions, for example, a person can see to what extent such an institution will go to maintain power and control, especially when it feels threatened by what it does not understand. Furthermore, the dark history of Christianity represents the fanatically narrow-minded side of it that has continued to the present day in the form of fundamentalists thinking that if a religion or culture is not Christian, then it must be of the devil. Or at least its followers will not go to heaven. Such people are often ready to dismiss or criticize other spiritual paths and cultures without understanding them. They may see a ceremony or ritual of another religion and immediately say it is heathen or devil worship, without realizing that it is the worship of the same Supreme Being that they worship.

The point is that all people have to have the freedom to find themselves to the fullest extent on whatever path it takes, providing it is a genuine and uplifting path. So how do we make sure we can continue to have this freedom? By understanding each other and other cultures of the world and the different paths of self-discovery, and by recognizing the value that they have to offer. We must also bury our preconceived prejudices that are based on our immature feelings of superiority because, spiritually speaking, we are all the same. We just have to attain that spiritual vision to see the reality of it. And the path we take to do that is the only difference among us.

A true religion paves the way for everyone to become spiritually aware, and to establish his or her own relationship with the Supreme. And the Vedic system is an ideal means for supplying that. If a religion is not based on the higher principles of self-realization, but is merely based on dogmatic rules and regulations that it forces on others, then it becomes a trap based on fear, guilt, oppression, and intimidation. One must not be afraid to break free from such a trap. It is greater to see God's love manifested in many sages belonging to different traditions at different times and places, among different people.

The premise that all spiritual knowledge must be connected with one distinct or localized savior is itself a stifling factor in allowing individuals to progress in spiritual understanding. There is so much more that could be learned if they did not feel that if something is not connected with their particular savior or scripture, then it must be Satanic. In this way, if it is not in the Bible or Koran, for example, they refuse to acknowledge the value of any additional spiritual knowledge if it comes from a different culture or source. Thus, they act with fear or contempt toward anything outside their own sphere of familiarity or acceptability, or like people who are proud of their own ignorance and narrow-mindedness.

The straightjacket of Western theological dogma keeps a person from looking at additional resources that could supply answers for questions not considered in western thought, or at possibilities that are elementary in Eastern traditions. What's wrong with learning newer ways of connecting with our higher selves, and with each other and with God? What's wrong with allowing our hearts and minds to expand with new vibrancy, new insights and confidence? Why not allow ourselves new hope and understanding in regard to the purpose of the universe and the nature of God, even if we look to different sources of knowledge? Who knows what additional information we can add to what we already know, or newer ways to incorporate and develop ourselves into people who are better and more aware and spiritually developed. This is natural for those who participate in the Vedic system.

For these reasons, India must remain the homeland of a living and dynamic Vedic culture. This will allow the world to retain some of the deepest knowledge and methods of attaining the most profound spiritual insights that have been known to mankind. India should defend itself from the risk of further partition or divisions. If India is divided up any further, Vedic culture could dwindle or even be lost over the long-term, except for small colonies of Vedic practitioners here and there. This may indeed be what many people would like to see. Yet, if Vedic culture is lost, the world will not even realize the treasure of human development that will disappear. Then such deep spiritual knowledge and insights will begin to permanently fade away from society.

Once India and Vedic culture is diluted or even gradually stamped out, along with other decreasing numbers of indigenous traditions, then the whole world will be fitted with the straightjacket of Western thought and monotheistic religion. Thus, it will be more easily controlled by the establishment that is connected with or promotes a single way of viewing human spiritual progress. Then individual freedom for the pursuit of higher understanding and spiritual happiness will be limited to the constraints as dictated by whatever regional monotheistic views reign in that area.

For this reason Vedic culture is the last bastion of deep and genuine spiritual truth and freedom. This is also why it should be clearly understood and preserved. And to help with this purpose and show the value and broad nature of Vedic knowledge is why this book is being presented.

The King of Knowledge

Robert Taylor

I believe that my own spiritual interest in life was already indicated when I was born in Carmarthen, Wales, the mythological birthplace of Merlin the Druid. My Welsh uncle informed me that I came into the world just 200 yards from Merlin's sacred oak tree.

My gentle, loving parents then raised me in the English country of Wiltshire within close proximity to Avebury, Stonehenge and Glastonbury, considered by metaphysicians as some of the world's most powerful sacred sites.

From early childhood, I had a definite spiritual inclination, but it was in my late teens that I began an intensified search for the truth of my existence in our universe. I was asking those very important questions which have tantalized the minds of spiritual seekers throughout "the ages".

"Who am I? Where did I come from? What happens after the death of my physical body? Is there a superior existence transcendent to the mundane plane? What lies beyond this planet earth? Can perfect happiness really be attained?"

Some of you who have also attempted such esoteric illuminations may have thrown your hands up in desperation, declaring that these impossible questions can never be satisfactorily answered by the limited human intellect and so have resigned yourselves to the concept that there is nothing beyond our present existence.

During my own philosophical search, I was very fortunate to discover Aldous Huxley's "Perennial Philosophy" in which he quotes and comments on the wisdom of great saints and sages from various spiritual traditions. Reading through the book, I found myself especially attracted to the segments from the ancient Sanskrit writings known as the *Vedas*. I instinctively felt that these sacred texts were not just someone's imperfect mental speculations, but the profound utterings of realized Truth.

I was so enthusiastic about my discovery that I searched out some of the Vedic literature which Huxley had quoted. These fascinating volumes, such as *Bhagavad-gita*, sparked an interest in my practice of yoga, mantra meditation and vegetarianism. These disciplines inspired me to eventually travel to India where I dedicated myself to the full time study of the *Vedas* in a monastic, contemplative environment.

These nonsectarian ancient scriptures are so voluminous that one cannot study them all in this one lifetime. Full of knowledge of both the spiritual and material realms, these gems of wisdom cover every conceivable subject necessary for man's harmonious spiritual, emotional and physical progress. Although 5,000 years old, the *Vedas* give elaborate scientific information on the nature of time, the mind and intellect, atomic structure, life on other planets and universes, medicine, physiology, aeronautics and mathematics.

In the social sciences, volumes of wisdom discuss economics, law, political science and military strategy and for the promotion of the creative arts exquisitely beautiful forms of dance, music, drama and sculpture are presented. The *Sthapatya Veda* discusses architectural knowledge including *Vastu Vidya*, similar to the Far East's Feng Shui, which instructs us how to build a home, town or entire country in harmony with the laws of nature.

The most fascinating and important knowledge for me, however, is contained within spiritually rich metaphysical texts which give philosophically satisfying information on the nature of God, reincarnation, karma, and self-realization with various practical yoga systems for our spiritual perfection.

The *Vedas* also teach a very advanced astrological system with astronomical calculations which would stun our modern day physicists.

Originally only accessible to erudite scholars of Sanskrit, the Vedic literature has recently been translated into English and many of the world's languages. This has been through the tireless and dedicated work of compassionate Vedic spiritual masters, such as the distinguished authority A. C. Bhaktivedanta Swami, who personally wrote 80 volumes of books to expose our needy world to sources of authentic knowledge. Many of his students are similarly translating important texts, following in his footsteps.

These spiritually realized masters have carefully handed down their wisdom to qualified students in an unbroken chain of succession known in Sanskrit as the *guru-parampara*. The four major disciplic lines trace their origins to the first teacher of Vedic wisdom—the Supreme Personality of Godhead. Because of the omniscient nature of God, perfect knowledge of the Absolute Truth has been transmitted to us through these disciplic lines from an untainted, perfect source. By hearing this pure transcendental knowledge from realized, exemplary teachers and practicing the precepts in our daily lives, we are assured of the spiritual success which is the inherent birthright of all living beings.

It is my purpose and hope through the mercy of these great spiritual preceptors that I can relate some of this invaluable Vedic knowledge, and share a wonderfully enriching experience which has been the joy and fulfillment of my own life.

DISCOVERING THE DIVINE SELF

It was a beautiful August morning of 1970 in Amsterdam, Holland when my life's direction took a revolutionary turn. As I strolled in the sunlight, contemplating the knowledge I had absorbed from the "Perennial Philosophy", I was immersed in a spiritual quest of self-discovery to realize my true nature and identity.

The yogis and sages of India, who Aldous Huxley frequently quotes in his book, would tell us that the first step in spiritual life, which is a giant leap in terms of realization, is the understanding of the essential nature of the Self. It was this very essence that I was endeavoring to comprehend.

As I ambled along the picturesque canals of Amsterdam, I began to analyze the elements that make up our material world—these same ingredients that contribute to our physical bodies. I had what I felt was a most enlightening experience as I realized the Self could not possibly be a product of inert matter—that I was in fact a transcendental, spiritual being inhabiting the complex machinery of the material body. I further realized that my essential Self was pure consciousness, which is the energy of the soul and not some product of a material combination. Just as the sun and the sun's rays are one, so also the soul and consciousness are one and the same.

If we analyze our current life's situation we will see that consciousness is the only part of the Self which has remained constant. Science tells us that the cells which constitute the body are in a state of flux, going through the material process of birth and death in a seven year cycle. The cells which made up the baby's body will be different from the ones in the youth's or adult's body. We also observe the same cycle of change on the atomic level. After a short while of sitting in a room, some of the atoms which make up the body will have changed. During a one year period 99.9 percent of the atoms will be replaced, so how can we consider the physical body to be the self?

Not only is the physical self constantly changing, but so is the more subtle self which we call the mind. I have a very different mind as an adult than I do as a child. It's desires, comprehensions and concepts have all radically changed.

The only constant in this temporary world of change has been the consciousness, which as a non-material element existed prior to the current body and will continue to exist after its demise. It is this element which is the permanent self, the true individual and our real identity. As the soul, we continue to exist eternally. It is because of material desires and attachments that we take birth in temporary material bodies.

This is eloquently expressed by Teilhard de Chardin in his immortal words: "I am not a human being having a spiritual experience, I am a spiritual being having a human experience."

To illustrate this difference between the self and the body, I like to give the example of an automobile. I have a very nice vehicle which I use to go from one place to another. It sits dead in the parking lot until I, the conscious being, get in it and turn on the engine. The physical body works in the same way. It is a most remarkable machine. Just one of its billion of cells is more complex than the communication system of a large city, but is only operable and alive whilst the individual soul resides within it. What we call death is simply the moment when the person, consciousness, or soul leaves the body. Death is therefore the great illusion. We do not die! We simply leave our current existence to be transported to our next existence.

The *Vedas* call this consciousness the Brahman, which is the essential life of all creation and is the determining factor in all life forms. Wherever we see the symptoms of consciousness—a being who has the faculties of thinking, feeling and willing—there is a soul present. The *Vedas* do not, therefore, make the spiritual error of limiting souls to only human bodies. Plants, insects, birds and animals, even germs, where consciousness is present, are souls in different levels of evolutionary progress. The *Vedas* inform us, in fact, that there are 8,400,000 levels of life through which the soul can transmigrate.

The Vedic texts also inform us that the soul is transcendentally situated within the region of the heart and pervades the body with consciousness through the medium of the bloodstream. The soul is so infinitesimal, atomic in size, that it is impossible to view through even the most powerful microscope. Being a non-material energy anyway, it is not possible to detect with material senses. Just to give us an idea of its atomic nature, the Vedic texts describe the soul as being one ten-thousandth the size of the tip of a hair. It is a wonder that a self-realized, enlightened soul becomes so humble upon realization of something so infinitesimal?

One of the beautiful qualities of the soul is pure love. Love is our very constitution, just as sweetness is the quality of sugar. We are loving beings by nature, and the more we manifest our original pure consciousness, the greater our love will become.

I have always marveled at the fact that the heart is so much connected to this most important of sentiment. It is just an organ after all, like the liver or kidney. I would suggest that the heart is associated with the love principle because it is the seat of the soul.

We are not only full of love, but are naturally complete with knowledge and bliss. These are all qualities of the illumined self. Everything that we are searching for in our external world for fulfillment already exists within. The more we free ourselves from material concepts, desires and attachments, the greater will be the experience of love, knowledge and joy.

Due to our identification with the material body we view our selves in terms of mundane designations, such as black or white, male or female, Palestinian or Israeli, American or Chinese, Hindu or Muslim, etc. These are simply bodily labels which have nothing to do with the soul. We change these identities from one life to the next. So what is their value? In one life I may be a Hindu, the next a Muslim, or I can take birth in China, emigrate to the United States and become an America citizen. I could even have the operation to change my sexual identity.

My own self-realized spiritual master, A. C. Bhaktivedanta Swami, said many times that the only problem in the world today is that we are all suffering from "skin disease" due to our false identification with the material body. We are in essence all the same—pure souls inhabiting human bodies. But due to our material conditioning we see each other according to material designations.

An enlightened soul does not discriminate between humans, plants, insects or animals, for he (she) sees all beings with the transcendental vision of spiritual equality. Such a spiritually aware individual sees the same divinity in all of God's greatness and treats everyone and everything with the same love and respect. If we could enlighten the world's population with this knowledge, that we are all equal souls coming from the one same source—the Supreme Personality of Godhead— we would have a much more peaceful and harmonious planet. I would suggest in our present world that the sectarian religious fundamentalists and political extremists, who in their anger and hatred cause so much violence and pain to their fellow souls, need to realize these A B Cs of metaphysical knowledge.

On an individual basis, as we realize our self-identity as the eternal consciousness, the soul, we simultaneously decrease the most negative of emotions—fear! It is due to a lack of self-realization that the fear element literally paralyzes our existence. In many ways it is the opposite of the love principle. As we realize our soul identity, we automatically know that we are eternal beings. We have existed prior to this body and will continue on forever. We are indestructible, immutable and eternal souls. So what do we really fear?

Armed with this invaluable knowledge that we are spiritual beings who belong in the transcendental realm of God, our life takes on a new meaning and perspective. The ultimate goal of our lives then is to completely surrender our existence into the loving arms of God and to live with full faith that our existence is in divine order and has a great purpose.

Vishnu, the Wish for Sustainability

Jeffrey Armstrong

Although I was born in Detroit, Michigan in the United States, the last 35 years of my life have been dominated by a passionate study and practice of the Vedic knowledge of India. The *Vedas* are an extensive library of ancient spiritual and material knowledge. Whereas most religions or traditions trace themselves back to a single book, teacher or prophet, the Vedic culture, or as it is now called Hindu culture, derives its wisdom from a large body of knowledge contained in a great collection of sacred texts. This is one of the reasons for the diversity of practices and viewpoints that make the Vedic Hindu process seem confusing to people used to only one book.

To make a comparison, if each of the great wisdom traditions of the world are mountains and their practitioners are climbers of those mountains, then the *Vedas* appeared to me the way the Himalayas would to a seasoned mountain climber. As a seeker of the truths to be found in the rarified atmosphere of the mountains of truth, I found in the *Vedas* a Himalayan range of philosophy, science, poetry, wisdom, history, cosmology, genealogy, astronomy, medicine, martial arts, religion and much more. And so I have dedicated my life to the living exploration of this great range of ideas. This article is only a small glimpse of those amazing peaks. It is an inadequate report from one small climber of the range of great ideas that are the legacy from India's spiritual past.

As with any expedition to unknown peaks, the guide is absolutely essential. The "sherpas" or "gurus" of my climbing have been many. Without their blessings and guidance, this report and life as I know it would have been impossible. "Fools rush in where angels fear to tread." In order to understand the *Vedas*, one must have a guru as a guide in order to climb the slippery slopes of truth that transcend ordinary experience or reason. So first I bow to them all with humility and gratitude as the prelude to writing this small travelogue. If you will, think of this as a brief excursion into the hill country of those mountains, from which place one or more of their peaks may be seen in the distance. There are so many great visions to be had in the Vedic countryside. No explorer has seen them all. What follows are just notes along the trail of Eternal Truth. May it serve you in your own journey.

At the heart of the Vedic knowledge is an ancient history of life on planet Earth. According to that history, the Supreme Being, Vishnu, or God, exists eternally in a realm that is currently beyond our sight. From that undying abode the temporary material world in which we are living is created, exists for some time and is then destroyed. The substance out of which this world is made is called the "unconscious energy" whereas the spiritual world as well as all living beings are made of a "conscious energy" that never dies. In the Sanskrit language in which the *Vedas* were written, the unconscious energy is called "prakriti" and the eternally conscious energy is called "Brahman". The Brahman energy is further divided into two kinds of beings, the unlimitedly powerful beings and those who, though divine in Nature, are limited in their power. One of the names of that God energy is Vishnu and the numerous eternal Brahman beings or souls are called "atmas".

According to the *Vedas*, the material world or unconscious realm is periodically created by Vishnu's command to accommodate the desires of the countless souls to visit that place. In other words, all of us souls have come to the material world to collect experience, stay for some time and then finally return to the spiritual realm which is our original home. Since the realm of matter is unconscious, it is dark and temporary by nature, whereas the spiritual worlds, Vishnu and the souls, are all light or enlightened by nature.

You can immediately see that the Vedic view of material nature and her laws is that they were all preceded and created by intentional acts of Divine Will. Think of the whole of material nature as an amazing science and art museum in which we are living. According to the *Vedas*, the original inventor of all these exhibits is God or Vishnu. Actually, at this point we should remember that the Vedic view of God is both male and female as one permanently connected reality. Let's just call them Mr. and Mrs. God for the time being. In the *Vedas*, one name for Mrs. God is Lakshmi. For this article, think of Vishnu and Lakshmi as Mother and Father Divine, who are the great parents of all beings. It's a little like the way we say that two people who marry become "one flesh" even though we know they are also individuals. So Vishnu and Lakshmi are one God and yet act also as individuals.

The first step of understanding then is that the Divine Couple, from within the Divine Brahman reality, create the world of matter by willing it to be so, for the specific purpose of creating a playground for the eternal souls to play in and gather experience. The *Vedas* say that this original wish, an English word derived from the Sanskrit "vish", meaning "all pervasive", is carried out within matter by three pairs of Divine Beings. Since matter is unconscious by nature, someone needs to bring it into manifestation. That someone is described in the *Vedas* as a Divine Couple named Brahma and Saraswati, the creators of life.

Whatever is created out of matter is temporary and must someday come to an end. The Divine Couple associated with the destruction of matter and who also act as Father and Mother Nature, are called Shiva and Parvati. In fact, as Mother and Father Nature, they are Shiva and Shakti, the original male and female, but when they destroy the material world they are known as Rudra and Kali. Finally, Vishnu and Lakshmi appear within matter as the Divine Couple who maintain life within matter. Since creation, maintenance and destruction are all necessary within the material, all three of these Divine Couples are equally necessary for life inside matter.

In order for this description to appear relevant to our personal lives, we need to connect this Vedic story to life as we know it. The two primary laws of material science are the two laws of thermodynamics: that matter is neither created or destroyed but merely changes form and that all created things go from a higher state of energy to a lower state and in the process give off heat and waste. These two laws are the basis of the world of matter. The *Vedas* agree that matter, though unconscious, is eternal. The second law of thermodynamics is only a succinct statement that all things within matter are created, at which point a certain quantum of energy is locked into their being. They then endure for a certain period of time and as they are destroyed (as their form changes) they release heat and create a certain amount of waste.

This is exactly the Vedic vision of Brahma/Saraswati, Vishnu/Lakshmi and Shiva/Shakti, who are in charge of anabolism, metabolism and catabolism; the building up of life, its maintenance and its breaking down. All life in the material world functions on the basis of these three principles. Now the question is, which of these three principles is most important in our life. Clearly, all three must be present in everything, but which one should we align ourselves with (worship) on a daily basis?

Let's examine this question in terms of our everyday lives. If someone chose destruction as their operating principle and their daily job was destroying everything indiscriminately, what would we call them? In society, a criminal; in nature, a disaster; in our body, cancer cells. We would applaud the destruction of an old building, surgery to remove a tumor or repair a tooth, and the necessary destruction to grow crops, but uncontrolled destruction would quickly ruin all we hold dear.

What about creation or procreation? If every family had a few children, that would be fine. What if every family had twenty children? What if you were an artist who only created art and nothing else? What would happen to your life? What if the cells of your body reproduced and kept creating beyond the number needed? So creation and destruction or the Brahma/Saraswati and Shiva/Shakti principles in nature must be held in check by a third principle. That third principle of Vishnu/Lakshmi is the principle of maintenance, balance, metabolic integrity, system integration, holistic thinking, ecological balance, homeostasis and is best expressed as sustainability.

Actually, the word Vishnu means "all pervading, in support of all". The Vishnu/Lakshmi principle is the integrating force that uses distributed intelligence and all pervasive consciousness to maintain life for the maximum period to benefit as many as possible. The Vedic culture says that life was consciously created by Father and Mother Divine as an opportunity for all living beings to evolve. The Divine Couples' consciousness pervades everything as the laws of Nature. They are the Divine lawmakers. The responsibility of human beings is to worship (work with) Vishnu and Lakshmi while sharing their wish for the maximum good for all beings in a sustainable lifestyle. Therefore, anyone, anywhere at anytime who behaves in such a way as to serve this Vishnu/Lakshmi principle of the preservation of life is worshipping Vishnu and Lakshmi through their intention and actions. Conversely, anyone whose lifestyle is causing the needless destruction of life, even if they say they are worshipping Vishnu/Lakshmi, is in fact not doing so.

In the Vedic view, just as the material world is composed of a dark unconscious principle (matter) and a light conscious principle (the souls and God), so the numerous souls here decide to align themselves with one of the Divine principles. Those souls who seek to associate with and serve the light principle are called "devas" and those who identify with and serve the dark unconscious principle are called "asura", which means against the light. In our body, cancer cells are asuras. In the social body, those who destroy the lives of others are asura and on the planetary body, those who adopt a means of living that is destructive of present and future generations are also asura. The principle of sustainability and fighting against the violent asura culture is the basis of Vedic culture and history.

This brings us to one of the most remarkable and unique features of the Vedic knowledge. Not only are the persons of the Divine described in great detail with their various functions, their historical appearance on Earth has been recorded. The descent of the Divine Persons to the Earth from the Transcendental Realm is known in Sanskrit as "Avatar". According to the *Vedas*, Vishnu/Lakshmi not only work to maintain the balance of Nature on an ongoing basis, they also descend to Earth at various times when the balance is threatened by the destructive actions of asuric beings.

One of the unique contributions of the Vedic literature to the rest of the world is that they contain the historical record of the descent of the Avatars of Vishnu/Lakshmi to Earth. The most recent visits of Mr. and Mrs. God to Earth arc recorded in the two great epic poems, the *Ramayana* and the *Mahabharata*. In the *Ramayana*, Vishnu/Lakshmi appear on Earth as Rama and Sita, and in the *Mahabharata* they appear as Krishna and his wife Rukmini. In both stories, Ram and Krishna are not depicted as prophets or enlightened souls, but rather they declare themselves to be the Person of God, or in Sanskrit, "Supreme Purusha", appearing to fight the asuras and bless the devas. These great epic stories are the "user manuals" for aspiring souls who want to serve Vishnu and Lakshmi in the struggle to create a sustainable lifestyle on Earth through right livelihood, correct action, protection of the innocent and conserving the precious resources of Mother Nature.

Now, let's apply this concept of Vishnu/Lakshmi to our "modern" world. How are we doing on sustainability? Endangered species? Love and respect for all beings? Protecting our land and water from contamination? Is the world population being fed and educated? Are the goals of sustainability the first priority for our elected officials and corporate leaders? Are we creating a world we would be proud to leave as a legacy to our great-great-great-grandchildren? Do our scientists speak of the Divine purpose as the basis of the great creations of Nature? Do we see all living beings as eternal souls and show them respect and kindness in spite of racial or cultural differences? These are the qualities of a Divine Being whose intention is to serve and please Vishnu and Lakshmi by assisting them in their job of sustaining life.

This perspective is one of the many challenging and beautiful summits in the Himalayan range called the *Vedas*. A mountain may exist in a country but it is the property of no one. Whoever we are, it may be our privilege to walk in sacred places and see Divine vistas. Vishnu and Lakshmi are not "Hindu Gods", they are the embodiment of important eternal truths which are true when called by any name. Either within our hearts or as an Avatar on Earth, let us hope that the spirit of Vishnu and Lakshmi appears everywhere, inspiring all to build a life that will be a gift and bring joy to future generations. May everyone hold this noble wish as the ancient Vedic culture devoted to Vishnu and Lakshmi once did. May all be fed. May all be happy. May all find peace.

Introduction to the Roots of Kundalinin and Kundalini Yoga

Yogi Harinam Baba Prem Tom Beal (Vedakovid)

My life began in a small rural community; I came from a poor uneducated family. My parents divorced when I was not yet born. It seems it was a karma my father had faced in his youth, and it would manifest in this life for me as well. My mother worked for minimum wages, barely above poverty as she struggled to rear a boy alone in a region of the world and time period that frowned on such things. I spent most of my time with friends or learning to cook at a young age. I was cared for by my grandmothers much of the time.

My grandmother on my mother's side was stern, and her solution was to whip or slap me across the face if I did not behave properly in her eyes. My grandmother on my father's side did not share the same view, and she would often take me for walks through the forest showing me rock crystals and telling me about herbs that were traditionally used in our area.

As a child I had a strong connection and appreciation for nature. We had several dogs, and they were among my closest friends. On one occasion I became lost in the forest and my dogs found me and lead me from the forest back to my home. To this day, I still have a close relationship with animals and their suffering.

As a child I would go into many yoga type postures as numerous children do, with the exception that I would enjoy spending periods of time in shoulder stand. I would practice it frequently in my room. As I approached the age of 12, a spiritual desire began to manifest with me. It was a desire to connect and understand spirituality and religion. I searched throughout our community, visited the local public library in search of books, studied the Bible, would explain the Bible to others, but nothing could satisfy my need to connect with spirituality. At times I would sit in my room and close my eyes, a man with long hair, beard, and thin build would appear before me. We would just sit with one another, but there was little conversation. On occasion we would talk, or he would put his hands into "funny" positions (*mudras*). This seemed to help with my spiritual thirst, but it still could not satisfy my longing or need. After time I began to slip into the same challenges that most people face in life. In the back of my mind, my spiritual need continued to surface, but my Christian fundamentalist upbringing only inspired me to try and run away from it.

As I neared graduation from High School, I realized that I needed to go to college somehow or I would spend my life working in a "sweat factory" just as my mother did. So I decided to go to college. My mother has never forgiven me for leaving.

I found a community college to attend and began to work my way through school. I majored in radio and television technology, and discovered that I had skill in radio. I started working for many stations and moved several times eventually moving to Albuquerque, New Mexico.

As time passed in Albuquerque I realized if I did not stop my lifestyle I would eventually die from it. Each day on the way to work, I would pass by a little yoga center with mauve awnings called the "United Yoga Institute". I felt compelled to stop in, but I was afraid due to my fundamentalist upbringing. As the months past, eventually I gathered the courage to walk in. It was a small shop with a few books, crystals, and items of that nature. I quickly saw that they had a yoga philosophy home study course. I grabbed it quickly, paid for it, and ran out the door.

One of the first books I read in the course was from Swami Vivekananda. It touched me so. It was like arriving at my 'real' home. It was everything I had been looking for in my youth. I studied everyday, digesting each of swamiji's words. I began to stop destructive habits and patterns in my life, and started the study and practice of yoga. I completed my teacher training at the institute after 4 years of study in 1988. Once I received my diploma in yoga studies, I remember standing outside and realizing that I have prepared myself to really begin the study of yoga and meditation. And I began the journey that I started so many lifetimes ago.

Within my yoga and meditative practice I found peace, harmony, and healing. From the Indian philosophy I found knowledge and wisdom. I found my consciousness expanding into deeper areas of awareness. But is there more, I wondered.

Eventually I was led to Ayurveda and spent a number of years studying this important system. It has been a tremendous aid to maintaining health and wellness over the years. But the spiritual voice was back and now, the words and terms of what I spiritually needed were coming to mind and they began to fill my thoughts. I began the study of Sanskrit, though to this day I still consider myself a beginner due to the complexity of the language. Sanskrit opened the doorway to mantra. And mantra opened the doorway to experience the mind of the deity. As this process continued, I began to realize that I was a Hindu, and that I had always been a Hindu. It was Hinduism I was looking for my entire life.

All of the study and experience was preparing and equipping me to study the *Vedas*. I started with the *Atharva Veda*. I was most touched by its relevance to our daily lives. It was not the obscure meaningless text that I was always told. It was alive! It offered practical insight into many areas of life. I then moved to the *Sama Veda* and found it to be a powerful text. Then to the *Rg Veda*. I found the mantras to be powerful and spiritually uplifting and healing. Using the mantras of the *Rg Veda* and with grace of God and guru I have healed myself many times and on many levels, mentally, emotionally, and physically.

I eventually began to study with Pandit Vamadeva Shastri (David Frawley) and with the American Institute of Vedic Studies. I studied Ayurveda, Vedic astrology and was accepted into the Vedic studies program, eventually receiving the title of Vedakovid.

Looking back over my life, what has always been there for me was the Vedic teachings, and the deities taking form from the eternal Brahman. Krishna and Arjuna have ridden through my heart. Shiva has protected this body, and Kali has held me when I was alone and hurting. She is and has always been my mother. When everyone one else deserted me, the teachings, and my Guru, Mahavatar Babaji, have remained. For me the Vedic teachings and other systems have been there when I needed them most. They have never judged me; they have only supported me in my journey to consciousness.

The *Vedas* have often served as a powerful reminder of the spiritual heritage I come from, and the spiritual essence I return to. I am eternally grateful to untold 'heroes', saints, sages, and all others that have worked to preserve these vital teachings for mankind, so I would have them this day. It is my attempt to participate in this preservation of the most important spiritual teachings that have survived for mankind for the future souls to use in finding their way just as I was touched by the grace of the teachings and awakened in my journey. This is also how I began my study of kundalini, which I will introduce in this article.

The Kundalini, the ancient mystery of Indian culture, feared, avoided, dark, and mysterious. While this is still a common teaching in the east and west, the kundalini energy is nothing more than our dynamic essence (*shakti*) that appears in a variety of teachings and systems. The kundalini is often misrepresented and misunderstood. A variety of factors contribute to this, *avidya*[1] being the most prominent, and western competition between yoga systems is another intriguing possibility. Whatever the reason, the kundalini has often been approached with fear and misinformation.

---

1 Avidya: a Sanskrit term that literally means ignorance.

Does this mysterious energy belong exclusively to Tantric yoga or does it appear within a variety of teachings veiled with different names? Is the kundalini to be feared? And of what benefit is it for human spiritual potential?

ROOTS OF KUNDALINI

Kundalini yoga is often associated with Tantric yoga. A variety of explanations are provided for the meaning of the word, ranging from literally meaning serpent or snake to a verbal root meaning "coiled". Hence the reason kundalini is always referred to as the serpent energy (*kundalini shakti*). The kundalini appears under a variety of names within different Indian systems and traditions, a sampling of these names would be *nagi, avadhuti, atma shakti, sarasvati*, and many others.

While almost exclusively associated with Tantra yoga, or packaged as kundalini yoga, in reality Hatha yoga is a kundalini yoga system as well; especially when one considers that the main Hatha text called the *Hatha Yoga Pradipika* contains numerous kundalini techniques including some of the key techniques to "awaken" the kundalini energy.

Within the *Hatha Yoga Pradipka* (HYP) we find references such as the "Bhastrika" breath (59), Shitali breath (57), "…it awakens the kundalini…"(66), "kumbhaka awakens kundalini…" (75). The channels of the body and the nadi's most associated with the kundalini are common within the HYP, namely Ida, Pingala, and Sushumna. The *Bhandas* or chakra locks common to kundalini yoga appear within the HYP (69-77). The sacred mountain of Hinduism, Meru[2], is mentioned within the HYP as well as a variety of Vedic terms indicating that the kundalini would have a Vedic association.

The Vedic battle between Vrtra and Indra is in essence the human struggle to "awaken" the kundalini energy by "releasing the waters" (*Rg Veda*)[3]. The reference to the Vedic Sun (Surya), which is hidden, can be a reference to the awakened kundalini, which is often described as having the brilliance of a thousand suns (HYP). This indicates the kundalini references as some of the oldest spiritual

---

2   From a yogic perspective the sacred Meru is represented physically by the spinal column. In a variety of ancient texts Meru is given a specific height, located within an ocean and surrounded by 7 islands. These islands, in yogic teachings, are the chakras. So one yoga teaching is that Meru is the Sushumna of the astral body. Meru can have additional meanings within different traditions.

3   This is a yogic interpretation of these teachings, though it is not the only interpretation or truth behind these multi-dimensional texts. See "Vrtra the Spiritual Adversay" VFA Journal www.vedicfriends.org

references known to humankind still practiced today. *Shakti*[4] and *shaci*[5] are both found within the *Vedas* also. There appears to be references to a kundalini awakening within the *Ṛg Veda* itself, as Agni and its earthly representation is the kundalini. Worship of Agni is a form of kundalini yoga, though the postures not evident within the *Vedas* are often taught as a precursor especially in western society and within the yogic traditions. But the Vedic tradition can be a separate kundalini system, possibly the mother to kundalini yoga.

There is a direct association between the kundalini and the Ashvins[6], which appears in later times as the Ashvin mudra is a powerful tool in yoga. A strong indication of the kundalini within the *Vedas* and in reference to the Vedic Ashvins is a reference to the Ashvins raising the water from the bottom of the well (1.116.22). This verse indicates the release of raising energy up the spine. The Ashvins and their powerful association with healing and *prana* strongly link them with the kundalini, though they are not limited to the kundalini energy.

Within the Indus valley, a variety of seals have been located. On a few of these seals there has been identified an image of a man sitting in a cross-legged position with serpents rising up the sides. This could be a reference to the kundalini, though it is only speculative at this time.

Kundalini energy is referenced in a variety of systems and under different names such as the Tantric union of Shiva and Shakti. This manifests on the lower physical form with sexual Tantra, which is a physical representation of the union of Shiva and Shakti. The actual union of Shiva and Shakti occurs not on a physical level but on the level of the astral body. The kundalini (*shakti*) becomes "awakened," travels up the *Sushumna* and merges within the *Sahasrara* chakra (Shiva). Shiva represents the masculine attribute at the crown chakra, as Shakti is the kundalini shakti located within the tailbone area of the astral body. In the higher stages this is a personal internal process, merging our personal masculine and feminine qualities together as one. This actually occurs on the level of the Chakras as well, as one-half of each chakra is masculine and the other feminine.

Astrologically within Jyotish or Vedic astrology, the kundalini is represented with the planets or nodes Rahu and Ketu. Rahu and Ketu represent the head and the tail of the serpent, with Ketu embodying qualities such as liberation, and Rahu representing the lower *tamasic* qualities of the dormant kundalini energy. These two planets are associated with the *sushumna*, with Rahu being the base of the spine and Ketu representing the top of the spine. Clearly they both are associated with the kundalini and the astral body.

---

4   Divine power.
5   Divine grace.
6   The Ashvins are Vedic deities strongly associated with healing, prana, Vedic astrology, and the movement of the sun.

Within the Vedanta, Yogic, Vedic and Shaivite systems we see a merging of terms that clearly describes the kundalini concealment. Maya becomes a common term and is one of the 36 *tattvas* of Shaivite religious teachings. Maya, in the non-intelligent form, manifests as three attributes: Sattva, Rajas, and Tamas[7]. The non-intelligent form of maya is concealed by *avarana shakti. Avarana Shakti* is the concealing force of Vritra within the *Rg Veda*. This keeps the kundalini within a *tamasic* state, commonly referred to as sleeping or dormant.

Within the *Shiva Samhita*, the sun is referred to as being at the bottom of Meru (II. 10), which is a reference to the kundalini. Within the same text, the *bhandas*, or chakra locks, appear again. This is clearly a Tantric teaching, but one that has been discovered, shared, or known between a variety of different groups. These techniques also appear within Nath teachings such as the *Gheranda Samhita* which includes teachings on classical techniques such as Bhastrika, Shitali, mahamudra, such as seen within the *Hatha Yoga Pradipka* and other teachings dealing with the kundalini shakti. It is important to note that Nath teachings are most likely much older than their recorded dates.

In light of this, it is difficult to make the kundalini owned by one sect, cult, group, or series of teachings. Clearly the kundalini belongs to the realm of mystics, and has been recorded in a variety of writings spanning a four to five thousand year period, possibly longer.

IS THE KUNDALINI SLEEPING?

Another common misconception is that the kundalini is sleeping and must be awakened. While these terms are good for illustrative purposes, they do have their limitations and can be misleading to western readers. The term sleeping, in reference to the kundalini, would be better classified as a static state. The most proper term would be a *tamasic* state. An awakening of the kundalini would involve moving from a *tamasic* state to a *rajasic* state. Or in modern terms, the kundalini would move from a static state to a dynamic state, though the *gunas* would be a clearer example keeping with tradition. The kundalini rising to the crown chakra, under proper situations, results in a *sattvic* state.

This process has lead to much confusion regarding the awakening of the kundalini energy. Eastern teachers that have traveled to the west often viewed any experience as a small movement of the kundalini energy, more properly classified

---

7   Sattva, Rajas, Tamas are referred to as the three gunas or attributes. They are an important teaching in a variety of systems, and worthy of much additional study. A quick interpretation would be Sattva-harmony, Rajas-activity, Tamas-inertia.

as a small release of *shakti*. This is represented as the "bulb" suddenly going off in someone's head. Though this experience does come from the kundalini, it is not a true kundalini awakening.

In classic texts, the experience of the kundalini was equated with various animals, with some animals holding gentler qualities than others. So the kundalini is not sleeping but is an active part of our self, and the human existence. It is the essence of spiritual awakening and transformation, belonging to the realm of the modern mystic, though other systems have developed their own paths to cosmic truth that are just as valid. All these systems fall under the umbrella of *Sanatana Dharma*.[8]

ILLUSIONARY KUNDALINI AWAKENINGS

One of the greatest illusions present within the modern new age movement is the kundalini awakening. Many people mistake their initial awareness of the spinal upward and downward flows to be a full kundalini awakening. It is for this reason that detachment and discrimination are so important on the spiritual path. It is easy to conjure up experiences that have attachment to this, or to desire the kundalini experience so much that any experience is mistaken for a kundalini awakening. This has lead to much confusion, it is wise to have one's experience verified by a qualified teacher, Guru, or other spiritual authority. As the true kundalini awakening is a rather rare event amongst the masses, the importance of consulting an authority cannot be underestimated. It is important to remember that the ancient sages have provided numerous texts and yoga systems for the sole purpose of preparing the mind and body for enlightenment.

The student should be prepared mentally, emotionally, spiritually, and the body systems should be prepared. Without proper preparation the kundalini experience can be a challenging event. If properly prepared the student is engaged in powerful spiritual transformation. A classic example exists for the importance of preparation. In the United States it has become common to see someone shake violently when the kundalini becomes awakened. While this might be common place, it is a serious warning sign that the subtle nervous system of *nadis*, chakras, and the physical nervous system has not been prepared for the increased energy released by the kundalini energy as it travels up the *sushumna* releasing energy via each chakra. With proper preparation using yoga, mantra, meditation, and guidance from a qualified teacher there is no such shaking. The lack of shaking indicates that the body had been fully prepared for the kundalini shakti. Few students are

---

8   The ancient name for what later became known as Hinduism. Literally meaning "eternal knowledge".

equipped or prepared to awaken the kundalini without training, though I have met some, clearly the preparatory work was completed in the previous life.

CHALLENGES OF KUNDALINI AWAKENING

Pre-requisite considerations for kundalini awakening would be the quality of the student. In the west, the common mentality is often, "I have some money, give me what I want, and now." This mentality actually can slow spiritual progress. Traits such as humility, grace, and qualities according to the *yamas* and *niyamas* should be cultivated within the student. While it is uncommon to find students that possess all of these qualities, the other practices of yoga can cultivate those qualities within the practitioner. In fact, this should become the primary role of yoga in western culture. Once the initial pre-requisites are met, to the degree required by the yogi, then one may proceed to the more disciplined practices.

The goals are quite simple and well defined within kundalini yoga:

1. Purification of the *nadis*. Purification of the three primary *nadis* should eventually lead to the purification of all remaining *nadis*, providing the appropriate lifestyle and activities are followed.

2. Purification of the chakras, in concert and resulting from purification of the *nadis*.

3. Strengthening of the subtle nervous system and glandular system.

4. Preparation of the aspirant on a psychological level for spiritual transformation.

5. *Sadhana*. The challenge for the average western student is to begin a strict *sadhana*[9]. While most students change their practice, within kundalini yoga, and numerous other systems, the key is to stay with a practice for a period of time. While the term *sadhana* is usually associated with Tantra yoga, it does appear within the Nath teachings and within the Vedantic tradition.

6. Proper direction of the kundalini flow. The kundalini energy can flow in one of four directions.

    a. It can flow downward, which can result in serious health and psychological issues.

    b. It can flow into the *Ida*, which can result in serious health and psychological issues.

---

9   Sadhana means discipline or disciplined practice.

     c.   It can flow into the *Pingala*, which can result in serious health and psychological issues.

     d.   It can flow upward through the *sushumna*. This is the only direction that one would want the kundalini to flow. All three other directions can result in serious problems on a mental, emotional, or physiological level.

Aside from the preparation required and noted here and in the previous section; once the kundalini has awakened, the real work begins. As the kundalini may initially only rise to the second, third, or other chakra, the student and teacher must evaluate how well the student physically and emotionally performed during and after this process. The kundalini may return to the dormant state after this, in which it would require additional work. Then work begins, if appropriate, to re-awaken the kundalini again. This process will repeat until the kundalini rises to the crown chakra (7th, Sahasrara). It is important to note that kundalini yoga should be practiced under the guidance of a master, yogi, or other qualified teacher.

KUNDALINI MANIFESTATION IN OTHER CULTURES

My first teacher taught me that the kundalini was practiced within the Egyptian systems. He would often reference the appearance of the serpent on their head-wear as an indicator of the mystical kundalini teachings within the Egyptian and ruling castes. This is not a difficult concept to grasp, considering the widespread impact of the Vedic culture. The Vedic culture was the dominant culture within the region as evidenced by seals being distributed in Mesopotamia and other areas. David Frawley, in several of his books, references that the Greeks referred their culture as coming from a great civilization to the east. While this could be called "Aryan", it is not the Aryans of the outdated Aryan invasion theory, but would likely be the Vedic culture. It is interesting to note that the Greeks had a serpent god known as Ophiucus, who was the god of medicine. The Greeks also had *dragon* the serpent of the cosmos, a concept that is shared with the Mayan civilization under a different name.

While in Palenque, Mexico, my first teacher would comment on the feathered headwear of the Mayans as a symbolic indication of the kundalini rising to the crown chakra. This illustrates the kundalini mystical connection in cultures separated by vast oceans and continues to strengthen the mystical aspect of the kundalini. In other words, truth will manifest in a variety of cultures under different names such as Kukulcan (the Maya plumed serpent god).

The Persians were strongly associated with the Vedic culture as well. This illustrates how information regarding the kundalini could easily travel across a vast region. The kundalini also appears within the earliest teachings of the Judaic tradition as the *Holy Spirit*. In ancient teachings pertaining to Abraham, he appears to have some degree of fear of the Holy Spirit, and referred to it as being painful, shaking, and other difficulties. Abraham often described it as descending down upon him and then a series of difficult physical experiences. This does follow the traditional *Sanatana Dharma* teachings, as the kundalini can appear initially to move downward before moving up. In fact, Abraham's story appears to be a kundalini awakening within someone that has not been properly prepared for the kundalini energy. In modern history, the Holy Spirit or Holy Ghost has become almost meaningless to most people, as people are moving away from the realm of the mystic.

CONCLUSION

For the modern day student, Kundalini yoga is a focused attempt to awaken the kundalini energies. Though this is often the goal of most yoga systems, kundalini yoga takes a more forward and direct stance toward this process. Different schools and systems place the kundalini techniques with Tantra, Hatha, and other yoga systems, though it is clearly represented within the *Vedas* and Vedic teachings. This makes the kundalini among the oldest recorded yoga teachings in the world, and possibly dating as old as 6500 BCE or older, depending on the date given to the *Rg Veda*. It is important to note that the current *Rg Veda* dates are most likely at the end of the Vedic culture and the core teachings would be considerably older.

The kundalini is not something to be feared, avoided, or misaligned. It is the transformational power of divinity that resides within each individual. It is an accelerated program of spiritual awakening, perception, and understanding. Each awakening of the kundalini is the equal of years of spiritual work through daily methods. The awakening of the kundalini is the journey of the seen perceiving the seer, as stated in the *Yoga Sutras of Patanjali*. While it should be given respect, as it is literally the power of creation, it is an attribute of our true nature.

Sources, references, and recommended reading:

Beal, Yogi Harinam Baba Prem Tom "Understanding the Kundalini" Universal Yoga www.floridavedicinstitute.com.

Beal, Yogi Harinam Baba Prem Tom "Qualities of a Student" www.floridavedicinstitute.com

Beal, Yogi Harinam Baba Prem Tom "Vrtra: The Spiritual Adversary" Vedic Friends Journal #1 http://www.vedicfriends.org/vfa_journal_and_newsletter.htm

Feuerstein, George "The Shambala Encyclopedia of Yoga" Shambala: Boston 1997

Frawley, David "Gods, Sages and Kings" Passage Press: Salt Lake City 1991

Frawley, David "The Rig Veda and the History of India" Aditya:Nw Delhi 2001

Feuerstein, Kak, Frawley "In Search of the Cradle of Civilization" Quest Books: Wheaton 2001

Kashyap, Dr. R.L "Rig Veda Samhita: First Ashtaka Vol. 1,2,3" Saksivc: Bangalore

Worthington, Vivian "A History of Yoga" Routledge & Kegan Paul: London 1982

Schuhmacher, Stephan et al "The Encyclopedia of Eastern Philosophy and Religion" Shambala:Boston 1994

Feuerstein, George "The Shambala Encyclopedia of Yoga" Shambala: Boston 1997

Web Pages:

www.vedanet.com

www.vedicfriends.org

www.floridavedicinstitute.com

Sanskrit texts:

Hatha Yoga Pradipika

Shiva Samhita

Gheranda Samhita

Rg Veda Samhita

Yoga Sutras of Patanjali

Transcendence Through Story
In the Age of Kaliyuga

Andy Fraenkel

Back in 1968, while attending college in New York City, I found a book in the college library of stories from the Vedic literature. It was an old, out of print book. I think there's something about the feel and the smell of an old book that unleashes the imagination and allows it to soar to exotic places. The illustrations in the book certainly helped arouse my curiosity. But one story especially started me on a journey which I continue to this day.

The story was an enchanting tale from the *Mahabharata* of King Yudhisthira and a faithful dog. Toward the end of his life, the king leaves his palace and worldly riches behind and journeys into the Himalayas. He is followed by the dog. Together they roam the barren wilds. One crisp morning a chariot drawn by four white horses descends from the sky. It is the chariot of Indra, the king of heaven and the lord of the rains and storms. Indra beckons Yudhisthira to board the chariot, explaining to him that his dear brothers are waiting for him at the gates of heaven. But the dog, being a lowly animal, is not allowed to go. The dog has been faithful to his master. Thus Yudhisthira declines heaven itself, refusing to leave this dear friend behind.

This simple story stirred a notion within my being. It seemed to encourage its reader to move in this world with a greater purpose than just for the desire to secure immediate comforts and pleasures. It spoke to me of an intelligence that would certainly be misspent if we used it to prosper at the expense and pain of others. Rather, life was to be lived as a sacrifice for a higher good and for the welfare of all sentient beings. A Vedic injunction declares; *sarva sukhena bhavantu*, may all beings be happy. I was struck by the message the story contained for me; that we should act with kindness to help all beings live a life of peace and wellness.

In college I majored in theater, and at the time a group of us theater students were selecting materials for a collection of one act plays to tour elementary schools. I worked the story into a script and the short piece became part of our program. I felt that this story would be a valuable addition to our repertoire. And indeed it was. In discussions with students afterwards, children wondered why dogs wouldn't be allowed into heaven; after all they have feelings like everybody else.

It was twelve years later when I heard about an upcoming Asian-Indian Drama Competition to be held at Columbia University. By then my interest in Vedic spirituality had been aroused enough for me to become a disciple of A.C. Bhaktivedanta Swami Prabhupada, the founder of the Krishna movement in the West. The *Mahabharata* had lead me to the *Bhagavad Gita*, the book's most famous section. And the search for a comprehensible version of that text had brought me to *Bhagavad Gita As It Is*, translated by Bhaktivedanta Swami.

To find a suitable topic for the drama competition I turned again to Yudhisthira and the *Mahabharata* for inspiration. I was especially intrigued by a chapter in the story wherein Yudhisthira observes ill omens throughout his kingdom. He sees relationships being corrupted, people beginning to cheat one another, and husbands and wives quarreling over trifles. He observes a change in weather patterns and in the behavior of birds and animals. He notices that time itself has somehow shifted out of place. These omens indicated the dawning of an ominous age, the Kaliyuga, wherein people will descend into confusion and madness. Our performance of "The Pandavas Retire Timely" struck a chord and we walked away with the first place award in the competition.

In the Vedic literature, the four great ages, or *yugas*, are described as Satyayuga, Dvaparayuga, Tretayuga, and Kaliyuga. These ages are compared to the seasons of the year. Like the seasons, the four great ages come and go, with each age having certain characteristics. The first age, Satyayuga, is likened to the springtime bursting with creative energy. In that age people have extraordinary powers and spiritual aptitudes. But in each successive age both their spiritual, intellectual and physical potency is diminished. By the last age of Kaliyuga (the present age of quarrel, hypocrisy and greed), these potencies have been practically exhausted. Like the winter, it is bleak and cold. Of course, after the winter of Kaliyuga, the spring comes back. Together, one cycle of the four *yugas*—these four 'seasons'—totals 4,320,000 years.

Five thousand years ago the sages of India gathered in Naimisaranya Forest to perform a sacrifice to ward off the ill effects of Kailyuga, which continues to weigh heavily upon us today. They understood that the future inhabitants of Kaliyuga would be short lived, misguided, overcome with anxiety, and lacking in spiritual wisdom. When the venerable Suta Goswami arrived, they all rose in respect.

In his great wisdom, Suta was conversant with all fields of knowledge. Thus the sages asked him to explain the essence of all knowledge for the benefit of future generations.

One of the stories Suta Goswami began with was the account of Yudhisthira observing the ill omens. Yudhisthira was the first to become painfully aware of the impending Kaliyuga. His heart trembled at the shrieks of the owls and crows. As the story unfolded, the sages at Naimisaranya listened with rapt attention. Suta continued to tell stories for he understood that the people in Kaliyuga would have little interest in philosophical understanding or in performing austerities and penance, which had been the means of *mukti*, or liberation, in previous *yugas*.

The literature of India, whether in the scriptural *Bhagavata Purana* or the historic epic *Mahabharata*, or the fables of the *Panchatantra*, unfold with stories within stories. A story is often told in response to a question. But it doesn't stop there. Within that story another point is raised which leads to another story. That story might tell of a discussion between two mystics wherein a third story is related. Stories take a detour and come around again to themselves. They arise and disappear only to be resolved much later.

It would be impossible to consider the philosophy and spirituality of India without entering into story. These stories are a vital part of the sacred culture and heritage of all mankind. Vyasadeva and Valmiki are the foremost of storytellers and poets of ancient India. Their epics of *Mahabharata* and *Ramayana* respectively are considered the "fifth *Veda*" and expound the timeless teaching of *Sanatana Dharma*.

The Vedic literature reveals a world full of stories for young and old alike. The stories are entertaining, thought provoking, and soul stirring. We encounter divine personalities, demigods, heroes, mystics, and other powerful beings involved in extraordinary conflicts, romances, tragedies and intrigues. These stories have endured for millennia because they reflect the longings of the human spirit. They have been, and still are, important sources of inspiration for dance, drama, puppetry, poetry, and music.

In India, when the shows of *Mahabharata* or the *Ramayana* are broadcast on television, everything stops. Teeming city streets are deserted. I've seen it. And I've experienced myself that when I tell these stories people have readily stopped to lend a receptive ear. It seems that Hindus have embraced the *Mahabharata* and the *Ramayana* to an extent that no other culture has embraced their stories. Indeed, the stories themselves are patiently waiting to be attended to, and, like wealthy donors, they offer both gifts and blessings to anyone who would speak them and listen to them.

In our present day culture we have perfected the craft of transmitting stories through various technologies in the form of print, radio, theater, movies, and the internet. But in spite of our outward appearance of sophistication and tech-nological wizardry, in this age we are plagued by rapidly diminishing powers of mental awareness and recall. The sages of India knew this all too well. They also understood that in essence religion is not so much about doctrine and ritual as it is about story. The former two emerge from the latter. The ancient cultures understood that the stories themselves are a technology containing within them components of understanding the world around us. Stories hold people together, be it in the form of a family, a community, a street gang, a nation, or a religious tradition.

The Vedic culture, when stripped to its very core focuses on three things: creating a sacred space, awaking our sacred consciousness, and seeing the sacred in everything around us. A sacred space could obviously be a church, temple or mosque. One could also create a sacred environment in one's own home. However, the sacred, or transcendence, is not limited to a particular place or a particular building. Since time immemorial the sages have practiced the art of evoking tran-scendence. They understood that everything stemming from transcendence and connected to transcendence also induces the same transcendental atmosphere. So it is possible to take any empty space and transform it into a sacred space if you know the art.

By the use of sound vibration, either through mantra or chanting, or by *Katha*, the sharing of sacred stories and wisdom, the sages were able to evoke a healing, sacred atmosphere. At Naimisaranya Forest, Suta Goswami told the sacred stories describing the mysterious ways and manifestations of the Supreme Lord and the Lord's devotees. After Suta Goswami spoke of Yudhisthira, he told the story of Yudhisthira's grandson Maharaja Praksit, how he was cursed and of his ultimate encounter with the wandering mendicant Sukadev.

The wisdom of India has for millennia confirmed that the first sense a child develops within the mother's womb is the sense of hearing. Suta Goswami describes that while still in the womb, Sukadev had heard his father Vyasadeva giving discourses on the perilous nature of the material world. Thus, the child refused to emerge from his mother's womb for almost sixteen years. When he did come out, he immediately left home to avoid the attachments and comforts of family life since they lead to further entanglement in this world. Sukadev wan-dered into the forest with his father pursuing him, pleading with him to stay at home. Sukadev, feeling for his father, created an interactive hologram of himself. Taking the hologram to be his real son, Vyasadeva took it back home to stay with him and his wife.

King Praksit had been cursed to die by a brahmana boy when he inadvertently offended the boy's father. The king had been hunting in the forest when he grew tired and thirsty. He approached the dwelling of a brahmana, requesting water.

But the brahmana was deep in meditation and was unaware of his royal visitor. On being ignored, the king's anger flared up. In a mock gesture of respect, he garlanded the brahmana with a dead snake that was lying nearby. Upon seeing the snake around his father, the boy cursed the king to die of snakebite. Then the king became saddened that he had allowed himself to become angry at the brahmana. But the king accepted his fate. After placing his own son on the throne, Praksit renounced his kingdom and proceeded to the bank of the Ganges River. There, numerous sages and mendicants gathered in his support as he awaited death.

People especially love to hear about the triumphs, tragedies and follies of royalty, of the rich and famous, of politicians, baseball players, movie stars, and, if nothing else, then about the people next door. In this world there are unending topics of conversation and gossip. The sages tell us that the tongue is the most uncontrollable of all the senses. No one can stop talking for very long. But what is the result of all this talking? Often, we form stale patterns of thought and become trapped by a distorted view of ourselves and the world around us. The tongue is credited for creating a network of paths leading to death. Just like the croaking frog attracts the snake to come and devour it, so our time is consumed and our life energy is devoured by the trite and hollow subject matters of our myriad discussions.

Striving to transcend the limitations of speech and the raging of the false ego, mystics sometimes take a vow of silence. However, the Vedic science of self-realization uses speech and story, which would normally entangle us, as an aid to transform the consciousness. This is done by replacing mundane stories with transcendental stories. Thus in Kaliyuga, the stories that are especially of the *Mahabharata, Ramayana* and *Bhagavata Purana* are meant to direct and focus our consciousness on transcendence. The sages of India warn us not to think of these stories as ordinary or being from some fanciful imagination.

Some Vedanta scholars, however, will say that these literatures are not part of the *Vedas*, such as the *Rig, Sama, Atharva*, or *Yajur*. But still, the *Puranas, Mahabharata* and *Ramayana* are considered by the sages as the fifth *Veda* since they are actually vessels which contain all the Vedic wisdom for the people living in Kaliyuga. These literatures help us to more easily grasp and retain this knowledge. The stories offer us another important ingredient that the dry, philosophical and ritualistic *Vedas* don't offer—that is an emotional context. We can identify with the experiences of the persons in the story. We can see our own stories, our own struggles, and our own fears and hopes reflected in these timeless tales.

In his wanderings, Sukadev came to the spot by the Ganges River where Praksit and the sages gathered. The sages observed from his demeanor that the youth was an enlightened soul. Praksit inquired from Sukadev as to the purpose of life. The king also inquired as to how one should prepare for death. Sukadev revealed the eternal truths through stories. These sacred stories comprise the *Bhagavata*

Purana. The stories Sukadev told were of ancient kings, wandering mendicants, wild men, demigods, and of the Supreme Lord Within the Heart.

One story is of Lord Brahma at the dawn of time, awaking to a world of void and darkness. There is the story of Ajamil who, at the time of death, is confronted by hideous creatures waiting to drag him to hell. Another story tells of King Yayati who pleaded with his sons to give him their youth when the king was cursed to become very old. And, of course, in the tenth canto of the *Bhagavata*, the stories of Lord Krishna.

The sages had gathered at Naimisaranya Forest for a thousand year sacrifice of prayer and chanting of sacred mantras. Kaliyuga was upon them. Suta Goswami told them the very stories that Sukadev had shared with Maharaj Praksit. Here again, they resorted to story as the soothing balm for this troubled age. The sages concluded that no one can become free from the horrendous affects of Kaliyuga without hearing the pastimes and adventures of the wondrous activities of the Supreme Lord. There is a most definite science and technology at play here. In the Vedic stories the divine is revealed in magnificent transparency. The stories are a window into the spiritual realm.

In 1986, the theater community was buzzing with news that the director Peter Brook was bringing his staged drama of the *Mahabharata* to America the following year. The production had an international cast of close to forty actors and musicians and ran nine hours. Leonard Jones (Lokamangala Das), my long time friend and drama collaborator, and I decided to expand our one act piece of Yudhisthira, which we had performed several years earlier for the drama competition, into a full length drama of *Mahabharata*. Theater people and critics who were familiar with the Brook production could not believe that the two of us, playing multiple characters, would attempt to stage the same story.

In an interview, Brook compared the *Mahabharata* to the entirety of Shakespeare's works. The *Mahabharata* itself explains that whatever is not in its pages is found nowhere else. We find stories of abandonment, intrigue, betrayal, war, and love. One of the principal persons of *Mahabharata* is Yudhisthira's brother, the warrior prince Arjuna. Arjuna becomes overwhelmed and confused at the onset of a great battle. He wants to run away from his dilemma and retreat to the forest to live in solitude. In his confusion and doubt, Arjuna is each one of us at sometime in our lives. Lord Krishna reveals to him the eternal wisdom in the form of *Bhagavat Gita*, the song of God.

What made our production work is that we broke down the fourth wall, which, in theatre, separates the actors from the audience. This is one of the main distinctions between live theater and storytelling. In a staged drama the actors ignore the audience. In telling a story, the storyteller acknowledges the audience and speaks directly to them. In our performance we combined the role of actor and storyteller. As storytellers we connected each scene with ample narrative, and also reverted to the role of storyteller within some of the scenes themselves. For centuries in India the actor and storyteller have shared the stage together.

One critic wrote of our performance that "it is nothing short of amazing that Fraenkel and Jones would attempt a Mahabharata told by two actors in under two hours…Scenes of spectacle are done with narration, yet they tell these stories in such a way that one can 'see' the scene as if it were staged…the best thing about their Mahabharata is that so many things that could go wrong with it do not."

We toured with the *Mahabharata* for fours years. In the 1990s I came full circle by bringing the story of Yudhisthira and the dog back to the schools. In this recent incarnation I offer it as a dramatic, solo storytelling piece, along with other accounts from the *Mahabharata*. When Yudhisthira chooses the dog over heaven, the dog reveals his real identity to him. It is not an ordinary dog at all, but Yudhisthira's celestial father Dharmaraj in disguise. The celestial had come to test Yudhisthira's forbearance and compassion. In the end, they board the chariot together.

When we truly listen, the sacred stories flood into our hearts to cleanse it of all misgiving, anger, fear and illusion. Transcendental vibration breaks apart these shackles that bind us and keep us apart from the Lord Within the Heart and the creation itself. We, as Yudhisthira, are held accountable for our actions toward all creatures. We cannot act whimsically even in our dealings with a dog, what to speak of Mother Earth or our fellow human beings. We have to answer to the celestials, to the ancestors, to future generations, and ultimately to that Divine Transcendent Personality residing as witness within the core of our hearts. Through the transcendental vibration of the Lord's name and activities, we acquire illumination, understanding, and happiness. And, as if coming out of a deep slumber, we gradually awaken to our true eternal nature.

Yoga and Cooking

George Vutetakis

THE ROOTS OF CIVILIZATION

Civilization can be defined as a culture based on traditions. It is appreciation for these traditions, rooted in fore bearers, that drives the creativity to excel. Whether a continuance or rejection, recognition of the power of tradition drives society to adapt and evolve.

One of the impressive aspects of East Indian culture is found throughout history. Indian culture enjoys an unbroken succession dating to the earliest findings of civilized man. Traditions, based on the *Vedas*, have been continuous, never conquered or usurped over millennia. According to many in India today, there are numerous temples where the shrines date back thousands of years and, in a few cases, millions of years. This is the culture that has been the heart of vegetarianism in the world and has given us Yoga, a proven method for physically fine tuning the body. From this point of view, the body is a vehicle for spiritual understanding. A vegetarian diet tunes the power train of the body to create a smooth ride into the spiritual realm. It helps to clear the path, removing blockage from karma and material attachment fostered by carnivorous behavior.

Ancient Indian civilization cut a broad swath into Afghanistan and parts of Persia and modern day Turkey. It had a huge influence on other cultures through trade and thought. We cannot underestimate the effect India had on our Mediterranean civilized roots. Ancient Mediterranean societies up to the first third of the previous millennium were very similar to Indian culture at the time. Religious rites and the consumption of meat only through sacrifice had continuity throughout the ancient world. Mythic tales of Gilgamesh from Babylon and Hercules from Greece had precise parallels in the Aukshohini warriors in the *Vedas*, especially in the *Mahabharata*.

46

The Persian Zoroastrian religion is an offshoot of the *Vedas*. Their main book, entitled "Avesta" is in a dialect of Sanskrit (language of the *Vedas*) and describes deities and worship in Vedic terms, even with the same names. Xerxes, the name adopted by a few Persian emperors, (Xerxes of Hellenic war fame and Artaxerxes defeated by Alexander the Great) is pronounced Kshatra in ancient Persian. Kshatriyas were the ancient warrior class of kings and heroes from the *Vedas*. Trade over the sea and through the land connected people in ancient times. Cinnamon, sandalwood, cashews, peppercorns and sugarcane all came from India and were integrated as part of daily culture in the Mediterranean region. It is said that classical Greece, where many of our cultural ideals stem from, was an eastern culture that spawned our western thought. India similarly created the foundations for our western views of vegetarianism, with many of the derogatory carnivorous clichés originating in the Darwinian justified racism and self proclaimed superiority of the British Raj.

EFFECTING CHANGE WITH FOOD

Political, religious, philosophical and social movements are normally viewed as the powers that change the world, for better or worse. Food has an unsung power, one that can affect the heart and soul of the individual as well as the community and the generations to follow.

Feeding hungry people is an obvious power. In India, it is said a person cannot think about spiritual issues while hungry. The traditional temples distribute food freely. In the fifties and sixties the communists distributed food to successfully gain power in Bengal and other places. By filling the stomachs of the masses, organizations have gained power and influence over the public.

Food changes people on a molecular level. It is the constant nurturing function in our lives. This is also how food and yoga are linked.

PRINCIPLES OF CULINARY YOGA

The first premise of Vedic thought is that we are not the body. We reside in the body, which is a gift (a direct result of our karmic journey) to be used for spiritual progress, or further entanglement if we choose. Between our body, mind and spirit, everything needed to attain the goal of spiritual perfection is at hand.

Normally the word perfection means without fault, or at least beyond mistakes. The Yogic perfection is not an aloof, ego-defined goal. The result of Yoga is to be in harmony with the cosmos, to work with that which is already defined.

The *Bhagavad Gita* explains the results of an egocentric identity of which the culminating actions further entangle the entity in the "Labrynthian Knot" of material existence. The *Gita* explains: "Lust, greed and anger are the three gates leading to hell". As defined in the *Vedas*, hell is not necessarily a specific place, but can also be a state of being. The *Gita* spends considerable effort explaining the nature of this world and the options available to go beyond the cycles of birth and death. In conclusion, the *Gita* says that dedication of all actions, thoughts and things we do should be done for a spiritual purpose. Spiritual is defined as anything to do with God.

The tongue is described as "the most voracious and difficult to control" of all the senses. Speech and the urge to eat combine to pull us in directions that the intelligence normally would not even consider. The urge to eat is tied to our gut emotions, our innermost thoughts and desires. A combination of perception, taste and smell create illusions of need, otherwise known as cravings. These cravings are fueled by lust and greed with a result of anger when a threat of lack of fulfillment is present. From the Yoga viewpoint, controlling the tongue is a major achievement. This is not done through abstinence, but through moderation. Hand in hand with common sense, the reason for eating is given perspective. In Bhakti Yoga, and most other forms of Yoga, the concept of *Prasada* is embraced. By offering the food to God first, the cooking and eating become part of the heavenly domain, and turns the food into *prasada*, or something sacred. Traditionally a Yogi will only consume enough to "keep body and soul together". However, when a person deals with stress and does physical labor, the amount of food needed increases. Judgments are made on a practical time and circumstantial basis. Extremes are not good and the positive swing of the pendulum is viewed the same as the negative. Attraction is the same as repulsion. The world is full of dualities. A Yogic goal is to find the "sweet spot", the place of balance. According to the *Vedas* this can only be attained with help from the spiritual energy. The mode of goodness (*sattva*) is not enough on its own, but can be a steppingstone or even a catalyst to reach the sweet spot.

True detachment is reached through a positive change in direction, not by denial. When the benefits are understood, we want to redirect the emphasis in our lives. This way we do not have to give up perceived comforts to enhance life through Yoga. We add Yoga, and through an organic process life improves.

SENSUALITY AND INDULGENCE

A good cook or a chef becomes a master interpreter of the common threads of cooking. Through intuitive understanding of the alchemy of ingredients, the cook masterfully combines ingredients to create sensational sensory experiences which add to life on many levels. The foremost of which is nourishment for the body, mind and spirit. This natural ability can mistakenly be thought to belong to us, thus creating ego and a blockage to true nurturing and healing cuisine. To have continuous success, the cook must be able to interpret the flavors, techniques and vital energy in the food.

When the cooks are in their element, it seems as though caution is thrown to the wind. But in reality, they are in a groove, moving in an inspired orchestration which becomes a vision of sight, sound, aroma and anticipation. This is the theater of food: A production that has been natural and fulfilling since time immemorial. To get there and to share it with others is one of the secrets to longevity and enjoyment in life.

These days, those who can cook like this are rare. They develop followings in their community and social environ. The power of the culinary flame has made people famous, influenced the course of history and changed the lives of many people. Culinary experiences have inspired the best of artists. Some of us owe our most innate happiness to a few great meals.

THE MAGIC OF FOOD

As the meal is prepared a symphony of sensual experiences come together with a rhythm and meter relevant to heat and the unique chemistry of ingredients. It is a wonderful dance, a sensuous ballet that builds to the finale as the food pirouettes on the tongue. Encore performances come with each course and the satiated palate rests in a sweet slumber. Similar to a wonderful massage, we wallow in a vitalized state of caresses and enthusiasm. This is the magic of food, which leads to its strong effect on our consciousness. And affecting our consciousness is a major goal of Yoga. Thus, the link between cooking and Yoga.

COOKING AS YOGA

For most of us, Yoga is a form of exercise that originates in India. Like acupuncture from China, western science has found and documented many benefits in the physical and psychological fields. After spending years studying Yoga, Vedic history and modern application, I have learned that Yoga encompasses much more than a physical and psychological regimen. Historically, the practice has been intimately connected with religion. After all, the Sanskrit word Yoga means "to link with the absolute". The premise being if we are able to connect with and understand the absolute, all aspects of life fall into place.

If only life was so easy. The traditions are vast and well documented. On a visit to the University of Chicago library, aisle upon aisle of Sanskrit volumes may be seen. Many Indian schools with different approaches and views are based on these Vedic Yoga traditions. The tradition of finding a teacher, or Guru, is the preferred method of understanding because it is difficult to place the volumes of information into perspective without a trained view of one who has practiced for years. This is much like the apprentice traditions in the guilds of old Europe.

In my own experience, it took years of practice under the tutelage of a Guru, along with the association of many *saddhus*, to open an innate understanding and to enable me to apply the principles daily and in a natural way. This experience helped to balance my background, heritage and religiosity. Most important, with the training in method and perspective, I was able to focus on and achieve goals that were in tune with my ideals.

This may sound like spiritual rhetoric and fluff to some. It would have to me. What Yoga has to offer that is beyond the floral speech and verbal mumbo jumbo is a well laid out practical application. Founded on thousands of years of study of the laws of nature, step by step the practices allow the student to become attuned to existing energies to create balance. The rhythm of the cosmos works under the laws of physics and metaphysics in cycles of action and reaction. Gaining insight about the nature of these cycles allows the practitioner to balance life with the help of earth's energies. The physical, emotional and spiritual synchronize to allow the person to function in harmony with nature and to gain perspective of humanity in relation to nature. Without this consideration we attempt to manipulate the energies and matter of the world to fit needs defined by limited vision. This creates a chain reaction that, in the long term, spirals out of control. The result is disconnection, lack of humanity and environmental crises.

Nourishment, and the cooking that enables it, is central to all ancient medicinal and cultural regimens. Hippocratic, Ayurvedic, Chinese, Buddhist, Tibetan, African, Native American and old European traditions utilize food as a primary healing tool. Just as genetic pre-disposition and the external environment affects us, the internal environment is determined by what is placed in it. Nourishment provided by food and how we eat it, is one of the most important things we can do to enhance health and quality of life. Yogic cooking as defined by the Ayurveda, has specific guidelines and principles to follow. For specific problems, illnesses and for those who strictly pursue a Yoga practice, it is recommended to consult an Ayurvedic physician. Currently, Ayurveda is one of the fastest growing alternative medical practices in the west. Many practitioners are available. I suggest doing a search on the internet for "Ayurveda" along with the name of your locale. For our purposes, Yogic principles may be applied to everyday cooking and lifestyle. Even with a simple approach many find that life is enhanced and the food has greater regenerative qualities. Incorporating Yoga relieves stress, helps us to see a bigger picture and enhances the ability to nurture.

The goal is to achieve a state of harmony and balance with daily life. Yoga removes stress and distractions allowing the practitioner to focus on living for the moment within the framework of life's goals. Since Yoga is based on natural laws, incorporating its principles works with any philosophy of life or religion. Historically, various principles of Yoga can be found in cultures throughout the world.

Physically, through *hatha* and *pranayam*, the Yogic practitioner seeks to center the body's energy in the higher chakra regions at the heart or above. There are seven chakras corresponding to the different energy centers in the body. The physical adjustments of *hatha* and the corresponding control of the breath refine the body's functions like a fine tuned race car. Fuel type and quality also make a tremendous difference along with the quality of the track one races on. Thus, a fine-tuned diet and the environment around us can make a difference in the quality of life. It helps us to live through the heart and intelligence, beyond the scatological and gut levels. As the practice of Yoga becomes incorporated into a daily life, we can see the subtle difference how each food affects the equilibrium of the body. For this reason, advanced Yoga students do not consume onions and garlic. They are *rajarsic* (in the mode of passion) and tend to lower the chakra energy to base levels. On the other hand, the Ayurveda uses them medicinally because of their stimulating and cleansing nature. Balance is the goal, thus too much in any direction is not productive. This is also why Yogis do not consume a high protein diet. Vegetarian protein options are used carefully because of the stress created in the digestive system. Complex carbohydrates aid the body's assimilation of protein so they are served together. The issue is absorption by the body and quality, not quantity.

What follows is a basic guideline for applying Yoga to cooking. While these practices may be applied to just the time of cooking, the best results will be derived from incorporating them into daily life. I only provide a brief synopsis here.

According to the *Vedas*, there are three basic modes of material nature: Goodness (*sattvic*), Passion (*rajarsic*) and Ignorance (*tamasic*). The ancient text of the *Bhagavad Gita* describes food in these three modes: "Foods in the mode of goodness increase the duration of life, purify one's existence and give strength, health, happiness and satisfaction. Such nourishing foods are sweet, juicy, fatty and palatable. Foods that are too bitter, too sour, salty, pungent, dry and hot, are liked by people in the modes of passion. Such foods cause pain, distress, and disease. Food cooked more than three hours before being eaten, which is tasteless, stale, putrid, decomposed and unclean, is food liked by people in the mode of ignorance." (*Bhagavad Gita*, Chapter 17, texts 8-10)

This is a good general outline for creating a balanced diet. The goal is to live in the *sattvic* mode, which is compatible with spiritual pursuits. *Rajarsic* foods, not to be confused with passion for life, are used in small quantities to balance the meal. They also may be used for healing purposes to stimulate weak areas and systems of the body. *Tamasic* foods, as can be seen from this description, are to be generally avoided. Since the *Bhagavad-gita* was written thousands of years ago, refrigeration and freezing were not considered. So the ideal is to cook with fresh foods only. This is the same ideal as Italian and French cooking (as well as most other traditional cuisines). Refrigeration slows the aging process, but does not stop it.

Meat is considered *tamasic*. This is from the digestive as well as the karmic implication of consuming items that are high on the food chain. From a Vedic point of view, some people may consume meat from different forms of sacrifice that are rarely practiced anymore. In all circumstances, meat from pleasure hunting and slaughterhouses is karmically poisonous and morally unforgivable. As a basic guideline, it is only consumed in life or death scenarios where no other food is available.

The *Vedas* also hold cows' milk in high regard. It is considered *sattvic* and called *amrit* or nectar. The cow is respected as a mother who shares her milk. The relationship between cows and humans is respectful and loving. This kind of milk, however, is only vaguely related to what we presently see on the grocery shelves. Modern dairy farmers term commercially produced milk as "monkey puke". Through the stress of not seeing the outdoors, with the addition of hormones, antibiotics, pesticide residues, homogenization and high temperature pasteurization, modern, store bought milk contains a different texture, nutritional balance and overall experience. The dairy industry in this country is also closely related to the slaughterhouse industry. Unfortunately, it is not economically feasible for most well meaning dairy farmers to maintain the cows after milking age. The cows and bulls (because we have no modern use for oxen) are sold to the meat packing plants. Without doing an "Upton Sinclair" kind of approach, it is safe to say (unfortunately) that to purchase commercial milk is to support the methodical slaughter of animals.

PERSPECTIVE

The benefits of applying yogic principles to cooking are increased health and vitality, a connection with the bounty of the earth and the enhanced ability to share with others. The first step is to determine for whom you are cooking. When we are disconnected spiritually, the purpose of cooking tends to be selfish. Like a drowning person only interested in our own breath, we do not think of others. The *Vedas* describe that we should not prepare food for ourselves, but should cook as if we are cooking for a king. The respect, honor and appreciation for what the food is should be constant. So the mind should be focused on the preparation, not on enjoying the preparation. The process itself is a joy and when we do it for others, we have a greater sensitivity to the nuances as well as being more careful while we work.

One French chef I met at a demonstration in Washington D.C. described to me that he never tastes the food. "A good chef should even be able to smell if the salt is right. A chef does not cook for himself."

SADDHANA

To help support the goals of Yoga, Saddhana is practiced. Saddhana includes the day to day rituals or sacred acts which are dedicated to regaining our spiritual nature and become a demonstration of sincerity to the cosmos while, in a practical sense, making Yoga second nature.

BREATH

Prana means life force. The practice of controlling breath is called *pranayama*. According to Yogic traditions, the life force resides in the breath. When we die, the life force leaves with the breath. If there is anything important in the body that should be identified with, it is the breath. Awareness of breathing is the first step. It is not easy to remember as we are always breathing in the background. Breathing should be smooth and full. Different body types breathe at different speeds, but during meditative moments, practicing slow deep breaths in and out through the nose helps us to be aware.

Many times we stop breathing to focus or to do something strenuous. Sometimes this stopping becomes a habit. With practice, awareness of our breath allows us to continue breathing during any activity. This reduces stress, allowing the body to function at an even keel.

COOKING MEDITATION

The Vaishnava culinary traditions in India are rich and colorful. Everything is cooked for God, offered to Him first, then served to people as *prasada* (the Lord's mercy), much like the host in the church. The difference is that all the food that Vaishnavas consume is *prasada*. A vivid example is the Sri Nathji temple in Nathdwar. The entire town centers around the temple. Pilgrims come from all over India to visit and special festivals are held a few times a year. The biggest one is the Annakuta ceremony which celebrates the story of Krishna lifting Govardhan Hill over the Vrndavan residents to protect them from torrential rains. The tradition is to build a mountain of *prasada* and to distribute it to the masses of pilgrims. They cook many metric tons of rice, enough for a hill that is 40 feet long and 10 feet high. Hundreds of thousands of people visit and partake of the *prasada*. It is an amazing sight that echoes in Vaishnava temples around the world. This kind of cooking, offering to the Lord and then sharing with the public is seen as a process of spiritual self-realization itself. The story of Nrsinganandana das bramhacari in the *Chaitanya Charitamrita* of Krishna Das Kaviraj (16th Century) helps to illuminate these traditions while demonstrating the power of meditative thought.

CLEANLINESS

"Cleanliness is next to Godliness" is apropos for the Yogic approach to cooking. The first step is personal hygiene. It is best to be freshly bathed before cooking. For this reason, Brahmins in India bathe three times a day. Of course, this is not always practical. The clothes should be at least clean that day, wash the hands, rinse the mouth and, in India (or if barefoot), wash the feet.

The kitchen should be free of as much clutter as possible. All the food surfaces should be freshly washed. Make sure there is an area that is dedicated to only washed foods and clean utensils.

Basic foodservice sanitation should apply. The most important is to treat hands like a surgeons hands. Be careful not to touch unclean surfaces, including clothes and face, without cleansing the hands before touching anything else. This helps to prevent cross-contamination. Another thing to consider is temperature. The general guideline is that it takes 2 to 4 hours for bacteria to start growing in an environment between 45 degrees and 140 degrees. If the intent is to leave something out longer, keep it under 45 degrees or over 140 degrees Fahrenheit.

TASTE

The kitchen is part of an altar to life. Keep this in mind and do not nibble. We are not the first to taste the results of the cooking, especially when we are cooking to offer the food first to God, and then in this way allow the food to become *prasada*, spiritual food.

TOUCH

Knives should be sharp as most accidents occur with dull knives. Rinse all vegetables with water before peeling. The principle is that water cleanses in more ways than washing dirt off. As is done in India, when ancient pilgrims would arrive at the Greek sanctuaries like Delphi, they would first cleanse themselves and their offerings with water. As in Indian Temples, a water supply was situated near the entrance to the sacred area.

SOUND

According to the *Vedas*, along with Pythagoras' Harmony of the Spheres and other ancient references, sound is the original element in the universe. From the vibration, movement is created. This set into motion the original creation (and makes sense whether one believes in the Big Bang or Creationism). The *Vedas* describe the sense of hearing as a direct connection to intelligence and the soul. The *Vedas* also prescribe Mantras (specific chants) to create a spiritual resonance to affect change in matter, and to connect with the energies of the cosmos. Sound is very important. We can see that music affects us in different ways, creating moods from exhilaration to apathetic aggressions. The sounds of the kitchen environment do the same. I prefer silence. If there is music, meditative or mild uptempo Jazz, Latin or World music is great. Devotional Indian *bhajans* also help set a more spiritual mood and atmosphere.

SIGHT

A clutter free kitchen that has uplifting colors and a well-lit work space is a pleasure to cook in. Consulting a Feng Shui reference or a Vedic Vastu Shastra reference can help for understanding the subtle psychological effects of placement and colors. The kitchen should be laid out for ease of use with a workspace next to the stove and a clear area to cleanse and prep. A trash receptacle and/or a bowl for compost should be readily available. As a matter of principle, do not eat in the same bowls and pans used for cooking.

AROMA

Often overlooked, but definitely noticed, the sense of smell is one of the most important when it comes to cooking. Conflicting scents in the kitchen should be avoided. Here is a list of offending scents: Mold, decomposing garbage, old food, scented candles, heavy chemicals like bleach and, especially, personal perfumes. Other scents enhance the culinary adventure: Fresh herbs like rosemary, basil, cilantro and thyme, open windows that allow the breeze to carry the scent of burning wood or the earth after a fresh rain, unscented beeswax candles and exotic aromas of a spice cabinet. Because seventy percent of taste is smell, the environment should be mostly neutral. The cooking process itself is full of aromas that keep us in touch with the cooking while enticing us to take it to the next step. Distracting scents sometimes remove us from the cooking flow, thus creating disconnected cuisine.

THE SIXTH SENSE

An ancient concept that has continued to this day in the Balkans, Mideast and Asia is the Evil Eye. The premise is that what other people think can effect us physically. Thinking negative thoughts can make people ill, cause calamity or worse. On a more tangible level, we see how some people are infectious with their great personality and others seem to spread negativity wherever they go. While people aspire to be around the former, they tend to cower and hide from the latter. The same principles apply to cooking. As a cook, we become responsible for the welfare of whoever consumes our fare. Food will resonate with the level of craft as well as the state of emotion and consciousness of the cook, which enters the food. This sometimes overcomes the earth's energy already in the food. Then whoever eats the food is also affected by the state of mind of the cook. Then one's consciousness can also become more positive or negative after eating the food. To complete the point, just as the French cook never allows the pot to stop cooking, no matter the ingredient added, so the good cook never allows the energy of the food to diminish, while the energy that is added enhances the final experience.

Furthermore, the body is a marvel of biological engineering that contains an electrical field, manufacturing, recycling and a power plant averaging 11,000 BTUs of heat. The same way these industries can effect the environment around us, our own body and mind can create change in a similar fashion. Physical sciences, both gross and subtle, are in play when we cook. Yoga helps us to get in touch with our subtle energies, the ones that become intangible to us on a daily basis. The result is the ability to consciously project (hopefully good) energy through our activities. Cooking becomes expression that nurtures and enhances life in longevity and quality. It bypasses stress by reaching to the core of the emotional state, spiritual identity as well as physical being. It can create fluidity where the stress normally creates blockage. That is why daily routine (*sadhana*) is recommended. Practice makes perfect and the more natural our actions are, the more fluid the results. When water flows without hindrance, the volume increases exponentially. Similarly, working with existing forces of nature is less stressful, therefore the food we prepare becomes packed with life giving, healing energy.

SPIRITUALITY

The first premise of spirituality in the *Vedas* is that we, the life force, are not the body. We reside in the body and it is a tool for attaining spiritual goals. For this reason, and for others not critical to our point, it is important to respect and take care of the body. It is a fine tuned marvel that responds to regular maintenance and attention. We reside in it temporarily, so it becomes important to take advantage of our stay.

Awareness goes hand in hand with attention to details. Sometimes we see that spirituality is substituted for responsibility in this world. It is used as an excuse to act beyond the laws of nature and the land. Thus basic issues of humanity are overlooked and food becomes just another unfortunate necessity. Enjoyment of food becomes a selfish act instead of a celebration of life.

The Yogic process utilizes food that is prepared in harmony with nature and with an appreciation for the source of the food. This appreciation is built into the cooking process so that the result is a "spiritualized" food (*prasada*) for the body and soul. Cooking, consuming and sharing *prasada* is listed as one of the processes for spiritual realization.

LOVE AND YOGA

Since Yoga and love affects our innermost being and identity, along with our physical vitality, love is entwined in every aspect. The basic concept of living in harmony with the natural laws of this world is about happiness and comfort. Sometimes the comparison is made between a fish in the water or out of it. In our lives, lack of stress along with a solid identity is synonymous with happiness. The next step is humility and selflessness, which allows us to share happiness without expectation. This is love or *Bhakti*, acts of devotion It is accomplished through generosity from the respect and appreciation for other beings recognized as parts of God.

APPLYING BHAKTI YOGA

Unlike other types of Yoga, Bhakti is incorporated on a daily basis and in every type of activity we perform. When practiced in addition to other forms of Yoga, Bhakti helps to give perspective and a way of interacting in the world with spiritual meaning. Srila Rupa Goswami describes six kinds of activities: "Offering gifts in charity, accepting charitable gifts, revealing one's mind in confidence, inquiring confidentially, accepting *prasada* and offering *prasada* are the six symptoms of love (*priti*) shared between *bhaktas* [those who practice Bhakti]." (*Upadeshamrita*, text 4, 16th century India). "Even in ordinary social activities, these six types of dealings between two loving friends are absolutely necessary…whenever there is dealing of *priti*, or love in intimate dealings, these six activities are executed." (A. C. Bhaktivedanta Swami, *The Nectar of Instruction*) These are basic principles of human interaction and etiquette. In ordinary dealings, they are the markings of a civil society. With a spiritual perspective, they are the hallmark of those who understand their relation to humanity and the earth we reside upon.

CHARITY

Giving to others recognizes that they deserve the same as us. It is a statement of human equality and a way of detaching ourselves from our external labors. Giving up something that is dear to us (like wealth) is also a recognition that we come and go in this world without our possessions. Giving to others, especially those who cannot help themselves, is an activity that works with the karmic laws to return the positive action of a charitable gift in many ways. The most tangible is the goodwill and respect of others.

ACCEPTING CHARITY

Many of us are good at giving. Not all of us are good at accepting gifts. The giving and receiving of charity is a selfless activity. When it is done as a method of furthering economic status, control over others or greed, the positive nature of the activity is counteracted. In traditional cultures the giving and receiving of gifts is an important part of the social exchange and is, most effectively, carried out in a humble and unpretentious manner. With Yoga, this exchange is part of the respect for the link with the higher energies of this world. It is about being part of the world, not about the world revolving around us. This is an important element in traditional cultures.

REVEALING ONE'S MIND

This is about honesty and being real. Living in the present while respecting the past and working toward the future is a noble approach. Honesty is always the best policy. It is listed here to emphasize the importance of sharing openly with those of like minds. Other parts of the Vedic works describe how we should be careful not to share too much with those who do not appreciate or understand. In simple terms, basic communication should be open, but we do not want to be boring or misunderstood.

INQUIRING CONFIDENTIALITY

The context of this instruction relates to those who are able to reveal the mind. Like the giving and accepting of charity, communication is a two way street. In India there is a saying "All Gurus are One." This is because there is consistency in the teachings. Other people on a spiritual journey are seen as potential *shiksa* (instructional) gurus. Since ultimately everyone is here for their spiritual journey, all people are respected for their spiritual potential. In Bengal a saying goes, "Instructions should be accepted from anyone, as long as they are true". The difficult part is to understand when they are true. The *Bhagavad Gita* says "The wise sage sees everyone as a spiritual soul". While we are all equals on the spiritual level, everyone has an individual relation to the spiritual. Keeping the *achintya beda beda tattva* principle in mind ("simultaneously one and different") while equals, we must be discerning about how we act and communicate. This is why one seeks out a guru (spiritual teacher). Historically an apprentice relationship is a confidential, or intimate, method of learning. By being in the presence of a teacher, it is easier to learn the mindset and approach. This especially holds true for cooking.

ACCEPTING AND OFFERING PRASADA

Like charity and communication, the sharing of food is a bi-directional endeavor. *Prasada* means mercy. It is foodstuff prepared for a higher cause. Like charity and communication, the result of such action is the food becoming mercy. In India, the food is offered to the deity of God. What is considered the most important part of this ceremony is the selfless sacrifice of cooking for God and the etiquette of not eating before honored personalities. Since God is seen as being within everyone and even within each atom, all food is first offered to God. This is similar to the prayers of other religions (like Christian grace) before a meal. The humble recognition that we are only a small part and parcel of the cosmos is the emphasis. Through this recognition, we are able to work with others and live harmoniously. It is a process of removing our artificial ego from the equation. This is the bottom line of yoga. As long as we view ourselves as separate from the world and the absolute, we cannot work in harmony with it. When food is cooked for a higher purpose, it is also consumed and appreciated for a higher purpose. It becomes a demonstration of respect for the whole Yoga process. We nourish ourselves and take care of the body because it is the vehicle for spiritual understanding. By feeding our body with the powerful and spiritual *prasada*, we also open up the door to our spiritual heart within and for cleansing our consciousness and karma. This is why pilgrims clamor to receive such *prasada* remnants from temples in India. Sharing it with others is considered one of the greatest charities. Temples in India widely distribute food. Everyone partakes, much like the host in the Catholic Church, but on a much grander scale.

In addition to these six activities, Sri Prahlad Maharaj describes nine processes of Bhakti Yoga in the Sanskrit text:

> *shravanam kitanam vishnoh*
> *smaranam pada-sevanam*
> *arcanam vandanam dasyam*
> *sakhyam atma-nivedanam*

"Hearing about and chanting the names of God, remembering, serving, worshipping the deity, offering respects, acting as a servant or representative of God, making friends with God and surrendering fully to Him."

The different schools of Bhakti Yoga concentrate on one or more of these activities. Each one is potent and considered a possible path to perfection. Cooking is certainly a part of this process and can bring one to higher levels of health, consciousness and spiritual perception. This is the art of Yoga and Cooking.

The Main Vedic Spiritual Paths: Something for Everyone

Stephen Knapp

In the Vedic system it is described that the Absolute Truth, the Supreme Reality, manifests in three forms; namely the impersonal and all-pervading Brahman, the localized expansion of the Supreme known as the Paramatma or Supersoul or Lord in the Heart, and then Bhagavan, the Supreme Person. These different traits of God are also presented in other religions as well, but the information they provide are only hints compared to the depth of understanding that we find in the Vedic knowledge. The Vedic information gives a full elaboration on the nature of the impersonal Brahman, as well as the localized expansion of the Paramatma, and Bhagavan, the Supreme Being.

There is not enough room to fully explain each aspect in this volume, but the Vedic system provides the means and methods so that any individual can realize any one or each of these aspects of the Supreme. In fact, it is said that until one realizes all three of these aspects of God, his or her understanding of the Supreme remains incomplete. The uniqueness of the Vedic system is that it expects that everyone should have their own realizations of the Absolute Truth. It is not enough merely to have blind faith in a dogma or whatever is propounded by a religion without the means to have one's own perception of the Highest Truth. To keep one bound by Faith alone without the means for furthering one's spiritual development is to keep people stifled, limited, undeveloped, or more easily controlled.

The Vedic system provides the means for the individual to decide how much spiritual progress he or she wishes to make, and thus gives the methodologies that a person can use to progress. It also provides the system that will allow a person to more completely understand and realize any of the three particular aspects of God, as mentioned above. So let us get a glimpse into the four main types of spiritual paths that are offered by Vedic culture. Let us not forget that other spiritual avenues are also offered and contained within the Vedic system.

THE PURPOSE OF RELIGION

Obviously, the purpose of religion is to raise our consciousness, to preserve our moral standards, and to further develop our devotion to God. This is, essentially, the way of piety. However, it does not necessarily provide one with the means of being truly spiritual. Being spiritual means to recognize one's spiritual identity and practically see the spiritual essence of all others. It also means to see that we are all parts and parcels of God and to respect each other in that light. But how can we be convinced that there even is a God?

We need to understand that all things that are spiritual function on a higher plane of existence, one that is hardly perceptible by our mind, intelligence or senses. The spiritual dimension can only be detected when our consciousness reaches a higher level of awareness. It is similar to radio and television waves. These are not perceptible by our mind or senses. They remain invisible, yet they are all around us. In our base level of awareness, or unawareness, we may think that such things as radio waves and television frequencies are not real. Of course, we may be viewed as quite retarded by those who are familiar with their existence. So the thing is, even if you cannot perceive them, if you have a receiver that can detect or even utilize such subtle waves or frequencies, then you will know that radio and television waves are not only a fact, but can be used for many practical purposes.

The same thing goes for religion, or a genuine spiritual path. They are meant to bring our consciousness up to a higher level of awareness, to fine tune it so that we can receive or perceive the higher vibrations of the spiritual strata. As we practice a genuine spiritual tradition, then our consciousness can become refined and focused enough so we can receive the subtle frequencies and perceive the reality of the spiritual domain. Then we can have our own spiritual experiences. The point is that the more spiritual we become, the more we can perceive that which is spiritual. As we develop and grow in this way, the questions about spiritual life are no longer a mystery to solve, but become a reality to experience. It becomes a practical part of our lives. And how to reach that level of perception is supplied in the methodologies that have been preserved and handed to us by the previous sages who have also used them for their own development and spiritual experience. And that is what the Vedic system has been giving to humanity for thousands of years.

The Vedic system is practically non-denominational. It is not for any one culture or ethnic group. It is for all of humanity and is called Sanatana-dharma and yoga. Sanatana-dharma is both a path and a state of being. It means, essentially, the eternal nature of the soul. We are all spiritual beings within material bodies, so the goal is to regain that spiritual identity. This comes by a reawakening of our spiritual identity and consciousness. It is through the process of yoga and the path of Sanatana-dharma that we can reach this higher awareness and percieve exactly who we are.

We mentioned in a previous chapter about the *Yoga-sutras* of Patanjali that comprise the essence of yoga practice. However, yoga itself is a deep and serious process, and there are a variety of forms of yoga that can be performed. There is the path of intellect (jnana-yoga), the path of action (karma-yoga), the path of inward meditation (astanga or raja-yoga) and the path of devotion (bhakti-yoga). However, in the preliminary stages, Yoga is, essentially, for controlling the flickering nature of the mind, and for developing one's finer qualities and expanding one's consciousness from material to spiritual awareness. When you progress in yoga you can feel the unwanted burdens of the mind fall away, such as anxiety, anger, greed, envy, hate, discontent, etc. Then other qualities like peacefulness, tranquility, contentment, and blissfulness will be felt. These are qualities everyone is trying to find and are some of the many things that can be accomplished with yoga, at least on the elementary level. As you make further progress, you may enter into the deeper levels of understanding and transcending the mind and gradually go so far as to attain realizations as to what your own spiritual identity is and what your relationship is with the Absolute. Becoming free from material life and regaining one's spiritual identity is the goal of all yoga. The Sanskrit root of the word *yoga* is *yuj*, which means to link or unite with the Supreme. And the word *religion*, which comes from the Latin word *religio*, means to bring back or bind to God. Thus, there is no difference between the goal of yoga and the goal of religion. So let us take a look at some of these forms of yoga.

HATHA-YOGA

There are thousands of people who practice hatha-yoga, some say more in California than in all of India. However, hatha-yoga is not a separate system of yoga as many people seem to think, but was developed as one of the eight steps of raja-yoga. It is described in such early texts as the *Hatha Yoga Pradipika*, the *Gheranda Samhita* and the *Shiva Samhita*. Lord Shiva is said to be the originator of the system found in the *Hatha Yoga Pradipika*. This is highly regarded by the

Nath tradition founded by Gorakshnath and his teacher Matyendranath, who was accepted to be a disciple of Lord Shiva.

In any case, hatha-yoga is one of the most popular forms of yoga, which can be done by anybody, regardless of how serious he or she may be about attaining higher levels of spiritual development. Although it is a part of a spiritual process, when taken as an isolated exercise technique it can be completely secular as well. It can be used strictly for physical and mental development, if that is all one wishes to do with it. It involves maneuvering the body through different *asanas* or exercises, along with breathing techniques for controlling the life airs within the body. This is the *prana*, the universal energy that comes through the body. *Prana* is divided into certain bodily airs that function in different ways. *Prana* is the incoming and outgoing breath; *apana*, is the air which expels bodily waste; *vyana* assists in the power of physical movement; *samana* distributes nutrition through the body; and *udana* is the air in the *sushumna* channel. Hatha-yoga is basically for helping keep the body in shape and free from disease, the mind peaceful and steady for spiritual pursuits, and the inner energy balanced and flowing. This, however, is very useful in whatever spiritual process we pursue because if our body is too diseased, and if our mind is too restless and unsteady, they become a hindrance in our quest for spiritual awareness or perfection. Thus, with the practice of hatha-yoga, the body and mind become healthier and our spiritual practice can continue with fewer impediments. Thus, it is beneficial regardless of what is one's spiritual discipline or even when there is no spiritual interest at all.

KARMA-YOGA

Karma-yoga is another system that many westerners often talk about. This is for attaining perfection through right action, which is something that this world could use more of. This sort of action is based on religious texts for one's purification and future happiness, such as entering heaven after death. These activities may include ritualistic worship of the demigods, as well as a variety of other things, such as avoiding the causing of any harm to all other living beings, and doing activities for the good of others who may be less fortunate, or digging public water wells, or doing other humanitarian work. The main interest of practicing karma-yoga is for oneself and in achieving good future results rather than transcendence. In other words, this path is for one who is still attached to materialistic fruitive activities. A karma-yogi works for acquiring good karma for himself so that he can get a better future, such as a birth in heaven or a higher status. But in the more elevated forms of karma-yoga, the results of whatever a person does are meant to be offered to

God as regulated by the rules in the Vedic literature. When one gives the fruits of his work to God, the work becomes yoga or linked to the Supreme, which makes such actions free of all karma. Without dovetailing one's work for God in this way, all activities that are performed for one's own interest or development simply cause one to accumulate more karma, not to be free of it. So karma-yoga is meant to be a means to work in the world but in a way that can rid oneself of all karma and establish a strong connection with God. Then work becomes yoga. By giving the results to God, one becomes freed from the reactions of such work and also begins to make advancement on the path of yoga. Thus, as a person becomes free from all karma, he becomes free from taking any more births in the material world. So karma-yoga is considered to be the transitional stage between material and spiritual life. Nonetheless, one's karma (as I have explained in my book *The Secret Teachings of the Vedas*) should be a concern for everyone.

JNANA-YOGA

Jnana-yoga is the path to enlightenment through the process of mental speculation and the study and acquirement of empirical knowledge. On a deeper level, *jnana* (pronounced gyana) or jnana-yoga is the process of discriminating between truth and non-truth, or reality and non-reality, *maya*, and understanding what is the Divine. This is the knowledge of the soul and God, and the relationship between them. Therefore, the acquirement of *jnana* or spiritual knowledge is one of the first steps in spiritual development.

The aspirant of jnana-yoga engages in long hours of study and discussion in the attempt to understand the highest truth. One following this path must also accept the authority of the great sages and study in their association. Without proper guidance along this path one can easily become confused about what is actually the Absolute Truth. By merely involving the cognitive intellect, which is the main activity of the jnana-yogi, one simply remains on the mental or intellectual platform. Therefore, it can be very difficult for the jnana-yogi to rise above material existence and enter the spiritual realm. The reason for this is that knowledge alone does not purify the consciousness, although it can help one understand the proper path to take. One should not forever remain a seeker of truth, but should reach a stage of following the path that will give one realization of what the Absolute Truth is and enable him to reach the spiritual strata. This is the level of *vijnana* or practical and realized knowledge. The spiritual strata should not always be a mystery to solve or a quest to reach, but through the proper perceptions become a reality to experience. *Vijnana* is this realized knowledge.

However, in jnana yoga much of what we find today is *advaita-jnana,* the knowledge of the non-dual impersonal aspect of God wherein the idea is presented that the individual soul and God are the same, and that God is the impersonal Brahman.

The preliminary levels of *jnana* may be acquired from books, but it is generally accepted that a person must receive the deeper avenues of this knowledge from a genuine *jnani*, a realized teacher. When a student has attained the means of accessing this knowledge, he must continuously absorb his mind in the concepts that are presented until his mind and consciousness completely adopts it. This is a long process and in earlier ages would generally take many lifetimes. Even if a student tries to do this with utmost sincerity, the conception of the Brahman for the *advaita-jnani* is inconceivable and unimaginable. So it can be difficult to actually get a grasp as to what the soul's identity is in connection with the Brahman.

After following this path perfectly, the mind is expected to become purified until it can perceive the reflection of the soul, which is beyond all *mayic* or illusory forms of experience, and thus beyond all external limitations. This level of perception is the stage of pure goodness or the pure *sattvic* level. Such a perception of the soul is when the *jnani* is said to have attained the stage of Self-realization. This level of enlightenment is as far as this process can take one. Though it is a major accomplishment, it still has not taken one all the way to God or to understanding one's relationship with God. Knowledge and the perception of the soul removes the attachments of materialism and ignorance from the mind, however this is in preparation for what must come next to continue the process, if a practitioner gets this far. So, although he may be considered Self-realized in his perception of the soul, he is not yet thoroughly liberated from material existence, which means this path is not complete in itself. There is another level of yoga which must be added to it. Therefore, jnana-yoga is often combined with other forms of yoga, such as raja-yoga or bhakti-yoga.

YOGA

From this stage of *jnana*, or jnana-yoga, many practitioners add or continue with yoga, if they have not already started it. This type of yoga may be in the forms of astanga-yoga, raja-yoga, kriya-yoga, or something of this sort. Yoga is the process to calm the mind and, ultimately, to become free of all sensual input and dictates from the mind. In that state lays the doorway to the spiritual dimension, higher ideals, inspiration and lofty states of being. In other words, it is the process of obtaining a perfectly thoughtless level of awareness in the state of pure *sattva-guna,* or mode of goodness, in which one can enter *nirvikalpa samadhi*—the thought-free form of meditation. In this state, the door opens to allow our consciousness to enter or at least have glimpses into the spiritual energy and the perception of it.

In this way, it is said that *jnana* is the theory or knowledge while yoga is the practice. By performing this perfectly, one can enter what is called *kaivalya*, the understanding of the Brahman, the impersonal form of God. The ancient Vedic texts, such as the *Yoga Darshana*, the *Yoga Sutras*, *Bhagavad-gita*, and others, mention that in order to be successful in this path, it normally takes years of continued practice without falling down from the proper standard, along with following all the rules correctly, such as the *yamas* and *niyamas*, which are the essential regulations of things to do and not to do. Only then can one gradually reach the *kaivalya* position, the perception of becoming one with the Brahman, which is the final stage of *advaita* or the impersonalist form of yoga. So the difficulty to reach the highest stage of this path in this age should be obvious, which also makes it suitable only for the most serious, yet anyone can gain insights from the practice of it.

RAJA-YOGA

To explain it more completely, raja-yoga, sometimes called astanga-yoga, is the eightfold path leading to liberation. It is also called the royal (*raja*) way. It is one of the most popular systems of yoga today. The process involves calming all mental agitation, which gradually helps the meditator to fuse with the objects of meditation by supraconscious concentration. The process is divided into eight basic steps.

The first step is *yama*, the essential moral commandments. This means to avoid violence, lying, stealing, greed, possessiveness, and a lack of celibacy.

The second step is *niyama* or preparation and discipline for self-realization. This involves austerity or undergoing physical hardships for a higher result, along with study of scriptural texts, purity of mind and body, contentment, and devoting all one's activities to God. *Yama* means the things to avoid and *niyama* means the practice one must do. Together they help keep the yogi's passions quiet and stilled and keep him in harmony with nature.

The third step is *asana*, or posture for meditation, often used in *hatha-yoga*. *Asanas* help steady the mind and promote health. *Asanas* are exercises, some simple and some quite advanced, that can be performed alone with minimal equipment, like a blanket or mat, fresh air, and room to move around, preferably outdoors.

Different *asanas* develop and affect different nerves, muscles, and organs of the body and keep the system strong, limber, and free from disease. Thus, the body becomes a fit instrument for spiritual development. Learning *asanas* can also help in other systems of yoga, too, and helps keep the body in a good, healthy condition. We will not elaborate on the different kinds of *asanas* one can learn since there are many books available that explain these.

The fourth step is *pranayama*, breath control for fixing the mind in concentration. *Prana* means life or energy, and also can mean spirit. *Ayama* indicates the length and retention of breath between inhalation and exhalation, and control of the *prana* within the body. Since it is considered that a person is born with a certain number of allotted breaths in a lifetime, the yogi learns breath control to strengthen the respiratory system, soothe the nerves and steady the mind for meditation, and prolong one's life. Simply by controlling one's breathing a person can steady the beating of his heart. When one's breathing is not smooth, the mind is also usually unsteady and easily agitated. So as one learns *pranayama*, the mind becomes equipoised and free from the pulling of the senses. It can also clean the *nadis* (subtle *pranic* channels) and open the *pranic* currents, as well as decrease the unwanted inner mental activity.

The fifth step is *pratyahara*, control of the senses and checking the mind's attraction to external objects. It is necessary to control the senses to advance in yoga, and in *pratyahara* the yogi analyzes the mind's attraction for external objects. By the use of his study and cultivated knowledge, he recognizes that sensual delights lead to one's destruction, and the path of sense control leads to his salvation. By intelligently adjusting his consciousness, the yogi gives up sensual desires in order to achieve the proper frame of mind and freedom from the modes of nature to pursue successfully the goal of yoga.

The sixth step is *dharana*, concentrating on the object of meditation. However, it is more than mere concentration. It is becoming so absorbed in one's focus on something that a person becomes oblivious to everything else. When the mind has been completely stilled by the previous steps, the yogi can totally concentrate on a single object of meditation. The seventh step is *dhyana*, when the mind is in a state of undisturbed flowing meditation. In this stage the mind takes on the likeness of the object being meditated on, and in his contemplation of the Supreme Brahman the yogi remains in that state of supreme bliss.

The eighth and final step is *samadhi*, in which, according to the eightfold path, the yogi becomes one with the Supreme. *Samadhi* means the absorption in the balanced, eternal awareness or knowledge. This is the state of Self-realization for the individual. It is when a person becomes free of ego, bodily identification, sense perception, mental activity, and all time and space. This allows for one's consciousness to achieve its natural state of nonduality. This is in reference to the way the mind interferes with our perception of things around us and, thus, rather than seeing everything as parts of the Divine energy of God, we see the world of names, forms, images, desires, goals, and temporary illusions. In this state of being, we become absorbed in the finite and unaware or forgetful of the Infinite. In reaching the state of *samadhi*, we attain the Infinite. In Kundalini-yoga, the state of *samadhi* is considered the union of the *kundalini* or *shakti*, the female energy, with Shiva, the universal male energy. This union takes place in the top *chakra*, the Sahasrara Chakra.

So in the state of *samadhi*, the knower and the known, the seer and the seen, the soul and the Supersoul, become one. Thus, the yogi loses all individuality and merges into the Supreme or in thoughts of the Supreme. This is the result of reaching perfection on this particular path of yoga.

We should point out, however, that the path to *samadhi* through this eightfold system is arduous. Each of the eight steps calls for its own rigorous discipline. As in any science, if you do not follow the procedure properly, you do not get the results. Furthermore, such practices of mechanically trying to completely subdue or control the mind and senses by long, difficult exercises in sitting, breathing, sense control, etc., are nearly impossible for anyone to perfect in this age in which there are so many sensual and mental distractions. Nonetheless, through such attempts the mind may indeed become tamer, quieter, and various minor insights are possible. And the practice of this form of yoga with the use of *pranayama* can still provide a variety of benefits, depending on how deeply a person can enter into it. It can still show how best to still the mind so that real meditation can take place. The point is that in this sort of yoga, as established in the *Yoga-sutras* of Patanjali, the real goal is to become free from the dictations and disturbances of the mind. This can help us distance ourselves from the external drama in which we always find ourselves and the constant conversation that goes on in our mind. And once you are free of the mind, real concentration and meditation can begin. It can also bring some peacefulness into our lives and insights into our real identity. It can even lead to experiences in which we can perceive a higher state of consciousness. In that state of mind, whatever system we use to meditate on God can be more effective.

Once the mind has been brought to a suitable condition for meditation by performing this type of yoga, still the goal of yogis may differ. Some yogis meditate on God with the intent of merging into the body of God, or to become God or equal to God, as explained in the *Yoga Sutras* of Patanjali. Others meditate on God as a form of service or devotion to God, which brings us to bhakti-yoga.

BHAKTI-YOGA

Bhakti-yoga, the process of simply developing devotional service to the Lord, is highly recommended in the *Srimad-Bhagavatam* as the ultimate end of understanding Vedanta. Bhakti is the unifying principle of all yoga systems, but in such texts as the *Bhagavad-gita* and *Srimad-Bhagavatam* it is the prime avenue for developing one's loving relationship with the Lord. This is what especially paves the way for freeing oneself from the attractions and attachments to the temporary material world, and, thus, provides the means for genuine liberation from the repeated cycle of birth and death in this cosmic manifestation. Bhakti-yoga is a system that is highly recommended for this age of Kali-yuga and is generally practiced by the followers of Vedanta called Vaishnavas, or worshipers of Vishnu or Krishna. It is by far the easiest of all the yoga processes and has fewer requirements for the practitioners than any other process. *Bhakti* is the yoga that begins, continues, and ends with love and devotion to the Supreme. There is no stronger binding mechanism than love, and spiritual love is the natural sentiment that emanates from God and connects the living beings to God. Thus, it is said that attaining this sentiment of devotion to God holds the sum and substance of all other yoga processes and religions. This path is so powerful that even married people may practice it successfully, while in other systems of yoga it is expected that one should be celibate. There are no extreme austerities to undergo; yet, the results are sublime. It is a scientific method of expanding one's consciousness to perceptions of unlimited joy and inner peace. Bhakti-yoga brings complete fulfillment to those who seriously practice it, and gives realizations and a perception of one's real identity as a spiritual being, and what one's relationship is with the Absolute. It also can be practiced anywhere at anytime.

In bhakti-yoga there is not much concern about the *chakras* and the practice for raising the life energy up the Sushumna *nadi* or freeing oneself of the subtle body, as we find in some yoga processes. The reason for this is explained in *Srimad-Bhagavatam* (3.25.33), which states that *bhakti*, devotional service, dissolves the subtle body of the living entity without separate effort, just as fire in the stomach digests all that we eat. In other words, being fixed in devotional service, which itself is a direct way of engaging in eternal spiritual activities, the yogi burns up the five coverings of the gross and subtle body, which includes the mind, as he or she becomes more and more spiritualized. Thus, there is no need to struggle in the separate endeavor of trying to open the various *chakras* within the subtle body or becoming free of it if the subtle body is automatically dissolved.

In this way, the bhakti-yogi naturally becomes free from ignorance, attachment to the body, false egotism, and material consciousness, and can rapidly reach the spiritual platform. In the deeper levels of bhakti-yoga, when the subtle body begins to dissolve, there is a decreasing amount of interference from the mind until there is unity between the spiritual dimension, in which the soul exists, and the loving devotional service to God that is performed by the body and consciousness. Thus, the physical and subtle bodies become spiritually surcharged as a vessel in which the soul serves God. Therein, whatever *anarthas* or faults and unnecessary attractions and distractions we have, or *samskaras* such as mental impressions or memories of both pleasant times and heartache that we may have experienced from previous relationships, all become dissolved by the overbearing ecstasy of our reawakened loving relationship with Krishna. It is like a slate wiped clean from all previous markings. In this way, a person becomes absorbed in pure consciousness and, thus, is said to become a pure devotee. This is confirmed in *Bhagavad-gita* (14.26) where it states that one who engages in full devotional service and does not fall down transcends the material modes and reaches Brahman, the spiritual strata.

So, this process merely uncovers and releases the true loving potential of the soul. This inherent potential for full and unconditional love lies deep within all of us and is our ultimate motivation for all that we do. Motivated by our need to love and be loved, when that need is interpreted through the body it becomes perverted and mistaken for the need of bodily affection or sensual desire, lust. When freed from this bodily and mental influence, the true needs of the soul stand revealed. This is an impetus for spiritual love, beyond all bodily desires, a pure love for God and all that is His.

The way this works is that within our material body and senses are our spiritual senses, which are lying dormant. They have no spiritual engagement while covered by matter. Devotional service, and the ultimate goal of any other yoga or religious system, involves freeing our real senses from the confines of matter and material consciousness, and engaging them in direct spiritual activities to the Supreme. When the contamination of materialistic consciousness has been removed and the senses act in purified God consciousness, we then have reached our eternal sensory activities which are spiritual and in relation with our real identity as an eternal spiritual servant of the Supreme Spirit. Eternal spiritual activities means to engage in serving the Supreme, our natural occupation, while temporary material activities means to engage in the attempt to satisfy our dull mind and senses, which keeps us a prisoner within matter.

While the yogis of other processes are struggling hard to control artificially their mind and senses, the senses of the *bhakti-yogi* are automatically controlled and purified by engagement in devotional service. When the mind and consciousness are attracted to the Supreme Being through the attraction of love and service, it becomes easy to remain in such concentration without any other regulations, austerities, or mechanical processes.

One example of this from the Vedic literature is of Visvamitra. He was a great yogi, seriously practicing and performing many austerities. However, even though in deep meditation, simply by hearing the tinkling ankle bells of a beautiful woman walking nearby, named Menaka, he fell from his yogic trance and had sex with her. After many years of living with Menaka he realized the futility of his position. He angrily gave up married life and again took to his yogic practices. However, when Haridasa Thakura was tempted by a prostitute while engaged in bhakti-yoga and chanting the Hare Krishna *maha-mantra*, he did not fall down. In fact, while the woman waited for hours in hopes of having sex with Haridasa, she became purified by hearing his chanting. She then gave up her interest in sex and also took up bhakti-yoga. Therefore, by experiencing a higher taste, Haridasa Thakura was successful. This is the advantage of engaging in bhakti-yoga. This is confirmed in *Srimad-Bhagavatam* (3.25.43-44), which states that those yogis who have spiritual knowledge and have renounced material interests engage in devotional service to the lotus feet of the Supreme Being for their eternal happiness. With their minds fixed in such devotional love and service, they are easily able to enter the spiritual kingdom. This, as it says, is the only means for one to attain the final perfection of life.

Therefore, those yogis or mystics who engage in devotional yoga are considered first-class because, while living in this material universe, they engage in the same devotional activities that are going on within the Vaikuntha planets in the spiritual sky. Thus, they have already attained their natural transcendental position. There is no higher perfection than this.

Presently, in bhakti-yoga the Vaishnava sect is one of the three major divisions of Hinduism, the others being Shaivism and Shakta. Vaishnavas have four major sects: the Ramanujas founded by Ramanujacharya; the Madhvas founded by Madhvacharya; the Vallabhas founded by Vallabhacharya; and the Gaudiya *sampradaya*, founded by Sri Chaitanya Mahaprabhu, who is regarded as an incarnation of Krishna Himself. This is the path that is most clearly enunciated by Srila Vyasadeva within the teachings of the *Srimad-Bhagavatam*, and is the process for the complete form of God-realization and liberation that is indicated in all the essential Vedic texts.

MANTRA-YOGA

To explain briefly, mantra-yoga is one of the oldest forms of yoga and is an easy system for enlightenment. It is recommended as the best means for focusing the mind on the Supreme in this age of Kali, so it is easily used in other forms of yoga and spiritual processes, such as in bhakti-yoga. The word *mantra* literally means to deliver the mind. The instrument used to accomplish this is the secret power of vibrations arranged in a particular formula, called a *mantra*. Different mantras have different purposes. Some bring happiness, some fulfill material desires, some are used in the worship of various demigods, some simply focus and steady the mind, some help raise the life energy up through the *chakras*, while others are incantations for casting spells and so on. But mantras used for spiritual enlightenment release vital energy, strengthen the mind, and prepare the consciousness for perceiving higher realms of existence.

Since it is especially difficult to void the mind of all sensual input in this day and age, and with so many distractions that invade our mind, the best way to concentrate on the higher vibrations and spiritual energy, making way for contact with God, is to fill the mind with the spiritual vibrations. This is the purpose and the advantage of mantra-yoga. By concentrating on the mantra, the mind associates with the energy within it and takes on the characteristics found within the sound vibration. The more powerful a mantra is, the more it can invoke the higher energies in the mind and consciousness. In this way, the mind can be purified by the spiritual vibrations within the mantra. One who chants a mantra generally repeats it a particular number of times each day while using a string of beads like a rosary. Mantra-yoga is a deep science and much more study can be given to it. It is especially useful in the practice of bhakti-yoga, and one of the most recommended mantras for this age is the Hare Krishna maha-mantra.

CONCLUSION

So with this brief introduction to the main spiritual paths that are offered in Vedic culture, not to mention many other types of yoga and philosophical outlooks found within the Vedic system, we can see that there is something for everyone. And this is regardless of a person's area of interest, type of consciousness, mental makeup, or what level of the Absoulte Truth or aspects of the Supreme Being a person wants to realize. In any one of these paths, a person is still considered part of the Vedic process or a follower of *Sanatana-dharma*. Furthermore, this also has nothing to do with the background, ethnicity, race, or country in which one lives. These are based on the universal truths that are applicable to anyone. The Vedic system respects that. Thus, this is practically non-denominational. Anyone can pick up whatever part of this path that fits one the best and move forward to become as progressed as he or she can be. This is the unique nature of the Vedic culture and its spiritual knowledge.

Vedic Sociology:
An Arrangement for
Everyone's Highest Potential

Parama Karuna Devi

At the beginning of this third millennium of the current era, sociology is certainly a very interesting subject because everybody is worried about social problems, locally and gobally. Even the more developed and advanced societies are troubled with unrest, dissatisfaction and uncertainty. Furthermore, alienation and an increasing percentage of suicides, serious physical and mental diseases, drug addictions, crimes, terrorism, unemployment, geographical and cultural displacement are also taking place. People seem to have more and more difficulties in respect to tolerance and cooperation, moral values, family and community support, and even satisfaction with their own position in life and society. In the meantime, the planet's resources are quickly getting depleted. The global financial situation is becoming more and more unstable, all kinds of pollution are on the rise, and even the global climate threatens to destroy people's lives and properties. These problems are all due to wrong choices at the social level, and the effects are felt by the entire society.

For example, the products of science and technology, to which people look for knowledge and solutions, are becoming more and more hazardous and unsustainable, and human beings are turning into the servants and victims of technology and science instead of getting real benefits from them. Developing countries are firmly determined to follow the footsteps of the "more advanced" countries, and increasing consumption, urbanisation and artificiality of life. They do not want to "be left behind" or "left without".

Commoners, politicians and even academics keep blaming "bad governments", lack of overall financial development or scientific progress, and inefficacy of the penal systems, but the problems remain unsolved or even become worse. So governments are falling one after the other, states and regions are fighting for separatism, inflation is growing, and the quality of life is becoming poorer.

So is human society really progressing? It would seem otherwise. Let us trace our steps to see where we have taken the wrong turn so that we may get on the right track again.

First of all, modern Western sociology was born around the middle of the 19th century together with modern psychology. Before Max Weber and his contemporaries, the concept of sociology as the study of interactions among human beings had already been cultivated in Europe during the Age of Enlightenment (18th century) by brilliant researchers and philosophers like Voltaire and Rousseau. Their work was considered revolutionary because it affirmed the value of the human being in himself, something that was largely ignored by the medieval conception of life.

The first spark of this understanding had been ignited by the cultural movement called the Renaissance (from 15th century) with its studies on politics and humanistic sciences. It provided a renewed enthusiasm for culture, arts, philosophy and science in scholars and thinkers. These were protected by powerful and wealthy patrons (mostly kings, aristocrats and bankers) from the persecutions of the Inquisition of the dark Middle Ages. In fact, this new cultural movement opposed the dogmatism of the Church, creating a secular development of knowledge that separated philosophy and science from institutionalized spirituality and religion, and was accused of heresy and paganism.

In fact, the inspiration for such flourishing cultural and scientific interest came from the study of the works of pre-Christian ("heathen") philosophers in the ancient Greek and Hellenistic culture, which were considered the civilizing force of the Roman empire. Unfortunately, such texts had largely been lost in the zealous destruction of "pagan" libraries and universities, and the salvaged fragments were further mutilated by the later scholars who dismissed as "mythology" all the archetypal, mystical and spiritual aspects forming the wholistic concept of reality that was characteristic of the ancient cultures. This was the "wrong turn" on the road of man's civilization that created a mechanistic science and a godless philosophy as the foundation of Western culture.

As a result of the fierce opposition of the Church to the free cultivation of scientific knowledge and their claim of a monopoly on the human soul, in mainstream Western culture the physical and metaphysical planes became more and more separated. They lost the wholistic character they had in ancient classical cultures (stemming from Vedic culture).

So science and religion became enemies, man rejected nature, spirit and matter lost their harmonious connection, the brain became alienated from the heart, and a mechanistic and artificial vision of the world was created. For some time people in the West have thought that such a development was progress, but in these last 50 years or so, it has become apparent that a better balance and a wider perspective are required.

One of the main problems in modern and contemporary Western sciences, including sociology, is this "loss of the soul" because mechanistic science denies the existence or relevance of spirit. Devoid of their common spiritual basis (the science that studies the "observer" of the world, called *atma vidya* in Sanskrit), all the sciences that study the world have become increasingly fragmented, separating ethics from knowledge, happiness from the creation of wealth and prosperity, and consciousness from action. This process had heavy effects on people, at the individual and collective levels, and serious social problems were created.

However, to solve such problems we can now reclaim the original balanced and wholistic knowledge possessed by the ancient civilizations by directly tapping into the source of the Hellenistic culture, the Vedic civilization.

Not many people know that ancient Greek culture had been powerfully influenced by the great centers of knowledge in India, especially the universities of Taksha Sila and Pushkala Vati (known in ancient Greek language as Taxila and Peukela otis). According to the tradition these had been founded by Taksha and Puskhala, the two sons of Bharata (the brother or Ramachandra).

Pythagoras, who was known to be a great traveler, spent time in India and then returned to Greece to teach a deeply metaphysical doctrine that united mathematics, philosophy, music, medicine and ethics. In fact, one of the main teachings of Pythagoras' school was ethical vegetarianism, so much that until the 19th century in the West all vegetarians were commonly called "Pythagoreans". Pythagoreans were also famous for believing in reincarnation or metempsychosis (a Greek word that traditionally defines the doctrine of reincarnation in ancient Europe, still used by many Western scholars who relate it to Greek philosophers).

However, ethics and philosophy were not the only things that the ancient Greeks learnt from their Indian universities. Medicine, architecture, metallurgy and chemistry, physics, astronomy and mathematics were major subjects there. We should note that the Vedic *Shulba-shastras* thousands of years ago explained what is today known as "Pythagoras' theorem". Similarly "Thales' theorem" on parallel straight lines was also well known before Thales was born, and taught in ancient Vedic universities where Greek scholars studied.

Alexander the Great, a student of Aristotle (the main disciple of Plato) was so inspired by the reports of the Greek historian and traveler Megasthenes about India that he decided to conquer that land. Although he was unsuccessful, he organized a group of scholars to translate "all the Indian books" for his famous

700,000 volumes library at Alexandria of Egypt, the city he had chosen for his capital and that took its name after him.

Let us examine now the basic concepts of Vedic sociology from the same texts that inspired the ancient scholars.

SOCIETY AS THE BODY OF GOD

A simple and clear metaphor about the nature of human society, also quoted by ancient Latin and Greek writers, is originally contained in *Purusha Sukta*, a Vedic Sanskrit text.

There human society is described as the material body of God, the Virat Purusha or the Universal Person, the Soul of the Universe. His head is represented by the intellectuals, his arms by the warriors, his belly by enterprisers, and his feet by laborers. Therefore the intellectuals' functions consist of thinking, speaking and collecting information, and coordinating the entire body for proper action. The warriors or government administrators protect the entire body from attacks (internal and external) and take care of each limb in difficulty. The enterprisers utilize material resources to produce wealth and prosperity and distribute it to each limb of the social body, according to the needs. And the general laborers and assistants practically carry the entire social body wherever is required.

These social categories, called *varnas* in Sanskrit, exist naturally in every society, even the most egalitarian. They are defined by the natural interests, talents and propensities of the four different human types: the intelligent and reflective, the men of action and courage, those who are able to manage things and make them work, and then the tradesmen, technicians, and unskilled workers.

From ignorance or misconceptions about the different duties and rights of the various positions in society, problems and corruptions will arise in any civilization. Then we will find that individuals are pushed to perform activities for which they are not suited by nature. Or they may be prevented from doing what is proper for themselves and for the social body in general. In such cases, usually intellectuals are either forced to serve and carry out the orders of narrow minded and ignorant people who hold the political and financial power, or are tempted to get and keep the material power and resources in their own hands. They are thus forced to prostitute their ideals and intelligence and cheat the masses with biased information, or engage in destructive research.

Similarly the protection of society (that should be normally the duty of generous and self-sacrificing heroes) is entrusted to ruthless cowards and exploiters who oppress the weak and innocent, repress and persecute intelligent dissenters and become easily corrupted by criminals. In the same corrupted way, business-oriented people will simply continue to accumulate wealth by any means, including unjust exploitation and cheating methods without using it for the benefit of all. This is because they begin to feel that greed and envy are the basis of economic development, and that money and property have a greater value if kept for themselves and not used for the benefit of society. Thus they plunder and consume the resources of the planet and enslave people in the name of profit. They also view work in itself as a curse and a suffering, something undignified, and therefore they pride themselves of not doing anything with their own hands.

In such a society, enterprisers do not take proper care of their employees' families, and birth, death, old age and diseases become even greater problems for the mass of people. Unemployment becomes a serious difficulty, and jobless people are left to themselves, pushed into alienation, degradation, drug addiction and criminality by neglect and by excessive responsibilities they cannot cope with. In this way, they may become a serious disturbance to the rest of society.

All these problems create a general feeling of frustration, rage, envy, and intolerance that pushes the mass of people to react in violence and extremism. Shrewd politicians stir the muddy waters with emotional discourses, propaganda and accusations against the ruling government. Or they may blame some kind of scapegoats (ethnic minorities, religious communities, etc.) in order to harvest votes. But once they get elected, their performance and use of power is often equally dissatisfying and corrupted. Emotional manipulation, media control and false promises are the methods by which politicians obtain their posts, when unqualified commoners are asked to choose the supreme leaders of the country and decide its policies.

The metaphor of society as a body shows the absurdity of such behaviors, comparing them to walking on one's head, thinking with one's feet or never taking care of one's feet, or having hands that refuse to protect the body, a mouth that only wants to keep the food for itself instead of sending it to the stomach, or a stomach that refuses to digest and distribute the food to the rest of the body according to the needs of each and every cell. The root problem is that each limb of society wants to get selfish benefits at the expense of the others, not understanding their close interdependence.

On the other hand, Vedic knowledge scientifically regulates the duties and rights, activities and requisites of every class and individual in a wholistic spirit of cooperation and selfless service. Something like that is being re-discovered recently by the movement of voluntary organizations, anti-globalization forums, non-profit societies, grassroot international cooperation, fair trade and so on. However, these movements have caught only a glimpse of the actual science of civilization that is represented by Vedic sociology.

When this scientific knowledge is ignored, the concept of social categories may be denied altogether, and anarchy and degradation ensue. In India, the proper knowledge of sociology was lost and polluted because of misconceptions, so it gave rise to the degraded caste system, creating immense sufferings and obstacles to the progress and happiness of the individuals and the community at large.

THE CENTRAL POINTS OF A VEDIC SOCIETY

The example of human society as the universal body of God is particularly effective to illustrate the following central points of Vedic sociology:

1. All positions in society are actually natural functions based on qualities and activities of the individual.
2. All classes of society must sincerely cooperate together and selflessly take care of each other in the clear understanding of a strict, mutual and active interdependence.
3. All members of society must be kept healthy and strong, satisfied, well cared for and nourished, to ensure a good functioning of the society as a whole; a diseased, aching or weak limb of the society must not be neglected, otherwise the other limbs will be affected.
4. Serving society by performing one's duty is service to God.
5. Each member of society has particular duties and rights that cannot be disregarded whimsically.

The correct and scientific functioning of society is not simply an end to itself, although it is a very desirable achievement. After all, even animal societies, like those of ants and bees, easily demonstrate social harmony and efficient cooperation. Human beings are capable of attaining much higher achievements, described by Vedic knowledge.

THE FOUR PURPOSES OF HUMAN EXISTENCE

Vedic civilization is based on the profound and detailed knowledge of the human needs and aspirations, individually and collectively. It is specifically geared to lead every individual in a gradual process of evolution, training and self-realization, from the lowest to the highest platform, and collectively create the perfect environment for everybody to be happy and useful.

The first purpose of Human existence is called *dharma*. This Sanskrit word is extremely difficult to translate because it contains a wealth of meanings. Generally it is rendered as "religion", but actually it indicates the "intrinsic nature and activity", or "natural function" of the living entity.

Thus we may say that the *dharma* or natural function of fire consists in heat and light, and similarly the *dharma* of the human being is described as "sacrifice", "sacred action", "duty", "work", "service", "law", "rightful position" and "relationship with the whole".

We can therefore say that in Vedic terms, "religion" essentially means "service" to the Divine. In this sense, religion is practically identified with the proper and sincere performance of one's social duties for the benefit of all, and this is why Hinduism is generally identified with the *varna* system. We could say that Vedic "religion" is a way of life equivalent to social work performed in divine consciousness.

Dharma is the specific and qualified aspect of *Rita*, the general cosmic order by which all the planets and stars revolve in their orbits and interact with each other, the material elements function and manifest their qualities, and all the universal laws have effect.

This cosmic order is based on duty: planets and stars simply do their duty (or execute their functions). Similarly, man has a specific function, duty or place in the cosmic order. By executing such function, he substantially contributes to the maintenance of the cosmos and finds happiness and satisfaction: it is the celebration of dutiful work—any dutiful work, from the university teacher to the street sweeper—at a cosmic level. Work is held sacred and enthusiastically lived as an opportunity for personal development, creativity, responsibility, and purification of human character. However, each individual must properly understand what exactly is his function and duty, because confusion can lead to trying to perform someone else's duty with negative results.

Thus the first step in human evolution is to understand and follow the universal law of *dharma*, or selfless service (duty) as sacred activity offered to God. According to the specific qualities and inclinations of each individual, *dharma* takes a specific form, or *sva-dharma*. All the *sva-dharmas* are inscribed within specific circumstantial frames (*varna-ashrama dharma*) contained in the absolute *Sanatana-dharma*, the eternal (*sanatana*) function (*dharma*) of the living entity in all circumstances: which means service to the Divine in love and selfless dedication.

Once the individual has properly understood theoretically and practically his or her sacred duty in society according to the specific circumstances and works sincerely and selflessly in the proper capacity, thus achieving the platform of correct *dharma*, prosperity ensues both at an individual level and collective level.

In Vedic civilization, women are not forced to work at a regular job for basic maintenance besides having to take care of the house and family. The rightful aspirations to marriage, comfortable living place, and child rearing are considered very valuable in themselves, and generally marriage matches are chosen so that husband and wife can work together cooperatively without compromising the quality of life for the entire family. Although housework is considered an important and valuable job in itself where they retain all power (financial and organizational, including the control of the servants), women in Vedic civilization are not disrespected, emarginated or banned from other spiritual, cultural or social pursuits. And the mother's order is always sacred for any son on any issue.

The second purpose of human life is prosperity or economic development (*Artha*, as it is called in Sanskrit, meaning "valuable or desirable things"). In Vedic civilization, this is acquired through the selfless service of each individual, by interdependence and cooperation, and not by selfish exploitation or accumulation of private material possessions, either by individuals or groups at the expense of others. The real value of being human is dutiful work, not mere survival or the pursuit of status symbols or unnecessary consumption of goods. By definition, *artha* means valuable things that favor health, well being, beauty, harmony and serenity: a simple but comfortable house, proper clothing, healthy food in proper quantities, a pleasant environment with clean air, soil and water. And the opportunity to cultivate the higher human faculties with creative and beautiful activities, as well as to pursue knowledge and wisdom.

As we already mentioned, in Vedic civilization wealth is considered a means and not an end. Since the social body is considered as the body of God or Vishnu, wealth (symbolized by Lakshmi Devi, the Goddess of Fortune, God's consort and internal energy) is naturally engaged in its service for the benefit of the total social body. Sociology is always strictly connected to economy, and Vedic civilization is an economy of "giving", not an economy of "taking" or "getting", which paradoxically makes "getting" much easier and more pleasurable for all.

The third purpose of human life: pleasure and enjoyment. From the prosperity created by the sincere, selfless and intelligent performance of the respective duties by the various categories of society, natural happiness and enjoyment (as full satisfaction of all material needs) are automatically derived for all groups of society. Actually the original Vedic culture is much more pleasure-oriented than contemporary western or westernized civilizations and puts no guilt in genuine and healthy pleasures, so they do not need to be substituted by the vicarious possession of unnecessary status symbols that give no enjoyment and just clutter our lives, forcing us to toil more and more to pay for them. The formula is simple living, high thinking, and enjoying the bountiful blessings of the Lord in the form of good food, good relationships, good environment, festivals, and a proper balance between work, rest and entertainment.

The artificial and dogmatic dichotomy of western culture between matter and spirit, body and soul, material and spiritual needs, pleasure and elevation of consciousness, has negated the legitimate needs of the embodied souls in this world and pushed them to cultural schizophrenia. Paradoxically, by negating the positive value of the body and matter in favor of an extreme abstraction of spirituality, western society has pushed people to gross and selfish materialism, hypocrisy and cynicism instead of elevating them spiritually.

When on the other hand work is a pleasure in itself, there is ample opportunity for the joys of family and friendship, and a beautiful and happy environment, life becomes very pleasurable.

The fourth purpose of life is when all life's necessities are successfully met and healthy pleasures enjoyed, and human beings become positively inspired to search for the higher purpose of existence: liberation from material conditionings. Since the acquisition of wealth and the satisfaction of material needs are not considered the most important goals of life, but rather a means to a higher end, they remain healthy and are not very likely to degenerate into lust and greed.

Vedic civilization presents regulated and healthy sense gratification (*kama*), properly understood and applied on the basis of *dharma* and *artha*, as the preliminary step to genuine liberation from material conditionings (*moksha*), that constitutes the fourth and highest purpose of human life. In fact, the regulated enjoyment of healthy pleasures is conducive to liberation from material conditionings, while artificial renunciation, denial and repression are the greatest enemies of liberation from material identifications and attachments. Artificially repressing or stifling the needs for enjoyment and happiness, without attaining a higher taste spiritually, merely creates difficulties in the psyche that come out and must be dealt with in other ways, which are often more problematic.

Those who attain liberation through the natural and easy process of Vedic civilization and society, utilizing the four social categories and the four stages of life, will become happily and safely situated for their own benefit and the benefit of all. This platform of genuine liberation is described by all Vedic scriptures and considered the highest achievement, the real purpose of human life. From this platform, the transcendental purpose of life (the fifth purpose) of direct and blissful God realization can be easily attained.

THE FOUR SOCIAL CATEGORIES

As we already mentioned, in all human societies, from the simplest to the most complex, there are basically four types of people:

1. Itellectuals who have a vocation and ability to teach, counsel and guide others in their personal evolution and duties; in Sanskrit called *brahmanas*.
2. Warriors who have a vocation and ability to protect and organize others and take responsibily for, and care of, others; in Sanskrit called *kshatriyas*.
3. Enterprisers who have a vocation and ability to create and circulate wealth and prosperity, develop businesses and manufacture things and objects (i.e. products), engage land, animals and resources; in Sanskrit called *vaisyas*.
4. People who need or would rather depend on others for their maintenance and work (employees, technicians, artists, laborers, agricultural hands, cleaners, servants and assistants); in Sanskrit called *sudras*.

It is very important to understand that each individual naturally belongs to one of these categories by dint of his personal qualities, talents, inclinations, and skills that have already been developed. In Vedic civilization occupational training is personalized and based on tendencies and symptoms that are already manifest in each individual, generally since a very early age, and evaluated by a qualified teacher in the social institution or school called the Gurukula. These are never determined simply by one's birth in a family or class of people.

Because each particular class of society only gets what is really needed and suitable for the execution of their duties, there is no artificial attempt to occupy a social position for which one is unqualified because such classes are not artificially privileged and/or artificially deprived of their genuine needs. The system of values is also very clearly established in the eyes of the public by an ethical and selfless demonstration, starting from the higher classes, and naturally the mass of people tend to follow the example and embrace the values exemplified by the leaders.

For example, according to the Vedic tradition the highest class of society, the intellectual class, by rule must live in a very simple, austere and humble way, without accumulation of money or property or material power. The greatest assets of the intellectual class are truthfulness and wisdom (the practical application of knowledge), and freedom from material attachments.

In Vedic civilization, an intellectual or leader who is attached to luxury and uses his influence to get personal advantages would be automatically disqualified from such a position. An immoral, greedy, or ignorant *brahmana* is an oxymoron, a contradiction in terms, just like a "sinful saint", "intelligent fool" or "dry water".

Proper knowledge helps society to avoid the danger of unqualified and greedy people trying to get a "higher" position in society only for the privileges it entails. In Vedic society higher positions have more duties and responsibilities than rights and facilities.

Each category naturally possesses all the qualities and abilities of the previous (lower) classes because they have already been developed in this or in previous lifetimes. In fact, the higher classes must be already fully qualified and expert in the activities and duties of the lower classes, otherwise it would be impossible for them to lead and engage others effectively. So each individual can and should progressively evolve up the social ladder because each subsequent step allows the individual to develop higher and more complete qualities and experience. This can be done in the course of several lifetimes, or sometimes in one lifetime only, depending on the determination and hard work of the individual. It is also very important to understand that each category has very precise rights and duties that ensure the perfect functioning of society.

As it is described, *Brahmanas* must be austere, honest, wise, fully knowledgeable, peaceful, tolerant and self controlled, unattached to material things, inclined to religion and pure. (*Bhagavad-gita* 18.42) Specifically, they must know the spiritual science and the purpose of life (*brahma-jnana*). Their natural activities (and obligations to society) consist in teaching and educating all the members of society, counseling, guiding, judging, writing and debating.

The only benefit they get is to be able to execute their duty or, in other words, be respectfully heard as teachers and advisors when they speak of knowledge, and rewarded with charity according to their needs. When engaged in priestly duties, they can manage the temple properties by engaging the necessary workers (administrators, cultivators, laborers, etc.) but they cannot possess, for themselves or for their families, more than the simple house where they live, the food they need and the simple clothing that is characteristic of the brahmanic class.

Kshatriyas must be heroic, determined, resourceful, brave, generous and powerful, capable to lead and inspire people. (*Bg.* 18.43) They do not need to be austere but they must be always ready to sacrifice themselves and everything they have for the protection of their subjects (*ksha-tra*). Their natural activities are within the fields of military and police, law enforcement, and state management at all levels.

The benefits they receive are respect and absolute obedience, and the offering of the best products of the kingdom, which they usually distribute in charity because of their innate generosity. They should exercise and practice martial arts, diplomacy, constantly collect intelligence about the situation of the kingdom and the surrounding states, go patrolling regularly and directly administer justice. In the event of attack from external forces, they must always be in the forefront, where the greatest danger is, inspiring their soldiers with heroic example. At all times, they must protect and finance artists, poets and philosophers, and make sure that everybody in the kingdom is properly protected, engaged and maintained, including the animals.

Vaisyas must be capable of farming, cattle raising and business. (*Bg.* 18.44) Their connection is with land, animals and laborers, and the production of wealth for the society in general; they have no other duty other than taking proper care of the laborers (*sudras*), animals, land and resources. The benefit they get is essentially the satisfaction of work well done. They also live simply but can possess what is necessary for their healthy and comfortable life.

They can also produce manufactured goods as per the requirements of society, based on the materials obtained from the land and animals. Sometimes they can travel to distant places to acquire rare goods because different geographical zones have different products. Depending on the needs of the society, the resources of their lands and their particular inclination, they can become grain merchants, perfume and incense dealers, manufacturers of clothes and house articles, traders, and so on.

Sudras in a truly Vedic civilization lead the easiest, most secure and most comfortable life among the four social classes. Belonging to this social category is not a shame or a misfortune, and they are never meant to be exploited, mistreated or insulted by the other groups.

Sudras are not required to perform any austerity and are constantly gratified by their employers with distribution of sumptuous foods, gifts, clothes and ornaments, and with the celebration of many festivals organized by the higher classes of society. Their employers are obligated to care for them in all circumstances and for all needs, including during the periods when they are unable to work due to old age, disease or other causes. *Sudras* are not required to handle money and therefore to pay for anything (housing, food, education, medical assistance) or to save money for the future (insurance, retirement funds, investments). This is according to Vedic standards, much of which has been lost in this modern society.

The benefits for *sudras* are basically assured employment and maintenance in all circumstances, opportunities for creative and pleasurable work, guaranteed proper housing and good food, and sufficient leisure and entertainment: a life free from worries. On the other hand, they are not supposed to get large amounts of money (which they generally squander) or excessive luxury (which becomes obstentation) and they are expected to remain faithful to their employer even in difficult times.

Any member of society, including *sudras*, have the right to demand justice and protection from the king or *kshatriyas* in case of difficulty. Unfortunately, to the degree which society becomes distanced from the Vedic standards is the degree to which all of this becomes lost.

THE FOUR ASHRAMAS OF SOCIETY

Together with the occupational duties in society, the Vedic system prescribes particular and personal duties that pertain to different stages in life, called *ashramas*, required to train and purify each individual in a progressive life. The purpose of such training is self-realization and spiritual elevation, the most important thing in human life.

In Vedic civilization, death is not considered an unspeakable tragedy but rather the natural conclusion of life, a passage that offers the opportunity for a better future. So besides their position and functions in society, all human beings are expected to work on their personal growth to understand the purpose of life and prepare themselves for the passage to the next life. This is the purpose of the *ashramas*.

Ashramas begin with the *brahmacharya*, the training period when all boys from all classes are sent by their families to reside in the house of the *guru* (*gurukula*, "family of the guru") to render humble service and learn about *dharma*. The *guru* must be an intelligent *brahmana* who is able to observe the symptoms of each individual, provide a basic education in the purpose of life and ethics, and help each student to develop his full potential.

When the boy has reached the highest possible education and training allowed by his talents and inclinations, he leaves the *gurukula* for the *grihastha ashrama* ("householder life") for starting a family and perfoming his occupational duty in society. The *brahmachari* training received makes boys honest, responsible, self-controlled and selfless persons, qualities that are essential to execute their duties in family and society, and to continue to cultivate their personal development.

Sudras and *vaisyas* usually remain in family life even in old age, more or less engaged in their occupation and guiding their children in their specific professional training. *Kshatriyas* and *brahmanas* are expected to retire from social ties as soon as their children are old enough to take care of their responsibilities. So they enter into the *vanaprastha* stage, retiring "in the forest", or free from social obligations to fully dedicate their energies and time to austerity and to the exclusive cultivation of spiritual liberation. Some of them, generally *brahmanas*, may take up a life of complete renunciation called *Sannyasa*, although in the present age such choice is very difficult to follow strictly.

Of the four stages of life, *brahmacarya* and *sannyasa* require celibacy; the first for training in self-control and selflessness, the last in preparation for death. Vedic celibacy is based on spiritual identification, giving up the false identification as a material body. It is not considered a "mortification of the flesh" as in Christian monastic ideals and does not create repression or denial of genuine needs with the ensuing psycho-physical problems.

The meaning of the word *brahmacarya* is literally "behaving like Brahman", or seeing all living entities with the equal transcendental vision of Brahman and treating them accordingly. This concept cuts the root of material exploitation and possession, as relationships are based on the spiritual level.

Grhasthas and *vanaprasthas* generally live with their wives, whose presence and participation is required to validate religious rituals. Husband and wife together create a good team for spiritual advancement in Vedic civilization.

Women as a group are not required to perform austerities or other duties except to work cooperatively with their husbands; however they may also choose a life of independent renunciation and spiritual pursuit (*tapasvini* or *yogini*) on the same level of their male counterparts (*tapasvi* or *yogi*).

Yogis and *yoginis* do not belong to the social orders of the *varnashrama* system because they are outside the material obligations of social life. They are directly engaged in the activities of Brahman that transcend circumstantial designations and their relevant duties together with all material limitations. However, since they are free from both attraction and rejection, they are also not averse to performing any service that may be required by the Divine Plan, even if they do not identify with such roles, and receive their instructions about their duty directly from the Supreme Lord, Vishnu. Therefore they are generally called *Vaishnavas* because they are fully dedicated to the service of the Supreme Lord, without any material identification. Therefore it is said that *Vaishnavas* are beyond all social designation, such as *varna* or *ashrama*.

Because they have a clear vision of the spiritual nature of reality, they are also called *rishis*, or "seers", and when they serve in the capacity of *brahmanas* they are called *brahma-rishis* (or *brahmarshis*). When they serve in the capacity of kings they are called *raja-rishis*, or *rajarshis*. Actually, however, they can play any role in society and establish a model of spiritual consciousness from any position. A society that is fully composed by such genuinely self-realized personalities is called *daivi varnashrama*, or "divine society", where all the members perfectly perform their duties not because they want to get some benefit or because they identify with their role, but simply to please the Supreme Lord.

THE FUNCTION OF THE KING

Even when he is not an extraordinary personality or *rajarshi*, the king is always considered in a special position above all the other social classes, just like the *guru*, or the teacher who takes personal responsibility in guiding people to the perfection of human life. Both the king and the teacher are considered direct representatives of God because they are taking care of the people, dedicating all their energies and ready to sacrifice themselves for the benefit of their subordinates.

The Sanksrit word *praja* does not simply indicate "subjects" or "citizens". It indicates all the living entities who have taken birth in the kingdom, and therefore are considered the direct "children" of the king, who is considered the father of the kingdom. In many examples, as described by Dasarath to Rama in the *Ramayana* and in many stories of the *Puranas*, genuine kings have shown a complete dedication to the protection of all the *prajas*, without any discrimination.

It is interesting to note that, in the Vedic society, the definition of *praja* also includes the animals who reside in the kingdom. They are also entitled to the protection offered by the king, as exemplified in many stories. In Vedic civilization the class of *vaisyas* employs animals like cows and bulls, the *kshatriyas* employ horses and elephants, and other animals like dogs and birds. Sometimes even deer are naturally found around cities and villages, and they are all entitled to protection and fair treatment.

Since the king is only the guardian of the law and not responsible for the spiritual advancement and religious activities of the subjects (which is the job of the *brahmana* or *guru*), material power and religious power are always independent, even in the case of a saintly king (*rajarshi*). This, along with the universal vision of faith presented by Vedic knowledge, can include and accommodate practically all levels of spiritual practice and development. This is what can ensure the greatest religious tolerance. The king takes the advice of the learned *brahmanas* but does not force anyone into religious submission.

The king is generally part of the class of *kshatriyas*, but he can also come from any other class, depending on the situation since the definition of "king" is "one who takes care of the subjects". Such a position does not require a great political power or a large dominion. Even a city or a village can be considered a kingdom when there is a person who is actually responsible and taking care of the inhabitants. In Vedic times each kingdom was peacefully coexisting with others, without imperialistic aspirations.

In Vedic history we also see that sometimes a very capable king (then called emperor) would become responsible for a larger area. He would take care of subordinate kings who in turn continued to directly take care of the subjects in their respective areas.

Kings and emperors were also always very near to the people. Anyone had the right to approach them to ask for justice or protection or charity, and they periodically organized large distributions of wealth and met the people, especially during the religious celebrations.

A Vedic monarchy is not a dictatorship. Although the king has the power to sentence and punish all those who pose a serious threat to society, he always has ministers and advisors from the class of *brahmanas* or intellectuals, and a general assembly of people that would meet whenever the situation required it. Even this was open to everyone. The *brahmanas* even have the power to depose the king in case he disattended his duties and endangered the society instead of protecting it.

Vedic society has no rigid centralization of power. All qualified *kshatriyas* are supposed to take direct and personal responsibility for a number of *prajas* under their care, so police duties and administration of the state are managed with competence, although there are naturally different levels of positions, according to the qualifications and activities of each member of the *kshatriya* order. However, all the members of this social order have a very precise code of conduct that they must follow, otherwise they are expelled by their social order.

THE FUNCTION OF THE GURU

As we already mentioned, *brahmanas* are teachers and consultants for the general mass of people, giving spiritual protection and guidance just as *kshatriyas* are the material protectors of the general mass of people. And just like the king has a special role to play above all social classes, so does the qualified *guru* as the representative of the Supreme Lord.

There are, however, different levels of *gurus*, according to the qualifications and activities or functions they perform. Apart from spiritual guides, anyone who is able to teach something—from mathematics to grammar to medicine, even the use of weapons—is considered a *guru* and comes from the social class of *brahmanas* who are expert in teaching. Knowledge must always come with a sense of ethics and spiritual vision, therefore the job of teaching must be entrusted to people who have the characteristic code of conduct of the *brahmanas*.

However, we should not mistake this spiritual awareness with a blind theocracy that is only interested to protect the selfish material interests of a dominant class or religious organization. This degradation of the original genuine system regularly happens in all societies and communities when unqualified persons are accepted as *brahmanas* merely on the strength of politics, birth right, superstition, etc. The problem becomes especially apparent when their position becomes unquestionable and defended by material power, such as laws or decrees of political figures, social or financial blackmailing, police actions, etc., against all reasonable objections.

Genuine priesthood is also a characteristic occupation of *brahmanas*. An ignorant priest is one of the greatest dangers in human society, just like an irresponsible politician. So the qualifications required to perform the religious duties for other people are extremely strict and elevated. Vedic knowledge is very vast and deep, covering also the relationship with the supernatural world and the study of the self in a very scientific way.

In Vedic society, priests are teachers who facilitate people in their approach to the Divine. Their duties include reciting the scriptures, performing rituals in public temples, and initiating people into private worship and the science of Brahman. All the members of society, from all classes, are expected to perform their private worship and meditation, and directly connect to the Divine in whatever way they can, depending on their qualities (*guna*) and activities (*karma*). Still today, practically all Hindu houses have a "Deity room" for personal worship and meditation, and people from all social classes sit there in front of divine images offering their prayers, glorification, and symbols of worship.

CONCLUSION

Much more can be said about Vedic sociology, about its approach to multi-cultural and multi-ethnic relationships, and international cooperation. It laid the foundation to cover numerous social and spiritual topics. Some of these include health and medical assistance, full and satisfactory employment, economic systems and the creation of wealth, selfless service and social protection, the position of elderly people, women, children, diseased people, unqualified manpower, animals, ecology and environmental protection.

Vedic knowledge and civilization is based on a perfect balance of physics and metaphysics, where the science of the self is considered the most important science of all, supporting and connecting harmoniously all the other sciences.

Vedic sociology, described in a great wealth of classical texts such as the *Vedas*, *Puranas, Mahabharata, Ramayana* and *Shastras* in general, can be described as a global project for the elevation of human beings up to the highest peak of consciousness and happiness. It provides the means so everyone can reach their highest potential and attain the spiritual goal of life. Vedic civilization easily accommodated many ethnic groups, cultures and religions, and had elaborated a social organization that guaranteed all-round harmony, well-being and progress to all individuals, from those who had very prestigious roles to those who had modest social positions.

By directly tapping into the wholistic physical and metaphysical science amply expounded in Vedic literature, we will be able to get a wholesome and comprehensive vision that is so urgently needed by our world today.

In this short essay we have tried to present the main original Vedic ideas for the most beneficial social arrangement in a very simple language. For further discussion we will be happy to correspond by email. Please write to:

Parama Karuna devi
Jagannatha Vallabha Vedic Research Center, Jagannatha Puri
paramakaruna@dharmaseva.net, or
paramakaruna@rediffmail.com

The One World Religion

Stephen Knapp

Religion is supposed to bring us closer to God, which should certainly uplift us and show us that we are all spiritual beings. In that way we are united. This understanding could give us a central focus for general intentions of goodwill and cooperation. However, this is not how it has gone. This is mostly because each religion implies, or comes right out and says, that it is the best or the only way to God. All others are inferior and should be ignored, dominated, pushed away, or even destroyed by force. In this way, the most difficult of all things to break down are the barriers between us that have been caused by our religions.

A first-class religion is not the one that claims it is the highest religion. The first-class religion is that which teaches or trains one perfectly how to love God. That is first-class. And in such a first-class religion, no one will claim to be better than any other. That is because he or she will naturally see that we all have the same Supreme Father. The only difference between any of us is in the level of spiritual understanding we have, and how united we are to the Supreme Being. Otherwise, spiritually we are all the same, and whatever our bodily situation may be is temporary. That also means that whatever our ethnic label, our social class, or the religion we may follow, is all changeable in this life, what to speak of the next.

If you feel that your religion is the best of all others, it is natural to be loyal or appreciate what it has done for you. However, if you feel *superior* to others because of being a Muslim, or Christian, or something else, then that is where your religion has failed. For you to feel that way means that it has provided you with incomplete knowledge. You have not made much spiritual advancement. If your religion has failed to bring you to the spiritual platform in which you can see the spiritual similarities between you and all other creatures, regardless of caste, creed, culture, or species, then your religion has failed. Or you have failed to follow it properly or to its ultimate goal. It may have brought you to the path of being

94

pious, but it has not brought you to the point of true love of God and spiritual vision. Real love of God includes the spiritual love for all others, without prejudice, bias, or condescending attitudes. If you have not attained this level, then you still have much progress to make either in your own religion or by adding the help of another more complete source of spiritual knowledge. Those who are not understanding in this way and criticize different systems of religion due to jealousy, envy, malice, or a sense of superiority, are simply revealing themselves to be very immature. They do not cherish love toward their own God as much as they prefer to show more regard for vain quarrels and contentions toward those who are different.

In *Ashoka's Edicts* it is rightfully stated, "Never think or say your religion is the best. Never denounce the religion of others. But honor in them whatever is worthy of honor." After all, what good is a religion which condemns everybody else's philosophy or symbols for God except its own? Some religions say that if God is represented in a form, beautiful or symbolic, or is established in a Deity, then it is heathen or superstition, so it is bad. But if God comes in the form of a dove, burning bush, or a pillar of fire, then they say it is holy. This sort of logic is completely contradictory to the understanding of the omnipotent ability of the Supreme.

In all religions throughout the world, the external differences are easily noticed. These may be in regard to rituals, posture, clothing, food, behavior, or sanctity. There will be differences in conceptions of God and the objects of worship, or in the name of God because of differences in language or traditions. So it is natural that religions of the world may become disunited because of these differences. But it is very improper that there should be quarrel among them on the grounds of this disunion. We should, as mature servants of God, think that the religion of others still holds the same worship of the same Highest Entity as my religion, my God. Their practice may be different and I may not understand it, so I appreciate my own religion. However, there is only one God, therefore I also respect this form of worship and offer my prayers to God who is being worshiped in a different way or called a different name.

For example, the Jewish tradition has always implied that a Jewish soul has an advantage over non-Jews to realize or love God, but Judaism itself provides evidence to indicate otherwise. One quote that affirms that anyone has the ability to realize God, regardless of his race, religion, or sex, is: "Elijah said, 'I bring heaven and earth to bear witness that any human being, Jew or Gentile, man or woman, freeman or slave, according to his deeds, can become worthy of *Rauch HaKodesh*, the Holy Spirit, the transcendental experience." (*Tana DeBei Eliahu Rabba* 9, *Bahir II.* 94)

God does not favor one sect or religion over another, but monitors one's sincerity, devotion, surrender, and willingness to help and love others. And God reciprocates with one to the same degree of his or her devotion and sincerity. God is not the kind of being who favors only one sect and allows all others to be damned. Everyone is a part of God, otherwise they would not be here, and He cares for all.

In order to show His concern, God sends not just one but as many messengers and representatives as it takes to help guide and deliver all beings from material existence. The essence of that message, and all genuine religion, is the same. They all teach that we should not get stuck in material life, but keep moving toward pure spiritual existence. The essential method in all religions by which this is accomplished is simple: Love God, love all others as parts of God, and act in that way at all times. The Supreme Being has made it simple. It is only humanity that has created the confusion found in the divisions of religions. This is clearly enunciated within the essential Vedic teachings.

From this it is clear that God is the Lord of all beings, and in many ways. God is a multi-faceted being, unlimited in knowledge, ability, character, and personality. If a person is so narrow that he or she can hold allegiance to one faith while condemning all others, he or she will understand God only through that way. They will not know, nor will they be able to understand, that they can realize different aspects of God through other religions or spiritual paths. It is often seen that the most fundamental religions are the most limited in their understanding of God, and also carry with it the extra luggage of prejudice and condemnation of all other religions and cultures. It goes back to the principle that people who know the least about something are also the most fearful about what they do not understand.

Only religionists who are inexperienced and not conversant with spiritual Truth consider their ways as good and superior while hating the ways of others. They may even destroy the temples and images of God of other religions. Thus, they actually show their hatred of God. They show love only for their own conceptions, however limited they may be. All good men will refrain from such actions, and all those who engage in such deeds show their improper and animalistic mentality.

However, those religions with real faults—such as being atheistic, materialistic, rejecting the soul or the existence of the Supreme, or using evil methods in its worship—should not be regarded as genuine religions. Their doctrines are antagonistic to true spiritual love and can never please the Supreme Being.

We also need to understand that there is no such thing as two Supreme Beings, or a God of one religion and a God of another. Such distinctions are made through ignorance. God is one. The Absolute Truth is one. So how can there be two religions? When followers of different religions quarrel about Truth, it is a sign that they have yet to experience Truth. Rather than seeking an experience of the Truth, they spend their time in quarrels, nurturing their prejudices against others. They are still far away from God. The word *religion* comes from the Latin *religio,* which means to bind to God. If a religion does not teach how to directly link with God, to love, respect, and have regard for all others as His parts and parcels, then it can hardly be called religion. Or the people who follow it have lost the point.

Once again, God is one. There cannot be two. If there is another, then there is competition. And the one God is neither Hindu, Muslim, Christian, or anything else. Such classifications relate only in the way God is worshiped. Real religion does not mean that we stamp this person a Christian, someone else a Muslim, or Hindu, or a Jain. Such designations are names that have nothing to do with the reality of the soul. Unity between us will never be established by emphasizing such designations on the material platform. So if God is one, why should there be quarrels between those who worship the one God in different ways? There should be no such quarrels, unless they think they are worshiping a different God and feel their God is superior to the God of others. Such a mentality is childish.

Religion means to understand God and to abide by His laws. It means to understand the nature of the soul, which is to love and be loved, and to serve the ultimate lovable object, the Supreme Lover—God. In this way, every living being is a servant of the Supreme Being. Religion means to understand that God is great. We are subordinate. It means to understand that God is the greatest friend and proprietor. He takes care of us by providing the facilities by which we can survive. Furthermore, the ultimate purpose of religion is to regain your love for God and to return to God. This means you rise above earthly desires and designations and transcend material life. This is the real unity and purpose of life that we all share. Based on this essential principle, we should all serve, understand and love God. There is no difference. We may pursue different religions, but that is diversity in unity because we all worship the same God. When we realize that, then there can be peace and harmony. Religion will no longer be a point of division. This devotion to God is the universal aspect of all religions. And the Vedic system elaborates on that devotional path to a most detailed level.

Another way of looking at our unity is in the concept described in the *Vedas* that explain that one form of the Lord is the universe. We all exist within this universal form of God. So none of us are disconnected from Him. Furthermore, none of us are disconnected from each other. Each and every one of us has a particular function in relation to the universal form of God. Although each one of us may have different responsibilities, nonetheless, carrying out our functions within this world in relation to the universal form of God gives unity and harmony between all living beings throughout the world. However, the disruption of discharging our spiritual nature is the cause of disharmony between the living beings. So in order to achieve real peace and unity, we should recognize the fact that everything in this world and everyone is a part of this universal form of the Lord. Everything is an expansion of the Supreme's energy. No one is independent. Everyone and everything is connected. There are many diverse manifestations of God's energy. And although our bodies may not all look and act the same, we are all one in being a part of the Supreme's universal form. This is unity in diversity. When life is based on living in this truth by understanding the universal nature of the Supreme and His creation, then embracing universal love and compassion is a normal state of being.

This unity in diversity can be seen in observing the essence of any culture or religion. What we first notice are the superficialities, such as the dress, the outward formalities, the customs, rituals, and festivals. But deeper than this we find the basis of the culture's origin, the history of its development, the explanation of its philosophy, and the meaning and purpose of its rituals and customs. Still deeper is the essence and goal of the religion. As already pointed out, that essence is based on the principle that the follower should learn and engage in the process of serving, glorifying, and loving the Supreme Being. This is especially elaborated in the Vedic spiritual process of bhakti-yoga, which means uniting with God through the means of devotion. So, on the essential platform, there is really not much that differentiates the ultimate goals of the world's major religions. They all advocate love and devotion to God. The only difference in the authentic religions is the time in history in which they appeared, the place where they existed, and the people who were taught. But due to these factors there may be lesser or greater differences in doctrines, beliefs, and rituals. And depending on the intellectual ability of the people who were taught, there may be more or less spiritual knowledge that was provided. Thus, there are different levels of scripture. Some are more direct and complete than others in the same way an unabridged dictionary is more complete than one that is abridged, though they both contain the same type of information. So once again we find the basis of unity in diversity.

The most important difference, however, is the depth of philosophical understanding and spiritual knowledge each particular religious process has to offer, and the level of spiritual realization the aspirant can attain by following that process. It is a fact that all true religious paths can lead to God, but such deep experience is beyond the grasp of fundamental and materially motivated religions that are based on national or cultural traditions and feelings of superiority because of race or geographical region. Such religions fail in their attempts to promote universal or spiritual brotherhood because they lack the spiritual knowledge, depth and potency necessary to do so. Furthermore, because of this deficiency, they cannot give their followers the process that will enable them to become fully spiritually realized. So they remain attached to their own misconceptions and biased against others because they cannot rise above the materialistic vision that causes them to focus on superficial differences, such as race, creed, cultural background, sex, or dress.

So how do we solve this problem that keeps people of different religions or cultures from accepting each other and working together? It is both easy and difficult. The easy part is to understand that the people merely have to be willing to share their spiritual knowledge with each other. They can all keep their own traditions, holidays, festivals, and rituals, but the essential knowledge and science of the individual souls, the Supreme Soul, and the relationship between them is what is important and what can be easily shared. This spiritual science is not explained more thoroughly than in the Vedic literature (as has been summarized in one of my previous books, *The Secret Teachings of the Vedas*). In fact, comprehending this knowledge of the Absolute Truth is necessary for everyone's spiritual advancement, regardless of which spiritual process one is inclined to accept. There must be this kind of open and respectful exchange across global and cultural boundaries in order for peace and unity between all societies to exist. The hard part is to get people to agree to do this. But in some cases you have to look at other cultures and their philosophical systems to get answers that are not provided elsewhere.

In fact, the Bible agrees with the idea of researching other scripture for answers. In *II Timothy* (3.16-17) we find the following quote: "All scripture is given by inspiration of God, and is profitable for doctrine, for reproof, for correction, for instruction in righteousness, that the man of God may be perfect, thoroughly furnished in all good works." Therefore, it is without a doubt that all scripture everywhere is meant to uplift our consciousness. Such being the case, it is not contradictory to see similarities in various scriptures and spiritual cultures, and it actually adds to and proves the glory of God amongst all nations. After all, there are obviously more nations than one, and God is the Supreme Creator of all. Thus, He remembers those who are upon the isles of the sea, or in the heavens above or elsewhere. And certainly He can bring forth His word unto all of His children and unto all the nations of the earth in His own way. So simply because there is a Bible or a Koran does not mean that they contain all of His words. Nor that He cannot cause more to be written for those in any other location, or any other period of history. For He commands all men, both in the east and in the west, and in the north and in the south, and in the islands of the sea, so that, if He wishes, they can write the instructions which are given or inspired by God which can lead mankind to a better and more peaceful life, closer to Him. For it is by the deeds and intentions that each person displays toward each other and toward God that will be judged, that will be viewed as the content of one's character. If men cannot have love toward each other, who are but parts of God, then surely love of God and recognition of God in all beings is absent in such a person.

The above point is not unlike the Bible verse in *Romans* (10.12-13): "For there is no difference between the Jew and the Greek: for the same Lord over all is rich unto all that call upon him. For whosoever shall call upon the name of the Lord shall be saved."

We herewith have the reasoning why all our petty quarrels, whether between Catholics and Protestants, Hindus and Muslims, or nation and nation, are nothing more than a sign of our ignorance and animalistic tendencies which actually disqualify us from making any spiritual advancement. We may think we are a chosen people, but if we have no spiritual vision to see the unity between all people, then the "promised land" is a lot farther away than we think. For God remembers all of us and, indeed, supplies all nations the knowledge by which they can spiritually advance and live peacefully, depending on their ability to understand and use it. After all, those who are sincerely trying to advance are all sons of God, as verified in *Romans* (8.14): "For as many as are led by the spirit of God, they are the sons of God." A similar statement is in *John* (1.12): "But as many as received him, to them gave he the power to become the sons of God, even to them that believe on his name." Thus, we are all God's children, as also confirmed by Lord Krishna in *Bhagavad-gita* (9.17-18) in which He says that He is the father of the universe, the mother, the grandfather, the object of knowledge, the purifier, the sacred *om*, and the *Rig, Sama,* and *Yajur Vedas.* He is the goal, the support, the master, the witness, the abode, and the most dear friend. Krishna also says (*Bg.*7.6) that He is the origin and dissolution of the entire universe, and (*Bg.*4.35) by knowing the Truth you will see that all beings are a part of Him and belong to Him. Thus, by understanding how we are all spiritually related, all sincere souls will find no difficulty in harmoniously working together and helping one another to understand the laws of the Supreme and advance accordingly, whether we are brother and brother, or nation and nation.

So if we are all spiritually related and can find similarities in the basic law of all religions, then what is the difficulty in cooperating with each other within the essential principles of all religions and spiritual paths? And what is the essential principle we are all meant to follow? The essence of the law, as found in the Vedic, the Judaic, the Christian, the Islamic, and other cultures, instructs us to surrender to God and work together to please Him according to His instructions. For example, when the Pharisees asked Jesus which was the great commandment in the law, he told them: "Thou shalt love the Lord thy God with all thy heart and with all thy soul, and with all thy mind. This is the first and great commandment." (*Matthew* 22.37-38) Lord Krishna taught the same thing in *Bhagavad-gita*: "Always think of Me and become My devotee. Worship Me and offer your homage unto Me. Thus you will come to Me without fail. Abandon all varieties of religion and just surrender unto Me. I shall protect you from all sinful reaction. Do not fear." (*Bg.*18.65-66)

In the *Koran* (9.112) we find it said that those who turn to God in repentance and serve and praise Him, and engage in devotion to God, who bow down and pray, who do good and avoid evil, will rejoice. So proclaim these glad tidings to the believers. We also find it said (19.65) that everyone should worship the Lord of the heavens and the earth and be patient in constant worship. For who is worthy of the same name as God?

In Zoroastrianism it is believed that a person must live according to the religious tenets if one hopes to joyfully go before the Creator in the next world. The best of all practices is the worship of God, for all are servants of God. So one must lead a righteous life since it is one's thoughts, words, and deeds that determine one's next life after death. Similarly, in Sikhism we find the precept that a true follower serves the Supreme Soul alone.

All of this information makes it clear that regardless of which religious system you choose, they all have the same purpose, and they all give the same principles based on devotion, *bhakti*, to God. In this way, they are all united in their essential goals, the most important of which is to bring the living beings to the stage of cooperation with each other in love of God. Obviously, our love for God will be shown by how much we cooperate with one another.

Unfortunately, before we reach this advanced stage we are in the lower levels of understanding, and the fundamental stage of devotion. This immature level of love, or fundamentalism as some call it, can take on the characteristics of a blind and fanatical allegiance to a particular belief or process of religious expression rather than attachment to real love for God. In this situation, one may proudly and unnecessarily feel that he or she is on the highest path, and then will denounce every other process and culture without the proper spiritual understanding of himself or others. This is nothing more than sentimentality and fanaticism. Real love of God, which also displays love for all other living beings, will not develop within a person if he or she harbors such a divisive mentality. *People who show their love for their own religion by hating all others will spiritually stagnate and cause disharmony and quarrels between those of varying sects within their own religion and those of other faiths.* Someone may be a kind, generous, and devout person amongst those of his own culture, while ready to howl, insult, hate, and do injury to those of another. This is love of the lowest level, similar to the way a dog may love its master and will show it by snarling at anyone else who comes nearby. Only those individuals and dry forms of religion that are bereft of real spiritual knowledge look at all others with hate and suspicion. Such conceptions within materialistic forms of religions must be stifled or they will create havoc wherever they go.

Only when one's consciousness becomes mature does this form of fanaticism or immature enthusiasm subside. Then real love and respect for all will naturally emanate from that person. As one becomes closer to the all-loving Supreme Being by the development of his own love for God, no longer can he be an instrument of hatred or prejudice because he or she will see everyone equally with spiritual vision. Thus, he walks away from the animalistic quarrels and wars that others take so seriously due to their ignorance of spiritual reality.

We have to remember that we are in this world but not of it. We are all spiritual beings who are temporarily residing in the material creation. It is futile to try and make a permanent home here, or attempt to be fully content and happy by being absorbed in material pleasures. This world does not and never will offer that kind of accommodation. A spiritual being in the material world, which is what we all are, is like a fish out of water: It is an incompatible situation. So we must understand the reality of our circumstance, that we are all transients evolving in a temporary situation on our way from one point of existence to another.

So what is this life? It is nothing more than a moment on our great path towards full enlightenment. The world primarily is a field for activity which we can use to evolve to a higher state of being, and the body is the tool or vehicle in which we engage in those acts. But if we forget that, then we get caught in the illusion that this world is the cause and basis of our happiness, and our temporary body is the basis of our identity. Nothing can be further from the truth, and anyone with some proper understanding will see this.

By uplifting our consciousness with genuine spiritual knowledge, one will realize his or her spiritual identity and know that the immaterial realm pervades everything within as well as outside this material creation. Therefore, one who has become evolved and detached from the material focus of life knows that he is a spiritual being and a part of the divine strata. In this sense, wherever he goes, he is already home. A person who lives in this consciousness knows that there are only three things that are eternal: (1) the Supreme Being, (2) all the individual spiritual entities, and (3) the relationship between them, which is based on divine love. This spiritual love is all that has to be reawakened. This is the real goal of life and the real purpose of any genuine spiritual process. The spiritual strata, or fully enlightened consciousness, is where that love can manifest to the fullest degree.

If somehow or other the people of the world could give up their superficial differences and join together in genuine spiritual activity, which is based on advancing in one's devotion to the Supreme, the consciousness of society in general could change to such a degree that this very planet could become spiritually surcharged. It is not that we have to work for a specific change to bring about solutions to the world's problems, but when the consciousness of the people becomes purified, the solutions to the problems will become obvious and the necessary changes will automatically begin to manifest. Therefore, entering the spiritual realm, or changing the world in which we presently live, is simply a matter of reawakening our dormant divine consciousness. It is not a matter of outward observation, but it is an inward process of transformation and development. This is what the Vedic spiritual knowledge has explained since time immemorial.

If the people of the world would be more inclined to recognize that spiritual advancement is a process of inner transformation and participate in this process, and share with each other the different levels of higher knowledge from other cultures rather than merely accepting one particular religious dogma and rejecting all other forms of spiritual growth, then it becomes possible for all of humanity to be a united people. After all, a true religion respects whatever level of universal truth is found in any other culture and religion. Everyone could band together with a common cause of helping each other become enlightened: A universal religion based on hearing about and glorifying the Supreme. Every religion does this, so why not do it together? The only difference then would be whether people were theists or atheists, and atheists are simply those who have no spiritual experience or cannot fathom the depths of divine knowledge.

Otherwise, a world full of isolated religious cultures and doctrines is a world full of scattered and incomplete portions of the universal path to the Absolute Truth. Thus, we must seek to unite these paths by finding the common source from which these portions have sprung. This would lead one to the core of Universal Truth, or the conclusion of all spiritual knowledge, otherwise called Vedanta. When you find that source, you will find the doorway that leads to full realization of the Absolute Truth and the clear consciousness through which we can see that all living beings share the same immaterial identity. Spiritually we are all one family. And on this level of consciousness it becomes obvious that all temporary material differences are superficialities. It is only people's own immature prejudice, caused by their spiritual ignorance, that stops people of the world from being united and cooperating together. Remembering that God is in everyone, and everyone is here by the will of God, and that God cares for all beings, you can respect anyone.

This does not mean that all religions should become merged into some impersonalistic and ineffective hodgepodge, but it means that each process should include the knowledge and system by which all followers can completely understand the science of the soul, their true spiritual identity, and attain their own realizations of the topmost levels of spiritual reality and the real nature of the Supreme Being. If a religion or spiritual path does not provide these things, then it is not complete. In such a case, a person should seek out the highest available level of spiritual science that does provide the above-mentioned factors and gives the connecting link between the fundamental principles of all religions.

So herewith, in this chapter, we have given evidence that throughout the world and within the essential teachings of all scriptures thereof, those who shall realize their true spiritual identity and be released from material entanglement and even enter the spiritual strata are those who have taken shelter of the Supreme through *bhakti*, devotion, and the process of *sravana* and *kirtana*, hearing about, glorifying, and chanting the holy names of the Supreme. On this path, which has been recommended the world over, other than one's own immature prejudice, there are no superficial differences, such as race, creed, nationality, tradition, sex, age, etc., that can stop the people of the world from being united and engaging in this process together, for this is the one world religion.

The Vedic Process for World Peace

Stephen Knapp

One of the primary Vedic principles is that we are not these bodies, but only temporarily residing within them. To think that these bodies are our real identity is called being in the bodily conception of life. We need to rise above this bodily platform if we ever expect to reach a stage of permanent peace and unity in this world. Even on an individual basis, real peace of mind can be attained only when one realizes that he or she is not the body. Otherwise, when you think you are your body you engage in the never-ending game of trying to satisfy your mind and senses, which always want new things for stimulation. The more you try to satisfy your senses, the more you will come under the control of lust, greed and anger. Lust is there when you want to satisfy your material desires. Greed is there when you want more than you need. Anger will always be there in some form when you fail to achieve what you want, or when you attain it but then lose it. The unmerciful masters of lust, greed and anger will never leave you alone. The only way you can achieve real peace of mind is by being free from your material desires, or at least most of them. That can only be possible when you realize you are not your body, and that working only to satisfy the mind and senses is not the way for real happiness.

Happiness based on the body is like the pleasure a person feels when he or she drinks a tingling soft drink. As long as there is tingle on the tongue, there is some pleasure. The pleasure is gone when the sensation stops. So in material life, we may feel some pleasure or happiness during a thrilling or stimulating experience, or when we forget whatever problems or troubles we may have.

We all know there can be many problems and concerns in life, and forgetting these problems can also be a form of happiness. To help reach this forgetfulness there are a variety of things that we may do. For example, one may engage in the drinking of alcoholic beverages, taking drugs, or other diversionary activities. These can bring on a state of temporarily forgetting one's problems, weaknesses, suffering, or fears. If people resort too much to these forms of escape, however, their problems may actually increase. This is false happiness. It is temporary. It does not cure any problems. The problems are still there when you come down from being high. So trying to satisfy the mind and senses in this way is not a means to real happiness. It is mostly a crutch to help get through life. Beyond that, these activities are frequently a cry for help.

Actually, identifying with the material body means suffering. There are so many temporary things we are forced to work for to satisfy the desires we have in our bodily concept of life. However, as soon as you actually perceive or realize that you are not your body, you can immediately become very jolly because you now have so many desires, goals and prizes for which you no longer need to struggle. That is because you have a clearer sense of what is relevant to your true happiness and real identity. In the material situation, we are always hankering for what we want and lamenting for what we have lost. This is anxiety. We suffer this way because we are always trying to possess that which is temporary. We may have something for a while, but then it is subject to wearing out, getting lost, or being taken away. Even when you approach a large, luxurious house of a wealthy person, there may be big fences and gates to keep others out, or a sign that warns "No Trespassers" or "Beware of Dog." This means that they may be so comfortable, but they are still in anxiety that someone will come and try to rob them and take away what they have.

So through our bodily conception of life, we are always hankering after material enjoyment and, therefore, trying to acquire and hold on to so many things in hopes of maintaining that enjoyment. The thought of losing our so-called valuables and what we cherish gives us great anxiety. So, in that state of mind how can there be real peace? Material happiness and anxiety are two sides of the same coin. They are superficial to the soul since they are essentially states of mind. In other words, it is only due to the mind's interactions with sense objects that determine the mind's pleasure, pain or anxiety. The spirit soul is actually above such miseries and temporary pleasures. Thus, the secret to attaining real happiness lies in reaching the spiritual platform.

One of the ancient Vedic texts of India, the *Srimad-Bhagavatam*, explains it this way: "O my Lord, the material miseries are without factual existence for the soul. Yet as long as the conditioned soul sees the body as meant for sense enjoyment, he cannot get out of the entanglement of material miseries, being influenced by Your external energy." (*Bhag.*3.9.9)

The miseries of life are caused only by the influence of the illusory energy which the living beings are subjected to as long as they refuse to understand their real identity. This is also confirmed in *Srimad-Bhagavatam*: "O my Lord, the people of the world are embarrassed by all material anxieties—they are always afraid.

They always try to protect wealth, body, and friends, they are filled with lamentation and unlawful desires and paraphernalia, and they avariciously base their undertakings on the perishable conceptions of 'I' and 'mine.' As long as they do not take shelter of You, they are full of such anxieties." (*Bhag*.3.9.6)

The Vedic literature explains that working so hard for that which is temporary is like working hard for nothing at all. Why? Because one day you may have what you have wanted, but another day it is gone. That is the nature of material objects and whatever happiness they provide. However, once you realize you are not your body, you become free from this anxiety. You become free to the degree to which you realize that, as a spiritual being, real happiness is not dependent on material objects and pleasures. If we want peace without anxiety, we must come to the spiritual position.

OUR REAL IDENTITY

We are the spirit soul inside the body. According to the Vedic teachings, in this body we are covered by two layers: One is the subtle body, the other is the physical body. The subtle body is the mind, intelligence and false ego. It is within this subtle body where all of our concepts of life and desires exist. The psychic activities, such as our thinking, willing and feeling, take place within the subtle body. The false ego is the subtle element which makes us feel that we are this body, and that we are a certain kind of body, such as white, black, American or European. Real ego means to understand that "I am," or "I am a spiritual being." False ego means that you think you are the temporary material body. The sense of designations comes from the false ego. The second and outer layer which covers the soul is the physical body, which holds all of our internal organs, muscles, nerves, and bones. These are made of blood, mucus and skin, but are essentially made of different combinations of the common material elements of earth, air, fire, water, and ether. Combinations of all these elements, both physical and subtle, make the multi-dimensional vehicle or container in which we presently reside.

Those who are content simply to pamper and provide comforts for this container or body are materialists. Their consideration for happiness is the body and the material conditions that surround it. That is the general purpose of the material world. Beyond that, some people want to satisfy the mind through various arts, philosophy, or other mental stimulation. But both mental and physical happiness are considered external and temporary, because they exist only within the realm of the material or subtle body and do not touch the spirit soul. It is like taking care of the person's coat or shirt while neglecting the person within.

Pampering the coat or even the shirt of the individual does not reach the person within. He or she does not feel real pleasure. Similarly, by taking care of the bird cage while neglecting the bird inside is not the way to make the bird happy. This is why people who may be successful, absorbed in material affairs, may still feel empty, unfulfilled, or unsatisfied within. Real happiness is that which touches the soul itself, the true identity of the living being.

The evidence that the soul is inside the body is the consciousness which pervades the body. We find that the best sources for explaining the characteristics of the soul are located in the ancient Vedic literature of India. Many such texts have information about this, but the great classic *Bhagavad-gita* (13.34) explains: "O son of Bharata, as the sun alone illuminates all this universe, so does the living entity, one within the body, illuminate the entire body by consciousness."

Elsewhere in *Bhagavad-gita* Sri Krishna relates the eternal nature of the soul: "Never was there a time when I did not exist, nor you, nor all these kings; nor in the future shall any of us cease to be. As the embodied soul continually passes, in this body, from boyhood to youth to old age, the soul similarly passes into another body at death. The self-realized soul is not bewildered by such a change." (*Bg.*2.12-13)

"Know that which pervades the entire body is indestructible. No one is able to destroy the imperishable soul. Only the material body of the indestructible, immeasurable, and eternal living entity is subject to destruction. (*Bg.*2.17-18)... For the soul there is never birth nor death. Nor, having once been, does he ever cease to be. He is unborn, eternal, ever-existing, undying and primeval. He is not slain when the body is slain. (*Bg.*2.20)...As a person puts on new garments, giving up old ones, similarly, the soul accepts new material bodies, giving up the old and useless ones." (*Bg.*2.23)

Here in these verses we get great insights into the characteristics and eternal nature of the individual soul. According to these explanations, the soul is completely beyond the influence of the temporary material nature. Furthermore, the size of the soul is also described in the *Svetasvatara Upanishad* (5.9): "When the upper point of a hair is divided into one hundred parts and again each of such parts is further divided into one hundred parts, each such part [one ten-thousandth of the tip of a hair] is the measurement of the dimension of the spirit soul."

According to the Vedic literature, the body is compared to a chariot in which the self is riding. "Transcendentalists who are advanced in knowledge compare the body, which is made by the order of the Supreme Personality of Godhead, to a chariot. The senses are like the horses; the mind, the master of the senses, is like the reins; the objects of the senses are the destinations; intelligence is the chariot driver; consciousness, which spreads throughout the body, is the cause of bondage in this material world." (*Srimad-Bhagavatam* 7.15.41)

The *Katha Upanishad* also explains the refined nature of the soul which makes it so difficult to be seen. It says that within the body, higher than the senses and the sense objects, exists the mind. More subtle than the mind is the intelligence, and higher and more subtle than the intellect is the self. That self is hidden in all beings and does not shine forth, but is seen by subtle seers through their sharp intellect.

Naturally, until our consciousness is cleansed, we recognize various beings according to their body. We may see a person that appears to be a man, a woman, a child, or a baby. Or we may recognize those who appear to be animals, insects, aquatics, or plants. However, once we can see beyond these material bodies, we will see that all these entities are the same. They are all spirit souls within temporary material forms.

The *Svetasvatara Upanishad* (5.10-11) states that the self is not man, woman, nor neuter, but appears in different types of bodies only due to previous activities and desires of the living entity. This is how the entity chooses whatever status in which one presently appears. But a person in divine consciousness can perceive that he or she is beyond all designations and activities.

"The humble sage, by virtue of true knowledge, sees with equal vision a learned and gentle brahmana, a cow, an elephant, a dog, and a dog-eater (outcaste)." (*Bg.*5.18)

So this is some of the information about the size and nature of the soul as described in the Vedic literature. These verses from the Vedic texts are provided because such details about the soul are not found elsewhere. No other scripture contains such detailed information about the soul or even the characteristics of the Supreme Soul. So from this information we can understand that the soul is completely separate from whatever labels or designations we give to the body. This is clearly explained in the following verse from the *Srimad-Bhagavatam* (5.10.10):

"Fatness, thinness, bodily and mental distress, thirst, hunger, fear, disagreement, desires for material happiness, old age, sleep, attachment for material possessions, anger, lamentation, illusion and identification of the body with the self are all transformations of the material covering of the spirit soul. A person absorbed in the material bodily conception is affected by these things, but the soul is free from all bodily conceptions. Consequently, the spirit soul is neither fat nor skinny nor anything else you may consider."

Only in this frame of mind, understanding that we are not these bodies nor bound permanently by their limitations, will we be able to reach a stage of peace within ourselves individually and go on to attain peace in the world. We must be full of peace with ourselves before we can be peaceful with others.

BEING FREE OF ALL DESIGNATIONS

There are two levels of existence; material and spiritual. Designations for the body and mind are material. To be on the spiritual level means to be free from the influence of bodily designations. Neither will you think you are the body, nor will you think that others are their bodies. You will see the individual soul within the body as if seeing a person dressed in clothes.

Our body may be European, or African, American, Christian, or Muslim. But that deals with the body and mind, like the dress or coat of a person. Someone may wear a white shirt and someone else a black or red shirt, but that is not who we are. Nor should it be the basis of our quarrels. If we see only the dress, then we think we are different. If we think we are different and that we oppose each other, then there may be fights or even wars because one side is wearing a white shirt and the other a red shirt. The dress is our covering or our body, it is not the real person. And the dress may even change in color, shape, size, design, and style. Anything material in this world is subject to change. Therefore, we have to look beyond the dress to see the real person within. The spiritual platform is eternal and absolute. Thus, the spiritual being within the covering or dress is the same as every other spiritual being. So where is the reason for fighting?

On the bodily platform we engage in defending our honor and reputation. But what are these? Whatever fame, power, or strength we have clings only to the body. We lose it all when we shed the body at the time of death. The soul is above such things. All material situations are temporary and have nothing to do with the eternal, spiritual self. We are all here in this world for a short time, like travelers on a bus. We have been given a seat or position which we have for a little while. Then we will be forced to give it up at the end of the journey; the end of life. Why, therefore, should we be so attached, so ready to fight, over a temporary seat?

It is obvious that as long as people are in the bodily concept of life, there will not be any real unity or harmony between us. Unity cannot be attained by resolutions, political platforms, social agreements, laws or military actions. It cannot be attained through force. It can only be attained through mutual realization and understanding when we reach the spiritual platform, centered on the fact that we are all spiritual sparks of the Supreme Being. This is the platform of real unity between us. As long as we see our fellow men and women as being merely human, we will continue to suffer disillusionment. Only by seeing the greater potential of the divine nature within all of us, beneath the weakness of the flesh, can we reach unconditional love. Then we can all unite in our constitutional and spiritual position of being eternal servants of the Supreme. That is real unity. Then we are properly centered. Then we can turn to each other with the proper respect and consideration, helping one another and treating each other as we would like to be treated. In such a condition, the whole world works for its own upliftment.

As explained in another of the ancient Vedic texts, the *Sri Isopanishad* (*Mantras* 6-7): "He who sees everything in relation to the Supreme Lord, who sees all entities as His parts and parcels and who sees the Supreme Lord within everything, never hates anything nor any being. One who always sees all living entities as spiritual sparks, in quality one with the Lord, becomes a true knower of things. What, then, can be illusion or anxiety for him?"

SEEING THE DIVINITY IN EACH OF US

Morihei Ueshiba, the founder of the Aikido method of martial arts said: "Above all, one must unite one's heart with that of the gods. The essence of God is love, an all-pervading love that reaches every corner of the universe. If one is not united to God, the universe cannot be harmonized. Martial artists who are not in harmony with the universe are merely executing combat techniques, not Aiki (*Ai*—uniting harmony and love with *ki*—the universal energy)."

This understanding is very important even in ordinary, everyday life. If we are not working in harmony with love and universal energy, we are simply going through daily routines that are ineffectual and empty. We need to practice the methods that also awaken the connection we have with God, the universe, and each other. This is the way we can fully grow and develop. Then our life will have meaning and purpose. We will be guided by our own upliftment and will be able to assist in the upliftment of others. We will be able to recognize the all-pervasiveness of the Supreme Being.

The essence of this perception has been related in the ancient Vedic texts, as we find in the *Svetasvatara Upanishad* (6.11) which states, "He is the one God hidden in all beings, all pervading, the self within all beings, watching over all worlds, dwelling in all beings, the witness, the perceiver." If one can truly understand this and become enlightened in this way, he will see that he is a part of the Supreme Reality and realize his union with all beings. Within that enlightenment one can reach Divine Love. This love is based on the spiritual oneness and harmony between all beings, which is sublime. It is a source of spiritual bliss. It is a love based not on bodily relations or mutual attraction, but it is based on being one in spirit, beyond the temporary nature of the body. This is the love for which everyone searches, from which springs forth peace, harmony, and unity, of which all other kinds of love are mere reflections. This state of being is reached only through spirituality. Therefore, a life without spirituality is a life incomplete. All have the need to fill their souls with spirituality, the presence of God, in order to feel fullness, peace, contentment, and unity.

As the Supreme says in the ancient Vedic text of *Bhagavad-gita* (6.30): "To him who sees Me in everything and everything in Me, I am never lost, and he is not lost to Me."

To begin seeing how things really are, and to recognize the Divinity in each of us, we have to start adjusting our consciousness. This takes place by being trained in spiritual knowledge and by the practice of yoga which purifies the mind. When the mind becomes purified and the false ego no longer influences our vision, we become sensible people. As the *Bhagavad-gita* (13.31-32) says, when a sensible man ceases to see different identities due to different material bodies, he attains the spiritual conception. Those with the vision of eternity see that the soul is transcendental, eternal, and beyond the modes of nature. Despite being within the material body, the soul is above material contact.

As the son is a part and parcel of the father, similarly, we are all individual parts of the supreme spiritual Father. In fact, the whole creation displays different energies which are expansions of the Supreme Energetic. Thus, there is diversity within the variegated material energy which expands from the Supreme Being. These expansions manifest in millions of species of life, as explained in the Vedic literature. Therefore, although we are in different material bodies, we are all expansions of the same spiritual energy. This is oneness and unity in diversity. On the spiritual platform, which is absolute, we are all the same. We are all spiritual beings, servants of the Supreme Being, undergoing life in the material creation. That is real unity. This perception is the perfection of the spiritually conscious person. He sees all living beings as reflections of the One, the Supreme Being. Thus, in a broad sense, there is one interest. Spiritually there is no clash.

We are all but small reflections of the Supreme Consciousness. When we put the greater whole above ourselves, and realize that we all contribute to the condition of this planet, then uniting with a common cause and with that Supreme Consciousness will be easy.

This planet does not allow us to be isolated. We all must work together and interface with others on some level. One lesson that this school of existence on this planet forces us to learn is that when we come together willingly to communicate, with a positive purpose, or to pray together, and to unite for the good of the whole, then harmony and peace can exist. That peace forms and manifests when we focus on our spiritual nature, which brings between us our unity in the Supreme. Making this the center of our existence will easily bring peace, unity, and harmony in this world because it brings in the spiritual vibration that emanates from the Supreme. That vibration is one of spiritual love. It is all that is eternal. All else is temporary. Therefore, focusing on and using our energy on temporary emotions such as envy, jealousy, and anger, will only keep us far away from the Supreme, and from reaching any peace or unity between us.

We have to recognize how similar we are in order to expand our heart toward others we may have previously rejected. This is how love and understanding can dissolve the boundaries that keep us stifled as a society and individuals, and keep us from entering higher dimensions of consciousness. There is no other way to grow spiritually. A lack of love for each other is a reflection of a lack of love for God.

When we think in spiritual consciousness, we do not recognize others by their differences. We do not see ourselves only as Americas, Russians, Iraqis, Afghanistanis, Indians, Muslims, Christians, Jews, Hindus, etc. We see our similarities. This is easy when we think in terms of being sons and daughters of the same Supreme Father. We all belong to the One. Only in this way can there be universal love among all living entities. Only in this way can we begin to think that we are all related to each other. Once we establish our relationship with the Supreme, then we can establish our true relationship with everyone else. Our spiritual nature is eternal, and our spiritual relation with the Supreme is eternal.

Therefore, our spiritual relationship with each other is also eternal. It is not subject to time and circumstances. This central point has to be established in order for there to be universal peace, brotherhood, equality, and unity in the world.

In essence, we are all bits of consciousness in material forms. Consciousness cannot be destroyed. It is the essence of God in each of us. We are all spiritual beings, reflections of the Divine. We are not our beliefs, our cultures, or our minds and bodies. We are all divine souls on a wondrous journey through Truth. We have all manifested from God, the Supreme Truth, and we are all evolving back to God. As the *Manu-samhita* (12.125) relates, "Thus, he who by means of Self sees the self in all created things, after attaining equality with all, enters into Brahman [spiritual consciousness], the highest place." That is the ultimate goal.

PART TWO

The Vedic Arts & Sciences

The Scientific Worldview—
Truth or Consequences?

Dhan Roussé

FINDING THE TRUTHS WITH SCIENCE

In a relative world, such as the one we live in, how does one find truth? That quest is undertaken by many young adults as they try to make sense of the world, and I was one such seeker in my youth. My experiences in college played an important role in guiding my search, providing a proving ground on which to test different concepts as I came across them. The "Arts" almost immediately failed my litmus test, as learning and attending to the subjective prejudices of my instructors were more important to getting a good grade than was any attempt to find or discuss universal truths. Nobody there seemed to be interested in such ideas, so I quickly abandoned the arts for engineering.

Engineering college seemed to be illumined in high contrast "black and white"—the confusing shades-of-gray missing. Test questions were either right or wrong and not influenced by the instructor's daily biorythms or other unknown or unknowable ephemeral influences too subtle for my developing understanding. I liked the fact that in engineering college 2+2 always equaled four, the second law of thermodynamics was as applicable on all continents, and that from theory one could extract principles that had the real-world results of dependable bridges, heavier-than-air flight, and communication using the electromagnetic spectrum. Here, I thought, I could find the genuine truths that applied everywhere-and-every-time, upon which to develop a reliable understanding of the world.

Likewise, I think that many people, probably even most, also consider science as that branch of study that has become *the* most powerful tool to discover and know the truths of our world.

THE SCIENTIFIC METHOD

Derived from the philosophy of rationality, and the principles of logic, scientific principles assert that the external world is real, that there is but *one* single reality, and the goal of science is to understand that reality. The scientific method requires the testing of ideas or postulates that are collected in a hypothesis, which will predict certain outcomes based upon logical deduction and known scientific principles. The hypothesis is then tested rigorously, and attempts should even be made to disprove it. After it withstands these challenges and its predictions are demonstrated to be correct, and as or even more importantly, not proven incorrect, the hypothesis may then be elevated to the status of a theory. Thus challenges, critiques, and testing of hypotheses are an integral and inseparable part of bona fide science.

At the time I felt reassured with such an ideal understanding of science. I also pursued graduate school as much as my own personal quest for the truth. However, not only was I learning more about material science, I was also maturing and developing my understanding of the world around me. In fact, I learned as much or more about people and the world in those years as I did about science, and there was one lesson that combined both that had a major impact on me. The research that I was engaged in was meant to replace a much older, and factually inaccurate, method of determining the physical properties of metals. Somewhere along the line, however, I was able to reason that just as my professor and I were working to upset a long-standing theory and assert a better one, someone at some future time would likely come along and unseat our theory with something better. Thus, I began to see that certain aspects of science were not rigid or fixed truths, but more practically they were a collection of facts that best represented what people at any given time could understand.

In fact, it is flatly stated in scientific theory that no aspect of "knowledge" can be considered as the conclusive or absolute truth, for exactly the same reasons as I was able to discern—at any time a better idea may come along that will disprove the earlier ones.

This developing perception created an existential crisis in which I felt myself floundering in a Nietzschean-like world that was not grounded by any fixed principle. Where then do we find truth, or do we find any at all? The world of "science" now seemed as uncertain as the Arts and seemed to afford little to no shelter or succor in an increasingly relative and uncertain world.

Serendipitously, however, it was just at this time that I was becoming acquainted with another approach to the truth—that of the Vedic perspective. Having learned about Vedic wisdom from a friend, I had acquired and began studying the

Bhagavad-gita As It Is by A. C. Bhaktivedanta Swami. The timing couldn't have been better. As the scientific rug was being pulled out from under me, I seemed to step onto a magic carpet that carried me to an epistemological firmament, and at the same time provided a meaning to life that superseded everything I had known. And all this despite the fact that I couldn't even pronounce many of the words within it. Over the years my continued study of the *Bhagavad-gita* has allowed me to better understand the nature of this world.

It is said that understanding a problem is 90% of its solution. And the great Einstein has instructed us that "problems cannot be solved at the same level of thinking that created them." This is the advantage of the *Bhagavad-gita*, or Vedic worldview—it provides a perspective that is distinctly different from Western experience, and allows problems to be reframed in such a way that solutions are more readily apparent. Further, it's a worldview that can account for *all* of the myriad experiences of human life. It is from theistic Vedic perspective that I have learned to view the world and its events, activities, and problems. In this paper I report on some of the deviations in the sciences and other areas of academia.

Although most non-scientists generally think that science is relatively straight forward in its approach, in many of its practices it is becoming increasingly at odds with its own bona fide methods. Social scientist Karl Popper[1] has analyzed the methods of science and his philosophical approach, called the hypothetico-deductive method, is widely accepted as the best approach to scientific logic. Despite the fact that the best practices are well-known they are not always used. Harvard Professor Emeritus Dr. Ernst Mayr, in his 1997 biology textbook writes that even among scientists there actually is a fair amount of confusion about what science really is, or how it should be practiced.[2] Some say that science is limited to that which can be known by observation and experiment. Yet others say that by its influence science consists not simply of the true facts of the world, but also includes what scientists may *say* about the world—regardless of what the true state of the world may be—because their mere assertions carry great legitimacy due to the authority that science has achieved within society.[3]

These ideas imply that science may be or is being used for purposes other than a search for truth. Indeed, some consider that beyond its usefulness in allowing us to create items helpful for our lives, science is being used as a system of power[4] and means of social control.[5] These uses of science are decidedly controversial, and are considered by many, especially in a democratic society, to exceed its legitimate boundaries. I share fully in this opinion and it is my premise in this article that science, especially within academia, flagrantly violates the legitimate limits of its domain and this has resulted in serious sociological consequences that go mostly unobserved by the general public.

SCIENCE AS A LEGITIMIZING TOOL

The foundations of every culture largely rest upon existential stories (worldviews) that explain how the world was created, who mankind is, and what our purpose is in this world. It is important that such existential explanations be offered because almost every individual requires answers for them. Every indigenous culture has a creation story that answers existential questions, and practically without exception these are theistically-based worldviews presented as historical truths within the culture itself. An intelligentsia, or priestly class, traditionally had the role of their interpretation for their general public. The creation story and nature of the answers to existential questions influence what types of activities are allowable, how the economies of the culture function, as well as the motivations and relationships of its people. Notably, many cultural religious worldviews that include a hierarchy of gods are often considered nothing more than myths by today's condescending anthropologists. As we shall see, there is a motivation for such an interpretation.

It is worth noting that in more recent years, in both the east and west, the authority of the intelligentsia lies not with qualified individuals as was formerly the case, but has become established within institutions through which it can be passed on to others: the authority of the institution now replacing the qualification of the individual, with significant consequences to the body politic. Thus we now often find that instead of through qualification, positions of authority are achieved by inheritance or through some other mechanism of transfer of power. All too often these posts are acquired by persons unqualified for the position, and who may have ulterior motives for power and control. In the Roman church power was held by and transferred to the popes in repeated succession. Their declarations, issued as papal bulls, were the authoritative conclusions regarding any important matter. During the later half of the second millennium the locus of authority and source of the dominant worldview shifted from the Roman church and its popes to science and scientists respectively. Today it is the scientists and other academicians who have taken on the priestly role of defining the "true" nature of reality, and their declarations of today's truths are passed on to the rest of us through their professional journals.

An important difference exists between our scientific and previous authorities. The scientific worldview is not derived from a theological source, but is in fact a socially constructed concept of reality, thus it requires legitimization that is unnecessary for religions. This legitimization is possible if it assumes the mantle of transcendence inherent in religion. Harvard University Professor and geneticist

Richard Lewontin describes how an institution may do so in his book *Biology As Ideology*.

First "the institution as a whole must appear to derive from sources outside of ordinary human social struggle. It must not seem to be the creation of political, economic, or social forces, but to descend into society from a supra-human source"... second "the ideas, pronouncements, rules, and results of the institution's activity must have a validity and a transcendent truth that goes beyond any possibility of human compromise or human error. Its explanations and pronouncements must seem to be true in an absolute sense and to derive somehow from an absolute source. They must be true for all time and all place"...and third "the institution must have a certain mystical and veiled quality so that its innermost operation is not completely transparent to everyone. It must have an esoteric language, which needs to be explained to the ordinary person by those who are especially knowledgeable and who can intervene between everyday life and mysterious sources of understanding and knowledge."[6]

It is not too difficult to deduce that these characteristics have actually been derived from religious worldviews and ideologies and applied to science. Consider that science claims to be objective, impartial, and nonpolitical, and that most scientists believe that science operates in an atmosphere free from political intrusion. The sciences such as physics and chemistry, are also seen to be universally true in all times and places, and the methods of science are constructed in such a way that they create a product or knowledge thought to be free from the ordinary human foibles of greed, envy or deceit. The scientific method (when properly practiced) is thus thought to result in universal truths, which we afford the title of laws, and which we must all accept simply as facts of life with nothing leftover to argue about. Science also uses an opaque language that is inaccessible to all but its members and which requires interpretation for the common man.

Writing with rare candor and openness for a highly recognized scientist, Lewontin unabashedly tells us that besides providing explanations of how the world works, and even irrespective of the practical truth of it's claims, science has served this purpose of social legitimization with remarkable success. He explains that science can be seen as a social institution whose job is to fight an ideological battle within people's minds, for the purpose of peacefully maintaining the existing social order.[7]

The fact is that Lewontin is not making idle claims because in many respects mainstream science is being used to support a political agenda. Scientific establishments both in academia and industry have settled into a fixed perception of reality that is not supported by scientific fact. Further, reputable and competent scientists are discovering and presenting sound scientific evidence that is being ignored and even suppressed. Where there should be controversy and debate we hear only the sounds of silence. And scientists who challenge this agenda are dealt with by derision, as well as loss of respect, jobs, and even careers. Next let's look at just some of a vast amount of evidence that demonstrates the deviations of science from its pure purpose of pursuing the truth.

THE FAILURES AND TRANSGRESSIONS OF MODERN COSMOLOGY

In modern cosmology a great deal rests upon what is called the red shift. Light from distant stars is shifted toward the red end of the visible spectrum. In physics this is called the Doppler effect and with sound it is the result of the increased frequency (higher tone) of the sound of an approaching object, and decreasing (lower tone) as it passes. In astronomy it is assumed that this shift of frequency is also the result of velocity, and a lot is riding on this assumption since the red shift figures prominently into many astronomical calculations. These include among others the distance of stars and planets, the expansion of the universe, and the age of the universe since the Big Bang.

So what's going on in the field? That depends on where you look. Inside of academia and other establishment institutions the Big Bang and the red shift are presented as final conclusions with only some minor details to be worked out. But look elsewhere and you will find a controversy raging over both the interpretation of the red shift and the Big Bang itself.

Astronomer Halton Arp was pushed out of his position at the Mt. Polomar observatory because he dared to challenge the prevailing interpretation of the red shift. He speaks to both the lack of professionalism in science as well as the limits on debate in his book *Seeing Red: Redshifts, Cosmology and Academic Science*. He says there, "What could be done, and is not done, however, is to use the observations to rule out a 75-year-old model [the Big Bang] which is presently unquestioned dogma. The mission of academia should be to explore—not perpetuate myth and superstition. Today, any newspaper, science magazine, or discussion of scientific funding, will take for granted that we know all the basic facts: that we live in an expanding universe, all created in an instant out of nothing, in which cosmic bodies started to condense from a hot medium about 15 billion years ago. The observations are not used to test this model…It is embarrassing, and by now a little boring, to constantly read announcements about ever-more-distant and luminous high-redshift objects, blacker holes, and higher and higher percentages of undetectable matter…For those who have examined the evidence on redshifts, and decided that redshifts are not primarily velocity…the important question arises as to how a disproved assumption could have become so dominant."[8]

These challenges come from many directions. In his article in *21st Century Science & Technology*, Grote Reber writes mockingly about the assumptions of the Big Bang Theory and how they are being handled: "The whole business of Big Bang Creationism is very shaky and based upon dubious assumptions. The under-lying questions have become lost in the sands of time and are no longer taught—even in astronomy schools! Lately, Big Bang Creationists have far overplayed their hand, making themselves look like fools. However, because the old-line scientific trade journals are also dominated by reactionary fuddy-duddies, there is not much opportunity for readers to examine the underlying issues."[9]

Are these examples of bona fide science that we thought our institutions were engaged in, or are these examples of propaganda and manipulation of public per-ception? Clearly they are the latter, and we are forced to wonder why. Nor are these two alone. There are many top-notch scientists who join in chorus with them challenging the reigning paradigm, but the public, and even students, hear nothing about the controversy. Further evidence of the deliberate false portrayal is provided by examining the Physics Department websites of many universities—none indicate any serious conflict surrounding the Big Bang Theory (BBT).

To be fair, the problems are mentioned by cosmologists, but almost without exception they are dismissed as being of little consequence, insignificant aberrations that will be cleared up with a little more tinkering, or else the theory is amended to accommodate what should be there, but isn't (such as the "dark matter" that we hear so much about). But the almost unlimited tinkering involved to adjust a theory that does not allow or provide for scientific observations cannot be considered sound science. Scientific method says that theory must be established based on observation, and that it is not good science to continually amend theory that does not initially provide for subsequently observed phenomena. Any hypothesis or theory that does not adequately provide for observation is generally thrown out after a while, and a fresh theory developed that can accommodate all of the observations. Another way of saying this is that in science and philosophy the rule is that postulations are not to be made beyond necessity, yet the long list of problems of the BBT indicates that at least some concepts have been postulated beyond necessity. William Mitchell, in his book *Cult of the Big Bang*, thoroughly-documents more than *thirty* significant problems of the Big Bang hypothesis that are minimized by the academic establishment.[10]

So why is all of this being allowed to masquerade in the name of science? Mitchell says that enormous effort had been spent, and continues to be spent, in support of the Big Bang in a way that is not the method of impartial research, the supposed hallmark of pure science, and he questions how could good and talented men participate in these endeavors. His conclusion is that other forces must be at work to corrupt the process. I couldn't agree more. Science is losing its scientific character, taking on the look and feel of *belief.* Geoffrey Burbidge, Professor of Physics at the University of California, San Diego, for one, is willing to admit it: "Big bang cosmology is probably as widely believed as has been any theory of the universe in the history of Western civilization. It rests, however, on many untested, and [in] many cases, untestable assumptions. Indeed, big bang cosmology has become a bandwagon of thought that reflects faith as much as objective truth."[11]

We wonder if these practices of "science" are unique to cosmology. Would that it were true. Manipulation of science can, unfortunately, be found everywhere—especially where the origins of life are concerned.

ARE CHEMICALS THE ORIGIN OF LIFE?

After the Big Bang resulted in the construction of the planets, the next major feature of the scientific worldview is that life arose spontaneously from the "primordial soup", a sea of chemicals that offered the unique circumstances for the constituent parts of living cells to self-assemble by chance combination. Darwin's ideas of evolution have subsequently achieved the same dogmatic status as the Big Bang Theory: an established fact that all scientists accept and over which there is little remaining controversy (allowed).

The suggestion is simple enough, but can chance chemical combinations actually form living cells? What is a cell? When Darwin first published *Origin of the Species* very little was known about biological systems and their complexity. One of Darwin's great admirers during the nineteenth century, Ernst Haeckel, expressed the prevailing idea that cells were a "simple little lump of albuminous combination of carbon," something molecular biologist Michael Behe says we might liken to a homogeneous blob of Jell-O. Given the limitations of the microscopes of the time it was an entirely reasonable deduction that the cell could easily have been produced from inanimate material and simply come together by a chance combination of chemicals. It's easy to assume something when you have no idea of the implications of the assumption. Much harder, however, when you actually understand what lies behind the assumption.

In the interim since the idea of evolution was first established, especially in the past twenty years, great advances have been made in understanding the inner-workings in the microscopic world of the living cell. The field of Molecular Biology has opened up the cell and exposed its fantastic workings, and we have learned that cells are made mostly of proteins, which are in turn made of amino acids. The twenty amino acids combine in chains of several hundred up to a thousand in very specific arrangements to form thousands of types of proteins, and in cells this is what we find—hundreds of thousands of proteins of hundreds of types—a typical cell contains ten million million atoms.

Since Darwinian theory assumes that life forms were created by the chance interaction of chemicals, how reasonable is it to assume that just one single protein molecule "self-assembles" by chance combination? By chance combination we mean that if the required amino acids were in the proximity of each other they would combine to form proteins. And now that we know the number of cell components that must be specifically ordered, this becomes a rather easy statistical calculation. Consider that even if all the atoms on the earth's surface, including water, air, and the crust of the earth were made into conveniently available amino acids and 4 to 5 billion years were allowed, the odds are 10^{161} (1 with 161 zeros after it) to one that not one usable protein could have resulted from chance combinations, and it becomes even more impossible when we estimate the probability to develop a cell.[12]

Morowitz has determined the probability for the origin of the organic precursors for the smallest likely living entity by random processes…The chances for producing the necessary molecules, amino acids, proteins, etc., for a cell one tenth the size of the smallest known to man[13] is less than one in $(10^{340})^6$ or 10 with 340 **million** zeros after it.[14] Noting that mathematicians consider that any event with odds of less than 1 in 10^{50} to be flatly impossible, people such as Nobel Prize winner Francis Crick, who, along with James Watson, determined DNA's molecular structure, have come to this conclusion:

> "If a particular amino acid sequence was selected by chance, how rare an event would this be?…Suppose the chain is about two hundred amino acids long; this is, if anything, rather less than the average length of proteins of all types. Since we have just twenty possibilities at each place, the number of possibilities is twenty multiplied by itself some two hundred times. This is conveniently written 20 and is approximately equal to 10^{260}, that is, a one followed by 260 zeros. This number is quite beyond our everyday comprehension. The great majority of sequences *can never have been synthesized at all, at any time.*" (emphasis added)[15]

Now, either the mathematical science of statistical probability is wrong, or else chemicals did not self-assemble by chance alone to create proteins, or cells or life. Since statistical probability is one of the most well-developed and tested sciences, we then come to the conclusion (if we are going to use the scientific method) that life did *not* arise from the chance combination of molecules. It *can't* have happened by *chance*. Period. Full stop. Something else then must have been involved. That something is pointed to again and again in dozens of books over the past decade that demonstrate the impossibility of the now Neo-Darwinian theory. But has establishment science considered this evidence to throw out a discredited theory? No, biology walks in lock-step with cosmology in denying any scientific evidence that can upset the ruling paradigm that matter alone is the cause of all causes.

Amazingly, the controversies within biology follow the same pattern of obfuscation and denial that is found in cosmology. Like the Big Bang, Darwinian evolution has plenty of controversy, but it is not given an adequate intellectual or scientific response from the biology establishment. Instead of addressing the issues they are dismissed with scant attention often simply because of the source—Behe, Dembski and others are Christian creationists. It is falsely claimed that their ideology influences their science too much. Thus their arguments are shunted to the "fringes" of science and are given short-shrift in academic and professional journals. The only time that these challenges get a fair hearing is when the authors take their case to the public via the popular press, and now scores of books offer legitimate and sound scientific challenges to evolutionary theory.

Any intelligent individual who reads the above arguments can reasonably conclude that the chance evolutionary creation of this world and its immense biological diversity is impossible. One need not have a long list of letters after his name to understand these concepts. Yet, although the controversy has been raging for decades, very little is changing. Even as far back as 1986 chemistry professor Robert Shapiro criticized several aspects of research on the origin of life. "We have reached a situation where a theory has been accepted as fact by some, and possible contrary evidence is shunted aside". He concludes that "this is mythology rather than science".[16]

SCIENTIFIC MAKE-BELIEVE

What to speak of discounting scientific challenges, it has been found that the biology community actually participates in scientific fraud by perpetuating and teaching evolutionary concepts in college textbooks that have long since been proven false. In *Icons Of Evolution* author Jonathon Wells demonstrates that even advanced college textbooks, and publications from such esteemed institutions as The National Academy of Sciences, contain patently false and deliberately misleading statements about evolution. In his introduction he writes: "The following chapters compare the icons of evolution with published scientific evidence, and reveal that much of what we teach about evolution is wrong. This fact raises troubling questions about the status of Darwinian evolution. If the icons of evolution are supposed to be our best evidence for Darwin's theory, and all of them are false or misleading, what does that tell us about the theory? Is it science, or myth?… The implications for American science are potentially far-reaching."[17] More than you probably knew.

In discussing what science does and how it does it, Lewontin describes how science is being used to legitimate an entirely *fictitious* story—that of human sexual preference. It is worth quoting him at length. He says: "Thus, the entire discussion of the evolutionary basis of human sexual preference is *a made-up story, from beginning to end*. Yet it is a story that appears in textbooks, in courses in high schools and universities, and in popular books and journals. It bears the legitimacy given to it by famous professors and by national and international media. *It has the authority of science.* In an important sense, it is science because science consists not simply of a collection of true facts about the world, but is the body of assertions and theories about the world made by people who are called scientists. It consists, in large part, of what scientists say about the world whatever the true state of the world might be.

"Science is more than an institution devoted to the manipulation of the physical world. It also has a function in the formation of consciousness about the political and social world. Science in that sense is part of the general process of education, and the assertions of scientists are the basis for a great deal of the enterprise of forming consciousness. Education in general, and *scientific education in particular, is meant not only to make us competent to manipulate the world but also to form our social attitudes.*" (emphasis added)

I am willing to bet that you didn't know that the function of a scientific education was to convince your children that sexual preference, a disingenuous way of saying homosexual inclinations, is written in their genes, and therefore such inclinations must be "normal".

E. O. Wilson is the father of a theory called sociobiology which says that sexual and other human behaviors are determined only by our genes. This tells us that "human beings are absurdly easy to indoctrinate. They seek it." Further he says that they are characterized by blind faith: "Man would rather believe than know."[18] I ask then, who is it that has given science (including Wilson) permission to determine what social attitudes we should be indoctrinated with? It certainly is not 'mom and pop' because the overwhelming majority of people in most cultures consider homosexuality a social deviation and unacceptable. Who then is making such socially significant decisions in the name of science?

It becomes easier to see where this is all going by examining the conclusions of several fields of study together, so we'll look at just a few more.

BOTANY

The story of prehistory from the field of Botany offers another interesting arena where we find lots of evidence of scientific make-believe. Since evolutionary theory demands that everything can only have evolved from a common ancestor, wild plants must have been the precursors of domesticated ones. When asked to explain the origins of our current domestic grains, botanists offer the miraculous solution that with time and patience Neolithic farmers created them by cross-breeding wild species over hundreds of generations. That's an entertaining answer, especially since doing so even defies our current bio-engineering abilities. The Botanical Garden Bin Ras in St. Petersburg, Russia, has not been able to cultivate wild rye into a new form of domestication in more than 165 years of effort, even with the tools and understanding of modern biology.[12] Their rye has lost none of its wild traits, especially the fragility of its stalk and its small grain. The hypothetical suggestion of Neolithic bioengineers is science? In the hypothetical-deductive scientific method it isn't. It is simply a speculative story with many unscientific assumptions. As in biology, the "science" of botany attempts to go beyond the limits of its domain to explain events that cannot be tested. In this manner both fields are using the authority afforded them by their bona fide scientific findings to present a philosophy of life and legitimate a particular worldview.

LINGUISTICS

Not only do the "hard" sciences give evidence of a fixed worldview, but the social sciences are pressed into service to support the scientific worldview as well. In the field of Linguistics languages are traced by what is called etymology, or the history of words through time and cultures. Uses of a particular word can be traced to their earlier counterparts from neighboring cultures. In this way changes in all languages are recorded—except for one—the language of ancient India, Sanskrit. It is a well recognized fact that the phonology (the speech sound) and morphology (the science of word formation) of the Sanskrit language is entirely different from all of the languages of the world, and that changes noted in all other languages are not to be found in Sanskrit. This is the actual history.

Yet, on 2nd February, 1786 Sir William Jones, in his Presidential speech for the Asiatic Society, presented a fabricated theory about a "proto-language" that was supposed to have been the mother of all languages. This unknown language, "Indo-European" in origin, was designed to provide ancestry to Sanskrit language, and to provide a cover-story for the theory of the Aryan invasion.

It was Franz Bopp (1791-1867), a German linguist, and close associate of Jones who was the main person to popularize the term 'Proto-Indo-European' or 'Indo-European'. Bopp rejected the arguments of earlier linguists who considered Sanskrit to be the original language of the world. He was an active member of the Asiatic Society, and interestingly, the *London Magazine* gave excellent reviews of his works. The Proto-Indo-European language, despite the fact that it has never been shown to exist, is accepted today by academic linguists as the root of languages in Europe, the Middle East, and India.

INDOLOGY

The history of India as presented in its *Puranas* and other texts such as the *Mahabharata* or *Ramayana*, is accepted as truth by hundreds of millions of India's native population, but academia regards them simply as superstitious myth. In place of this history, British 'Indologists' have created a history for India suggesting that there were simply barbarians in the subcontinent before the hordes of the Aryan Invasion brought culture along with them. The attempt was made to have the Aryan invasion turn India's ancient *Vedas* into little more than primitive poems of uncivilized plunderers. The articles of the Asiatic Researches were intentionally derogatory and presented false descriptions of Indian society, its history and religion. In 1828 an atheistic society was formed in Calcutta, and its founder and coworkers received great appreciation by the British. They were welcomed in England and praised by the writers of the Asiatic Society. In 1847 Max Müller was appointed by the East India Company to misinterpret the theme of the *Vedas* and construct a false history of India.

Recent scholarship is gradually correcting these attempts at revisionist history, so much so that even establishment scholars are now beginning to question the whole idea. In fact, there was no Aryan Invasion. India's culture is the oldest on the planet, and the mother of all other civilizations as supported by recent archeological finds in Orissa. On the banks of the Subarnarekha River was found evidence of a continuous culture extending from 2 million years ago to 5,000 BCE without a break.[20] Why then all of the revisionist history? Because the history of India as the seat of the world's theistic culture had to be altered if the materialistic worldview was to become the dominant paradigm of thought.

ARCHEOLOGY

As reported elsewhere in these pages by Michael Cremo, a great deal of evidence demonstrating the great antiquity of human existence has been discarded from acceptable academic discussion and even hidden from public knowledge. This has been necessary to support the idea that mankind is the recent result (the last 25-50,000 years) of evolution. The fossil record in fact not only challenges that theory, it destroys it—if the evidence is admitted into academic consideration, which it is not.

Cremo and associates collected over 900 pages of evidence formerly published in professional journals, but allowed to slip into oblivion by the establishment archeology community. Remarkably, where establishment archeologists restrict human presence in the Americas to the last 15-20,000 years only, there is abundant evidence of older human presence. In the Americas evidence of human presence has been found from 125,000 years (the Sheguiandah, Canada artifacts) to over 600 million years (Dorchester, Massachusetts metallic vase).[21]

Of course, the immediate question that comes to mind is that if Cremo and team, a two-person research organization, have uncovered so much bona fide evidence of extreme human antiquity,[22] then why hasn't the remainder of the *entire* archeological profession acknowledged the same? Why, as in the case with cosmology, is there no debate within the profession about this evidence and the failure of the accepted theories to accommodate it?

CONNECTING THE DOTS

In each of the areas reviewed above, the conclusions of all academic studies and research have something in common. That is, they all attempt to squeeze a square peg into a round hole in their efforts to support the scientific worldview, or dominant paradigm. Let's remember that the scientific worldview follows something along these lines:

In an instant after the Big Bang all matter was created and the stars and planets gradually coalesced as matter cooled. On our planet only, by the sheerest of chances, chemicals self-assembled from a chemical primordial soup to spontaneously generate simple living creatures. Over vast spans of time and by individual chance mutations, one-at-a-time, one living thing gradually gave rise to another until the planet was filled with millions of varieties of life—fish, birds, plants, insects, animals, and ultimately, in only the last 25-50,000 years, your ancestors—homo sapiens sapiens—human beings. At first hardly distinguishable from animals, we gradually became more and more civilized. We now stand at the pinnacle of evolution, and it doesn't get any better than this. Remember—enjoy it as much as you can, because when you die, that's it—game over.

This worldview is thought to be created in a composite manner, with the conclusions of all areas of study added together to complete the general picture. Cosmology tells about the beginnings of creation and planetary formation. Biology tells us about how life was formed and how life processes work. The archeological record tells us how species evolved from one another and where and when mankind appeared and how he populated the planet. History gives us the story of various civilizations and tells us about our social evolution, and this picture is aided by the study of linguistics which map the social intercourse of civilizations. Anthropology (including Indology) tells us about primitive peoples and how they became civilized. Add it all up and the equal sign after it will tell you who we are, how we got here, and where we are going. It's the modern West's answer to the existential questions.

What's wrong with this picture? *It's a Myth.* Each field of study has somehow amended its conclusions to conveniently fit with this worldview, and irrespective of the practical truths of their claims, academia legitimizes this story. If you are an educated person who lives in the 'real' world, and have given up other 'myths' of life, this is what you are supposed to believe. However, it would appear as though academics have, as of yet, only convinced themselves, since 90% of Americans still believe in a creation story involving God. People tolerate this being taught to their children because of the authority of science, yet they continue to take them to church. However, it appears that the relentless indoctrination campaign is showing results and that Americans are becoming sociological schizophrenics in an effort to reconcile science with religion. In a Gallup survey 38% of Americans believe that man has evolved from lower species but that this process was guided by God, and college indoctrinated students favor the story of godless evolution by 2 to 1.[23]

If each field of study were to include all of its findings (that are now suppressed or re-interpreted) to create the composite picture, we would have a very different story.

ESTABLISHMENT DENIAL AND CONTROL

There are a number of methods used in controlling the debate, none of which in the least fall into the category of bona fide science. Brian Martin, a senior lecturer in the Department of Science and Technology Studies, University of Wollongong,

Australia has studied what happens to scientists who challenge the dominant paradigm, and has written extensively on the subject. Rather than look at their actual findings and discuss their work on its own merit they become labeled as dissidents, and he says there is a standard set of ways for dealing with them: "Methods include denial of tenure, blocking publications, withdrawal of research grants, official reprimands, referral to psychiatrists, ostracism by colleagues, spreading of rumors, transfer to different locations or jobs, and dismissal...Initially I hadn't even thought of suppression as a problem in science. Now I realize that it is pervasive."[24]

It can be argued that suppression, while effective in silencing individual dissidents, is even more effective in signaling to others what they might face if they step out of line. Observation of the treatment meted out to dissidents is enough to make most university professors and professional researchers use 'professional discretion', or 'balanced judgment' in choosing their research topics and how they write about their findings. Over time they internalize their fears of loss of status, income or career in a way that leads to self-intimidation. Real restraints, such as external prohibitions, are then simply replaced by the 'agreements of academic gentlemen'.[25]

A specific example of such un-scientific treatment is provided by the response science writer Richard Milton received upon publication of his book *Shattering the Myths of Darwinism*. The book set about challenging the evidence presented for evolution in establishments such as natural history museums all over the world. He writes in the preface to the 1997 reprint: "I didn't expect science to welcome an inquisitive reporter, but I did expect the controversy to be conducted at a rational level, that people would rightly demand to inspect my evidence more closely and question me on the correctness of this or that fact." He was shocked that although a leading article in the London Times praised the book saying that it could shake the 'religion of evolution', a review elsewhere by the Darwin evolutionist Richard Dawkins painted a darker picture: "the book is 'loony,' 'stupid,' 'drivel' and its author a 'harmless fruitcake' who 'needs psychiatric help.'"[26] Milton replies that "these intemperate responses betoken more than a squabble between an inquisitive journalist and a couple of reactionary academics. They raise a number of important questions of general public interest."

Indeed they do. They bring into question the ability of establishment scientists to practice bona fide science, as well as the motives for such reactionary treatment of scientists, or others, who present ideas that appear to lie outside the boundaries of acceptable debate. They also raise questions about what those limits protect or defend.

FAILURES OF MODERN SCIENCE

Looking deeply into these issues, the following points show themselves: 1) sound scientific evidence is being ignored in many fields, especially when it threatens the dominant scientific worldview and/or established powerful interests; 2) acceptable debate within each discipline is limited to that which supports the established "scientific" worldview, which appears to have become a rigid dogma. These are implications that the principles of pure science are being subordinated to support a political agenda. This dynamic also appears to be operative in many of the social sciences; 3) going beyond their legitimate domain of knowing nature, people of the scientific profession are introducing many assumptions that are *scientifically* untenable and fall outside of legitimate scientific method. They also bring conclusions in the name of Theory, that have no scientific basis in fact, being only unsupported speculations and mere assertions; 4) in many cases science is exceeding its legitimate boundaries of determination of facts of material nature and is being used to legitimate a worldview, and promulgate its philosophy—even to indoctrinate an unsuspecting public. Exactly who is determining that philosophy is unknown; 5) knowledge of such uses of science are generally unknown by the general public, and it is doubtful that they would approve of such efforts; 6) the acceptable limits of debate are those that result in or promulgate an ideology that is implicitly atheistic: academic and "scientific" discussions allow no room for discussion of a spiritual element. Moreover there appears to be an orchestrated attempt across all branches of study to deviate from correct and true research, findings, or history, in order to give mutual support to the atheistic scientific worldview. Such efforts may be seen as attempts to control the thinking and understanding of the populace and may thus be considered propaganda of special interests.

The above issues are serious breaches of the authority and legitimate boundaries of science. In these cases science is indeed being used to support a social agenda as Lewontin claims. As this behavior becomes more widely recognized, the institutions of science will be seen in the same light as the Roman church formerly was at the advent of the Reformation—as a means to restrict the understanding of people and to impose a dogmatic and false reality. In other words, science is being used to support a political agenda. As people begin to understand the facts behind science's actions, the worldview of science will lose its position in the eyes of many people. Due to the above causes I predict that the failure of the atheistic scientific worldview looms on the horizon.

People want the truth and they don't like being controlled. When they find out that this is going on they will throw off the ideology of science and seek adequate alternative ways of understanding this world. If understanding the problem is

90% of the solution, we now stand at the threshold of the solution. The problem of the modern Western worldview is that it is artificially contrived to lead to and support atheistic conclusions. The solution is a worldview that can accommodate the theistic and spiritual concepts and forces that are present in the world and which make their effects known through a variety of phenomena. I suggest that the Vedic worldview is the only candidate that has the necessary complexity and depth to explain all of humankind's experience.

CONTROLLING THE DEBATE—TO WHAT END?

While biologists may claim chance in all affairs, practically speaking there is little experience of chance in human society. In law, commerce, and industry, all activities of strictly human endeavor, we get results only when a group of people set out with the intention to achieve them. Tell any lawmaker that the laws that he just passed happened simply by chance and he is likely to think that you are daft. He knows how hard he had to work to get the job done. Tell a businessman that he has been successful by chance and he'll laugh in your face. He's likely worked 80-hour weeks to make his business what it is, and at least he's convinced that that definitely didn't happen by chance. Similarly, since academia is an institution composed of people and managed by people, it is equally unlikely that any result happens there simply by chance. Therefore, I assert that it is not by chance that each field of study has developed limits on what is considered acceptable debate. These uniform results have been achieved only by the deliberate efforts of certain people. Who? And what is their motivation? Those are the next questions we want answered.

Interestingly for our case a similar phenomenon has been revealed in another area of human endeavor—the media. Just as we have trusted science to bring us the truths of the physical world, we have trusted journalists to investigate the matters of human affairs and bring us the truths of those events. Sad to say, it seems that our trust has been misplaced on both accounts.

A penetrating analysis of the media is told by Edward Herman and Noam Chomsky in their book *Manufacturing Consent*. Drawing on decades of criticism and research they report that the media, far from being impartial in presenting the news, defend the economic, social and political agendas of the privileged groups that dominate domestic society, the state, and the global order.

In the opening paragraphs they write: "It is our view that, among their other functions, the media serve, and propagandize on behalf of, the powerful societal interests that control and finance them. The representatives of these interests have important agendas and principles that they want to advance, and they are well-positioned to shape and constrain media policy. This is normally not accomplished by crude intervention, but by the selection of right-thinking personnel and by the editors' and working journalists' internalization of priorities and definitions of news-worthiness that conform to the institution's policy."[27]

The authors make no attempt to identify the powerful societal interests they speak of, yet we can take it that these are monied interests since money equates with power in our society. And why would the money interests want to control the media and scientific ideology? Again Lewontin gives us a clue. Throughout his book he claims that biology serves the purpose of legitimating a social order, and several times makes it clear that this is done intentionally to maintain the status quo. He frankly states that story of biology is meant to convince the public that the situation we now find ourselves in is inescapable since "the political structures of society—the competitive, entrepreneurial, hierarchical society in which we live and which differentially rewards different temperaments, different cognitive abilities, and different mental attitudes—*is also determined by our DNA, and that it is, therefore, unchangeable.*"[28] (emphasis added)

That is, genes make culture. As Lewontin puts it, "when we know what our DNA looks like, we will know why some of us are rich and some poor, some healthy and some sick, some powerful and some weak. We will also know why some societies are powerful and rich and others are weak and poor, why one nation, one sex, one race dominates another."

The implication is that whatever our station in life is, we are all born this way, so just accept it, since it's the natural order of things. Of course this is nothing more than a rigid caste system that justifies inequity and social discrimination by the religion of science.

WHAT IS MATTER AND WHAT IS LIFE?

Even assuming the self-assembly of atoms into amino acids, proteins, and cells, the sciences artfully avoid the discussion of what life actually is with yet another assumption—this time it is that life arises from the combination of chemicals alone. The scientific worldview would have us fully equate matter with life. This, perhaps, is the most grandiose assumption and it has even tripped up many Christian creationists who have bought into the idea. The question remains: can life arise from matter? In fact, while there is scant evidence that this is the case, there is a great deal of evidence that life exists independently of the material body.

Vedic knowledge does not sidestep this issue, but tackles it head-on, explaining that life stems from a transcendent source, and although temporarily encased within material bodies while on this earth, life has another dimension. Human beings having free will can choose in which dimension they want to live.

Presenting a fully developed philosophy that includes God, the living entity, karma, reincarnation, the material energies and world, etc., the Vedic worldview accounts for all of the many phenomena of this world, many of which are simply dismissed by materialistic science. Understanding these many dimensions of life puts us in a much better position to make informed choices about how to live in this world.

Failure to know our own nature and live accordingly has very real effects on the human condition, creating what the father of sociology, Emile Durkheim, has termed 'anomie' by which he means a situation that might be described as a sort of 'social emptiness or void'. Under such conditions suicide, crime and disorder are social behaviors that can be expected because our existence is no longer rooted in a stable and integrated social milieu, and our lives thus lose purpose and meaning.[22] We are already there. Suicide is the leading cause of death among teenagers in the U.S., and many millions, including children, take daily doses of psychotropic medication simply to be able to function under such conditions.

This condition is also predicted in the Vedic literature and is described as *sunyavadi*, or voidism, which indicates a purposeless existence or void. The consciousness and nature of persons absorbed in such a worldview is described by Lord Krishna in the sixteenth chapter of the *Bhagavad-gita*, as *asuric*, or demonic. The *asuras*, Krishna says, think that there is no God in control, and that the world has no personal or spiritual foundation. It has come about from sex only. Following such conclusions, the *asuras*, lost to themselves, engage in unbeneficial and horrible works that gradually destroy the world. Being bewildered by insatiable lust, pride and false prestige, they are attracted only by the impermanent material things of this world for sense gratification, which is taken as the ultimate goal of human civilization.

On the other hand, the *Bhagavad-gita* also describes the *sura*, or divine being, as a person who has purified himself by spiritual understanding and controls his mind with determination. Remaining free from lust, anger and false prestige, he becomes fixed in spiritual consciousness. In that state he is freed from hankering and lamentation, is equally disposed to every living entity, and is done with attachment, fear and anger. Being thus situated he achieves the highest stage of life—the realization of the transcendent Self, and the Supreme Brahman.

According to the Vedic worldview human life and consciousness is specifically created for achievement of this spiritual perfection, and a civilization arranged to facilitate this goal of life can as well realize peace and prosperity for each of its members. Such conditions have in fact been achieved by past civilizations as described in Vedic literatures. This is not a utopian dream, or a fanciful future never to be realized, nor a nostalgic idea of times gone by. This height of civilization can again be achieved in cultures whose members are committed to these principles, but this will never be achieved by cultures that deny their very nature.

WHAT PATH WILL WE TAKE TO THE FUTURE?

E. O. Wilson, while suggesting that there is a biological basis for morality, has written, "the choice between transcendentalism and empiricism will be the coming century's version of the struggle for men's souls. Moral reasoning will either remain centered in theology and philosophy, or shift toward a scientific material analysis. Where it ultimately settles will depend on which worldview is more widely perceived to be correct."[30]

Will the atheistic scientific worldview finally wipe-out all other theistic notions of life and purpose, or will the understanding of the spiritual dimension of mankind and the goal of his release from material bondage become the dominant paradigm? Will we bequeath to future generations the transcendent truth of the *Vedas* or the consequences of a bankrupt and dead-end, materialistic ideology?

NOTES

[1.] *The Logic of Scientific Discovery* (1968) and *Conjectures and Refutations* (1972)

[2.] Chap. 2 *This is Biology: The Science of the Living World* Belknap Press, Boston, MA 1997

[3.] p. 103, Richard C. Lewontin, *Biology As Ideology: The Doctrine of DNA*, HarperPerennial, NY 1992

[4.] Brian Martin. From his website: www.SuppressionOfScience.com

[5.] Lewontin, p. 9

[6.] Lewontin, p. 7

[7.] Lewontin p. 6-7

[8.] p. 257 *Seeing Red: Redshifts, Cosmology and Academic Science* Halton Arp, Apeiron, Montreal, 1998

[9.] p. 43-49 *The Big Bang is Bunk*, March-April 1989,

10. p. 220 William C. Mitchell, *Cult of the Big Bang—Was There A Bang?* Cosmic Sense Books, Carson City, NV 1995

11. Scientific American, February 1992, p. 96

12. p. 376 Harold Coffin, *Origin by Design*, Review & Herald Publishing, Hagerstown, MD 1983

13. Mycoplasm hominzs H. 39

14. p. 68 James Perloff, *Tornado in a Junkyard: The Relentless Myth of Darwinism*, Refuge Books, Arlington, MD 1999

15. p. 51-52 Francis Crick, *Life Itself: Its Origin and Nature*, Simon & Schuster, NY 1981

16. quoted on p. 27 *Icons of Evolution: Science or Myth,* Jonathon Wells, Regnery Publishing, Wash DC, 2000

17. Wells, p. 8

18. E.O. Wilson, *Sociobiology: The New Synthesis* Harvard University Press 1975; as quoted by Lewontin p. 91

19. from: www.lloydpye.com/A-literal.htm

20. United Press International, Calcutta, India, Sept. 8, 2003

21. p. xxix, *Forbidden Archeology: The Hidden History of the Human Race,* Michael A. Cremo and Richard L. Thompson, Bhaktivedanta Book Trust, Los Angeles, CA 1996

22. *Forbidden Archeology*, over 900 pages in length, offers dozens of examples of extreme human antiquity.

23. Gallup survey for Christianity Today, July 1982.

24. Article *Suppression of Science* by Brian Martin. From his website: www.SuppressionOfScience.com

25. Deyo, Richard A., Bruce M. Psaty, Gregory Simon, Edward H. Wagner, and Gilbert S. Omenn. 1997. "The Messenger under Attack: Intimidation of Researchers by Special-Interest Groups." *New England Journal of Medicine* 366 (16 April): 1176-1180.

26. p. ix *Shattering the Myths of Darwinism*, Richard Milton, Park Street Press, Rochester, VT, 1997

27. p. xi *Manufacturing Consent*, Edward S. Herman and Noam Chomsky, Pantheon Books, NY, 2002

28. Lewontin p. 87

29. p. xxi, *Ideology and Utopia, An Introduction to the Sociology of Knowledge*, Karl Mannheim, Harvest Books, NY 1936

30. *pages 53–70,* E. O. Wilson, The Biological Basis of Morality, from *The Atlantic Monthly;* April 1998; Volume 281, No. 4.

How I Discovered Vedic Science

Subhash Kak

My father was a serious yogic apprentice for several years before he married, so as a boy I heard many inspiring stories about the spiritual side of life. Our home was a magnet to swamis and householders on their spiritual path of devotion to Vishnu, Shiva, or Shakti. We would question the visitors, who would provide explanations for the more difficult passages in the *Bhagavad Gita* and the *Upanishads*. I was impressed but I don't think I fully understood all that I was told.

After school and college in various places in Jammu and Kashmir, I went to the Indian Institute of Technology (IIT) in Delhi for further studies in science and engineering. It was not before long that I became acutely aware of the limitations of the mainstream paradigm of science. For example, in the physical sciences, the past determines the future completely, but on the other hand, freedom of action is taken for granted at the level of the individual. Our lives are strung, so to speak, between these two extreme views. We make private adjustments to this situation, acknowledging that there are larger forces that define history at the personal level, and somehow our freedom matters.

I had also started studying mystical experience, and this led me to meetings with Gopi Krishna, who had become internationally famous for his yogic autobiography, *Kundalini*. Subsequently, I got to know many leading mystics and scientists. Meanwhile, I had begun teaching at IIT Delhi, where I continued with my meditations on science and self. It was clear that science must confront the mystery of awareness. Why is it to be found in the brain-machine but not in the computer? In what sense is the consciousness of animals different from that of humans? Although our bodies change with time, why do we feel that our person-hood remains unchanged? Many more such questions may be asked.

After I came to the United States in 1979, I decided to go beyond information and look at the problem of self and consciousness from the points of view of phys-ics and neuroscience. Meanwhile, my work on the history of Indian science led me to study Vedic texts in the original and not just depend on old commentaries, which I soon realized were not reliable.

My objective was to go beyond philosophy, in which there has been an unbroken tradition and for which one can find reasonable expositions in English and other languages, and explore the heart of Vedic knowledge. I began with an examination of the Vedic altar ritual, especially Agnichayana and Ashvamedha which were the grandest sacrifices. My discoveries were serendipitous. Perhaps they emerged out of my own spiritual advancement.

I don't wish to go into the arcane details of my findings, for which I would recommend my books such as the *Astronomical Code of the Rgveda* and the *Architecture of Knowledge* to the reader. Suffice it to say that Vedic ritual represented the astronomical knowledge of its times in the altar constructions and by virtue of the equation that the macrocosm is mirrored in the microcosm, this also was a representation of the spiritual self.

This explains why the number 108, which is the average distance the sun and the moon are away from the earth in terms of their respective diameters (the diameter of the sun is also 108 times the earth's diameter), shows up in unexpected situations in the Vedic lore. For example, the *Natya Shastra* claims that there exist 108 basic dance poses, the Hindu rosary has 108 beads, and God and Goddess have 108 names.

The *Vedas* recognize that the outer reality follows laws. They assert that there are two sciences: the lower, concerning the outer reality; and the higher, concerning the experiencing self. Since the self cannot be associated with any object, therefore one cannot have a multiplicity of it. But to speak of a self that is single invites the postulation of other selves, hence it is claimed that this self is non-dual. It transcends physical extension and time.

Ordinary language cannot describe the mystery, which is why formal descriptions are contradictory or paradoxical. The skeptic might say that all this sounds good and it may even be considered inspirational, but why should one take it to be the truth and not just an arbitrary belief system? The *Vedas* claim the proof of this science is the reality that one can obtain knowledge of the outer reality (a projection of the transcendent Brahman or Krishna or Shiva or Devi) by means of meditation.

There are at least three numerical values in the Vedic texts that support the view that knowledge is an uncovering of the potential within. They are:

- The age of the universe: 8.64 billion years in the current cycle, that is of the same order of magnitude as current estimates. This should be contrasted with the biblical view that the universe was created in 4004 BC.

- The speed of light: 4,404 *yojanas* in a *nimesha* found in manuscripts that are over 600 years old. This figure is almost exactly the correct value of 186,000 miles per second. Note that the modern value was found only over a hundred years ago, and even Newton thought its speed was infinite.
- The number of species on earth: Vedic thought conceives of 8.4 million species, which is impressive, considering that modern authorities (such as Graur and Li in their *Fundamentals of Molecular Evolution*, page 436) estimate the number of extant species to be 4.5 to 10 million.

One may look at these numbers as coincidences, but one is boggled by the odds against that view. On the other hand, the *Vedas* speak of rishis whose insight is so extraordinary that they can obtain knowledge from meditation alone. Of course, this intuition can only be expressed in terms of known linguistic associations, that is, in terms of concepts already known.

SURPRISING IDEAS IN THE VEDIC TEXTS

It was Herodotus who first spoke of the idea of the wonders of the ancient world. He was, of course, talking only of monumental art. There is a list of the wonders from the Greek world that was compiled in the Middle Ages. This list has the great pyramid of Giza, the hanging gardens of Babylon, the statue of Zeus at Olympia, the temple of Artemis at Ephesus, the mausoleum at Halicarnassus, the colossus of Rhodes, and the lighthouse of Alexandria. Only one of these seven survives.

There are other lists too that are not Greek-centric. We have marvels of art and architecture from China, Mexico, Europe, Peru, Iran, India, Indonesia, Cambodia, Sri Lanka, and other countries. Not all of these marvels are in a good state of repair. Some are under the threat of destruction. Three of the most magnificent creations were lost in Afghanistan just recently.

But here I don't wish to speak of wonders of stone and metal. Rather, I wish to propose a list of the 'Seven Wonders of the Ancient Mind'. These are revolutionary and astonishing ideas that have had a lasting influence on the world. Not surprisingly, it is hard for us to place these ideas in context. For most of them, we cannot name the originator.

Such lists are subjective, and mine is no exception. I had to leave out many obviously impressive ideas, such as airplanes, space travel, weapons that can destroy the world, embryo transplantation, multiple babies from the same embryo, space travel, and so on—from just the *Mahabharata* and the *Puranas*. (Lest I be misunderstood, we are not speaking of real planes, bombs, and biotechnology, but rather of the conception of their possibility.)

The ideas that I chose are perhaps more fundamental than those above that I left out. Ultimately, I used the criterion of not just originality, but continuing relevance and sheer improbability of the thought of it in the ancient world.

Here's my list of the seven most astonishing ideas:

1. *An Extremely Old Universe*:

   The idea that the universe is very old is quite startling, when one notes that humanity's collective memory doesn't go further than a few thousand years. The universe is taken to go through cycles of creation and destruction. This conception also assumes infinite number of solar systems.

2. *An Atomic World and the Subject/Object Dichotomy*:

   According to the atomic doctrine of Kanada, there are nine classes of substances: ether, space, and time that are continuous; four elementary substances (or particles) called earth, air, water, and fire that are atomic; and two kinds of mind, one omnipresent and another which is the individual. This system also postulates a subject/object dichotomy, which is a part of the systems of Sankhya and Vedanta as well. In these systems, the conscious subject is separate from the material reality but he is, nevertheless, able to direct its evolution. The atomic doctrine of Kanada is much more interesting than that of Democritus. It is the recognition of the subject/object dichotomy that led to the creation of modern physics.

3. *Relativity of Time and Space*:

   That space and time need not flow at the same rate for different observers is a pretty revolutionary notion. We encounter it in *Puranic* stories and in the *Yoga Vasishtha*. Obviously, we are not speaking here of the mathematical theory of relativity related to an upper limit to the speed of light, yet the consideration of time acting different to different observers is quite remarkable. To see the significance of this idea a couple of thousand years ago, note that modern relativity theory was forced upon scientists a hundred years ago by certain equations related to the transmission of electromagnetic waves. Here's a passage on anomalous flow of time from the *Bhagavata Purana*: "Taking his own daughter, Revati, Kakudmi went to Lord Brahma in Brahmaloka, and inquired about a husband for her. When Kakudmi arrived there, Lord Brahma was engaged in hearing musical performances by the Gandharvas and had not a moment to talk with him. Therefore Kakudmi waited, and at the end of the performance he saluted Lord Brahma and made his desire known. After hearing his words, Lord Brahma laughed loudly and said to Kakudmi, 'O King, all those whom you may have decided within the core of your heart to accept as your son-in-law have passed away in the course of time. Twenty-seven chaturyugas have already passed. Those upon whom you may have decided are now gone, and so are their sons, grandsons and other descendants. You cannot even hear about their names.'"

There are other stories, less dramatic, where an observer returns from a journey to another *loka*, and finds that people he loves have aged many more decades than he has.

4. *Evolution of Life*:
    The *Puranas* have a chapter on creation and the rise of mankind. It is said that man arose at the end of a chain where the beginning was with plants and various kind of animals. Here's the quote from the *Yoga Vasishtha*: "I remember that once upon a time there was nothing on this earth, neither trees and plants, nor even mountains. For a period of eleven thousand years the earth was covered by lava. In those days there was neither day nor night below the polar region: for in the rest of the earth neither the sun nor the moon shone. Only one half of the polar region was illumined. Apart from the polar region the rest of the earth was covered with water. And then for a very long time the whole earth was covered with forests, except the polar region. Then there arose great mountains, but without any human inhabitants. For a period of ten thousand years the earth was covered with the corpses of the *asuras* who roamed the world."

    Vedic evolution is not at variance with Darwinian evolution but it has a different focus. The urge to evolve into higher forms is taken to be inherent in nature. A system of an evolution from inanimate to progressively higher life is clearly spelled out in the system of *Sankhya*. At the traditional level this is represented by an ascent of Vishnu through the forms of fish, tortoise, boar, man-lion, the dwarf, finally into man. Aurobindo has argued that this evolution of intelligence is still at work.

5. *A Science of Mind, Yoga*:
    Yoga psychology, described in the Vedic books and systematized by *Patanjali* in his *Yoga-sutras* is a very sophisticated description of the nature of the human mind and its capacity. It makes a distinction between memory, states of awareness, and the fundamental entity of consciousness. It puts the analytical searchlight on mind processes, and it does so with

such clarity and originality that it continues to influence people all over the world. Several kinds of yoga are described. They provide a means of mastering the body-mind connection. Indian music and dance also has an underlying yogic basis.

6. *Binary Number System, Zero*:

A Binary number system was used by Pingala (450 BC, if we accept the tradition that he was Panini's brother) to represent meters of songs. The structure of this number system may have helped in the invention of the sign for Zero that, I believe, took place around 50 BC–50 AD. Without the binary system, the development of computers would be much harder; and without a sign for zero, mathematics would have languished. It is of course true that the binary number system was independently invented by Leibnitz in 1678, but the fact that the rediscovery had to wait almost 2,000 years only emphasizes the originality of Pingala's idea.

7. *A Complete Grammar, Limitation of Language*:

The *Ashtadhyayi* is a grammar of the Sanskrit language by Dakshiputra Panini (450 BC) that describes the entire language in 4,000 algebraic rules. The structure of this grammar contains a meta-language, meta-rules, and other technical devices that make this system effectively equivalent to the most powerful computing machine. No grammar of similar power has yet been constructed for any other language since. The famous American scholar Leonard Bloomfield called Panini's achievement as "one of the greatest monuments of human intelligence."

The other side to the discovery of this grammar is the idea that language (as a formal system) cannot describe reality completely. This limitation of language, the *rishis* tell us, is why the Truth can only be experienced and never described fully!

VEDANTA AND PHYSICS

Let me now talk of a savant who followed Vedic ideas and was inspired enough to create a modern theory that has transformed the world. I have in mind the Austrian physicist Erwin Schrödinger, who was arguably one of the two greatest scientists of the 20th century. If Albert Einstein is celebrated for his creation of the theory of relativity, Erwin Schrödinger is equally famous for his creation of Quantum mechanics, the deepest theory at the basis of outer reality. Quantum mechanics went so far beyond the already radical framework of relativity that Einstein refused to accept it to his last day. Without quantum theory, advances in chemistry and electronics that are the foundation of modern technology would have been impossible.

It is a fact that the great European scientists have searched for truth by first abandoning the narrow theologies of the religion into which they were born. But for Schrödinger, Vedic ideas provided the very foundation for his uncompromising search for meaning.

It is not generally known that before he created quantum mechanics he expressed his intention to give form to central ideas of Vedanta which, therefore, has had a role in the birth of quantum mechanics. In 1925, *before* his revolutionary theory was complete, Erwin Schrödinger wrote:

> *This life of yours which you are living is not merely a piece of this entire existence, but in a certain sense the "whole"; only this whole is not so constituted that it can be surveyed in one single glance. This, as we know, is what the Brahmins express in that sacred, mystic formula which is yet really so simple and so clear: tat tvam asi, this is you. Or, again, in such words as "I am in the east and the west, I am above and below, I am this entire world."*

Schrödinger's influential *What is Life?* (1944) also used Vedic ideas. The book became instantly famous although it was criticized by some for its emphasis on Indian ideas. Francis Crick, the co-discoverer of the DNA code, credited this book for key insights that led him to his revolutionary discovery. According to his biographer Walter Moore, there is a clear continuity between Schrödinger's understanding of Vedanta and his research:

> *The unity and continuity of Vedanta are reflected in the unity and continuity of wave mechanics. In 1925, the world view of physics was a model of a great machine composed of separable interacting material particles. During the next few years, Schrödinger and Heisenberg and their followers created a universe based on superimposed inseparable waves of probability amplitudes. This new view would be entirely consistent with the Vedantic concept of All in One.*

Schrödinger was born on August 12, 1887. He became a Vedantist, a Hindu, as a result of his studies in his search for truth. He kept a copy of the Hindu scriptures at his bedside. He read books on *Vedas*, yoga, and Sankhya philosophy, and he reworked them into his own words, and ultimately came to believe them. The *Upanishads* and the *Bhagavad-gita* were his favorite scriptures.

According to his biographer Moore, "His system—or that of the *Upanishads*—is delightful and consistent: the self and the world are one and they are all. He rejected traditional western religious beliefs (Jewish, Christian, and Islamic) not on the basis of any reasoned argument, nor even with an expression of emotional antipathy, for he loved to use religious expressions and metaphors, but simply by saying that they are naive."

Schrödinger was a professor at several universities in Europe. He was awarded the Nobel Prize in 1933. During the Hitler era he was dismissed from his position for his opposition to the Nazi ideas and he fled to England. For some years he was in Ireland, but after the conclusion of World War II he returned to Vienna where he died in 1961.

Quantum mechanics goes beyond ordinary logic. According to it reality is a superposition of all possibilities which restates Vedic ideas. It is quantum mechanics which explains the mysteries of chemical reactions and of life. In recent years, it has been suggested that the secrets of consciousness have a quantum basis.

In a famous essay on determinism and free will, he expressed very clearly the sense that consciousness is a unity, arguing that this "insight is not new…From the early great *Upanishads* the recognition *Atman = Brahman* (the personal self equals the omnipresent, all-comprehending eternal self) was in Indian thought considered, far from being blasphemous, to represent the quintessence of deepest insight into the happenings of the world. The striving of all the scholars of Vedanta was, after having learnt to pronounce with their lips, really to assimilate in their minds this grandest of all thoughts."

He considered the idea of pluralization of consciousness and the notion of many souls to be naive. He considered the notion of plurality to be a result of deception (*maya*): "the same illusion is produced by a gallery of mirrors, and in the same way Gaurisankar and Mt. Everest turned out to be the same peak seen from different valleys."

Schrödinger's ideas continue to be fundamental in a variety of new fields. The wonders of modern science, such as electronics, biology, chemistry, wouldn't have been possible without the insights of quantum theory. The possibilities inherent in quantum theory have not all been realized. Schrödinger remains one of the most discussed figures in modern scientific thought. His ideas will continue to inspire science.

Schrödinger was a very complex person. But he had a sense of humor and paradox. He called his dog *Atman*. Perhaps he did this to honour Yudhishthira whose own dog, an incarnation of cosmic justice (*Dharma*), accompanied him on his last march to the Himalayas. More likely, he was calling attention to the unity that pervades the web of life.

EVOLUTION AND RELIGION

The West has seen a Cold War between science and religion going back to Charles Darwin. His subversive thought that man evolved out of apes had a chilling effect on religion; it freed science from the meddling by church, giving birth to the modern age. Western religion has retreated from one defensive position to another. After a few decades it conceded that animals may have evolved, insisting man was special. By now that the idea of the Garden of Eden with Adam and Eve has been discarded, the fight has shifted from the creation of man to whether God created the first life. The church is certain that life couldn't have arisen without an intelligent designer.

In the West, evolution theory has led to a loss of the traditional religious belief. If nature could be explained naturalistically, then there is no place for an anthropomorphic God. The church having retired from the academic debate, the main fight in the academy is between those who believe that biology can determine human behavior to a great degree and others who claim that for man biology stands superseded by the world of culture, with its own laws of interaction and evolution.

Western and Indian thought are divided on the argument for design. In the West, thinkers from Aquinas to Newton maintain that nature manifests the design of a preexistent mind or the Creator. This idea helps to define the Westerner's personal sense of purpose and meaning.

In Indian thought, there is no separation between the Creator (the preexistent mind) and the universe. Consciousness is taken to be the fundamental characteristic of reality out of which material nature and individual minds emerge. Laws govern physical processes, but individuals remain free.

Evolution is basic to this view. Life is seen to have evolved over millions of years in a manner that makes the cell mirror the cosmos. This is expressed in the famous sentence: *yat pinde tad brahmande*, 'as in the cell so in the universe'.

From Consciousness arises matter (*prakriti*), and matter evolves as the balance between its three attributes (*gunas*) called *sattva*, *rajas* and *tamas* changes. This is the principle of Vedic evolution as given in Kapila's *Sankhya darshan*. Even mind evolves out of matter. The evolutionary sequence goes through many levels. There exist *tattvas* (principles) that lead to the emergence of life out of inert matter. These *tattvas*, which include the various sensory and motor capacities, are latent in matter. The chain of sensory organ adaptations may be seen amongst the animals.

The *gunas* are not to be taken as abstract principles alone. Indian thought believes that structure in nature is recursive, and the *gunas* show up in various forms at different levels of expression. For example, at the cellular level, the genetic informational flow is *sattva*, the metabolic activity is *rajas*, and the membrane that provides identity to the cell is *tamas*.

Texts such as the *Mahabharata* and the *Puranas* speak of evolution of life at many places. Earth is not considered unique regarding life. We are told that there exist countless planetary worlds, which go through cycles of evolution and decline. Hindu cosmology speaks of recursive cycles of creation and destruction.

The texts imply that ingredients for the growth of life are available throughout the universe. Infinite numbers of universes are conceived, so as a new one is created like a bubble in an ocean of bubbles, life elements from other existing universes migrate and at a suitable time lead to larger life forms. This idea supports the notion of an extra-terrestrial source of life on Earth. (On September 28, 1969, a meteorite fell over Murchison, Australia. Analysis of the meteorite revealed that it was rich with amino acids. The Murchison meteorite shows that the Earth may have acquired some of its amino acids and other organic compounds from outer space.)

The story of Vishnu's *avataras* is seen by some to represent evolution through the stages of fish, tortoise, boar, man-lion, dwarf, Rama the axe-man, Rama (the ethical man), Krishna (the spiritual man).

The Indic idea of structure showing up at different levels may be seen in the parallels between biological and linguistic evolution. Their analogies may be divided into four principal types. In historical and comparative linguistics, species with individuals capable of interbreeding are compared to the mutually comprehensible speakers of a language. In the study of animal behaviour, genes coding for physical and behavioural traits are compared to fragments of culture capable of transmission and expression. In evolutionary epistemology or history of ideas, competing scientific concepts are compared to interacting organisms in an environment in an intellectual ecology. Finally, there is an analogy between the processes in living cells and processes in the brains of persons. Each cell listens to and comprehends its own DNA speech stream; likewise, the human language helps to generate and maintain a stable network of mental reactions (mental metabolism) by means of the ongoing inner dialogue.

DRIVING FORCES IN EVOLUTION

The idea of evolution was originally taken to be a linear, ladder-climbing ascent from simple life to humans. Darwin assumed blended inheritance, in which if an organism inherits certain factors, A and B, from its parents, it passes a factor which is a blending of A and B to its offspring. But evolution cannot proceed with such a theory: the variation needed for evolution disappears rapidly as it is blended out of existence.

The next advance was provided by the Mendelian theory of heredity where the organism preserves the inheritance from the father and the mother, without blending it. The idea of such non-blending genetic inheritance is also in the *Garbha Upanishad*.

Mendelian ideas combined with Darwinian ideas provide a synthetic theory of evolution that has been called neo-Darwinism. In this theory, although mutation is recognized as the ultimate source of genetic variation, natural selection is given the dominant role in shaping the genetic make-up of populations and in the process of gene substitution.

In the 1960s, Mitoo Kimura proposed that molecular evolution was mainly driven not by natural selection but by random drift among equally well-adapted sequence variants. This theory (*neutral theory of molecular evolution*) contends that a neutral drift is the cause of most of the evolutionary change at the molecular level; also, much of the variability within species is caused not by positive selection of advantageous alleles, or by balancing selection, but by random genetic drift of mutant alleles that are selectively neutral.

Evidence supporting the neutral theory includes the discovery that synonymous base substitutions, which do not cause amino acid changes, almost always occur at much higher rate than nonsynonymous (amino acid altering) substitutions. Evolutionary base substitutions at introns also occur at a comparatively high rate. This is because the changes that are subjected to natural selection will include many that are deleterious and so unlikely to survive in later generations.

In contrast to phenotypic evolution, molecular evolution is characterized by two outstanding features. First is the constancy of the rate, so that for each protein or gene region, the rate of amino acid or nucleotide substitution is approximately constant per site per year (giving rise to the *molecular clock*). The second is that functionally less important molecules, or portions of molecules, evolve faster than more important ones.

Molecular evolution is like language change where grammatical markers and basic vocabulary changes much more slowly than the less basic vocabulary. It is providing new insights in biological evolution, and the molecular clock has been critical in helping reconstruct the history of life. Similarly, language evolution has helped in the understanding of ancient history.

Vedic evolution theory is like the neutral theory. If the gene function is seen through the agency of the three *gunas*, then evolution has a net genetic drift towards higher intelligence.

The *tattvas* are not discrete and their varying expression creates the diversity of life in and across leading different species. Each sensory and motor *tattva* is mapped into a corresponding organ.

Schrödinger, in his *What is Life?*, was the one to suggest that an "aperiodic crystal forms the hereditary substance," inspiring Watson and Crick to search for this molecule (DNA). He also thought that the *Sankhyan tattvas* were the most plausible model for the evolution of the sensory organs.

ALIENATION AND HEALTH

The world is in a crisis, not only because of religious conflict, but also due to the corrosive effect of materialism on the human psyche. There is violence in the schools, despair and depression amongst the young, and the fear that globalization will be destructive to social well-being.

In the midst of this, modern medicine is failing: not only because of the side-effects of drugs, but also because of the manner it creates drug dependency, so that most people are on one medication or other for stress, heart disease, cholesterol reduction, or pain. This has driven up the cost of health care so high that American companies are no longer competitive in the international marketplace, placing American prosperity at risk.

Perhaps this is because modern medicine seeks to look only at the body, without thought for the mind. The linkages between the mind and body are becoming apparent to science as a result of new research. For example, it is now known that stress caused reduction in the immune function. But, in itself, this knowledge is not helpful in creating new therapies. One needs a paradigmatic shift that takes as the starting point the Vedic conception of mind and body as a single entity.

Vedic science offers a vision of the world that is richer than that of materialist science, which it subsumes as a lower kind of knowledge. Unlike the Bible or the Koran, the *Vedas* are not in conflict with secular knowledge. They offer a way to obtain knowledge of the self that is essential for self-transformation, a knowledge that complements secular knowledge.

The challenge is to translate the categories that describe the nature of consciousness in the *Vedas* and the later books into a contemporary idiom that makes them accessible to a wider audience. Meanwhile, personal *sadhana* on the Vedic path is a way to obtain wisdom and insight needed to navigate through the present times.

Human Devolution:
A Vedic Account of Human Origins

Michael A. Cremo

In the *Bhagavad-gita*, the warrior prince Arjuna asks Lord Krishna about the fate of yogis who do not reach the stage of complete perfection. Lord Krishna replied that such souls, after taking birth again, will become automatically attracted to the yoga principles and make further progress. That appears to be the story of my life. I was born in 1948, and even though the place of my birth was America, as I grew up, I found myself attracted to essential aspects of the yogic way of life. I became a vegetarian. I felt much better, physically and mentally. I very much liked reading the *Upanisads* and the *Bhagavad-gita*. These books were very satisfying to my intellect. I developed a strong desire to visit India. Over the past 30 years, I have visited India over a dozen times. My voyages have taken me throughout the entire country, from north to south, from east to west. I have felt like a person coming home after a long absence. I became attracted to the teachings of one of the prominent gurus from India, His Divine Grace A. C. Bhaktivedanta Swami, and became his initiated disciple, learning from him the practice of one of the ancient Indian yoga systems, bhakti-yoga, the yoga of devotion. In so doing, my initial attraction and curiosity have matured into the commitment of a practitioner who has found a deep spiritual satisfaction.

According to the bhakti-yoga system, one's work can become one's yoga, one's transcendental connection to the supreme conscious personality behind all worldly phenomena. I have always had a tendency toward intellectual work, toward study, and writing, and speaking. I have always wondered about the origin and history of human beings. I am, of course, not unique in this regard. The question of human origins has always been a hot topic among philosophers and scientists. Today, most of them accept the Darwinian account that humans like us came into existence about 100,000 years ago, having evolved from more apelike ancestors.

I myself accepted that account during the early part of my intellectual life. And I probably would still accept it today had it not been for my encounter with the Vedic literature of India. Among this literature, one finds the *Puranas*, or histories. Had I not studied the *Puranas*, I would not have had any reason to question the evolutionary ideas I had grown to accept during my early education. In the *Puranas* I found another account of human origins. I call this account human devolution. To put it in its most simple terms, we do not evolve up from matter but devolve, or come down, from spirit.

The human devolution process, the process by which conscious selves enter human bodies on earth, has been going on for a very long time. According to the *Puranas*, or histories, humans like us have existed on earth for vast periods of cyclical time. The basic unit of this cyclical time is the Day of Brahma, which lasts for 4.32 billion years. The day of Brahma is followed by a night of Brahma, which also lasts for 4.32 billion years. The days follow the nights endlessly in succession. During the days of Brahma, life, including human life, is manifest, and during the nights it is not manifest. According to the Puranic cosmological calendar, the current day of Brahma began about 2 billion years ago. One of the forefathers of humankind, Svayambhuva Manu, ruled during that time, and the *Bhagavata Purana* (*Shrimad Bhagavatam* 6.4.1) tells us: "The...human beings...were created during the reign of Svayambhuva Manu." Therefore, a Vedic archeologist might expect to find evidence for a human presence going that far back in time. In our book *Forbidden Archeology*, my coauthor Richard L. Thompson and I documented extensive evidence, in the form of human skeletons, human footprints, and human artifacts, showing that humans like ourselves have inhabited the earth for hundreds of millions of years, just as the *Puranas* tell us. This evidence is not very well known because of a process of knowledge filtration that operates in the scientific world. Evidence that contradicts the Darwinian theory of human evolution is set aside, ignored, and eventually forgotten.

For example, in the nineteenth century, gold was discovered in California. To get it, miners dug tunnels into the sides of mountains, such as Table Mountain in Tuolumne County. Deep inside the tunnels, in deposits of early Eocene age (about 50 million years old), miners found human bones and artifacts. The discoveries were carefully documented by Dr. J. D. Whitney, the chief government geologist of California, in his book *The Auriferous Gravels of the Sierra Nevada of California*, published by Harvard University in 1880. But we do not hear very much about these discoveries today. In the *Smithsonian Institution Annual Report for 1898–1899* (p. 424), anthropologist William Holmes said, "Perhaps if Professor Whitney had fully appreciated the story of human evolution as it is understood today, he would have hesitated to announce the conclusions formulated, notwithstanding the imposing array of testimony with which he was confronted." In other words, if the facts did not fit the theory of human evolution, the facts had to be set aside, and that is exactly what happened.

Such bias continued into the twentieth century. In the 1970s, American archeologists led by Cynthia Irwin Williams discovered stone tools at Hueyatlaco, near Puebla, Mexico. The stone tools were of advanced type, made only by humans like us. A team of geologists, from the United States Geological Survey and universities in the United States, came to Hueyatlaco to date the site. Among the geologists was Virginia Steen-McIntyre. To date the site, the team used four methods—uranium series dating on butchered animal bones found along with the tools, zircon fission track dating on volcanic layers above the tools, tephra hydration dating of volcanic crystals, and standard stratigraphy. The four methods converged on an age of about 250,000 years for the site. The archeologists refused to consider this date. They could not believe that humans capable of making the Hueyatlaco artifacts existed 250,000 years ago. In defense of the dates obtained by the geologists, Virginia Steen-McIntyre wrote in a letter (March 30, 1981) to Estella Leopold, associate editor of *Quaternary Research:* "The problem as I see it is much bigger than Hueyatlaco. It concerns the manipulation of scientific thought through the suppression of 'Enigmatic Data,' data that challenges the prevailing mode of thinking. Hueyatlaco certainly does that! Not being an anthropologist, I didn't realize the full significance of our dates back in 1973, nor how deeply woven into our thought the current theory of human evolution has become. Our work at Hueyatlaco has been rejected by most archaeologists because it contradicts that theory, period." This remains true today, not only for the California gold mine discoveries and the Hueyatlaco human artifacts, but for hundreds of other discoveries documented in the scientific literature of the past 150 years, discoveries that contradict the Darwinian account of human origins.

There is also fossil evidence showing that the current Darwinian picture of the evolution of nonhuman species is also in need of revision. Beginning in the 1940s, geologists and paleobotanists working with the Geological Survey of India explored the Salt Range Mountains in what is now Pakistan. They found deep in salt mines evidence for the existence of advanced flowering plants and insects in the early Cambrian periods, about 600 million years ago. According to standard evolutionary ideas, no land plants or animals existed at that time. Flowering plants and insects are thought to have come into existence hundreds of millions of years later.

To explain the evidence some geologists proposed that there must have been a massive overthrust, by which Eocene layers, about 50 million years old and containing the plant and insect fossils, were thrust under Cambrian layers, over 550 million years old. Others pointed out that there were no geological signs of such an overthrust. According to these scientists, the layers bearing the fossils of the advanced plants and insects were found in normal position, beneath strata containing trilobites, the characteristic fossil of the Cambrian.

One of these scientists, E. R. Gee, a geologist working with the Geological Survey of India, proposed a novel solution to the problem. In the proceedings of the National Academy of Sciences of India for the year 1945 (section B, v. 16, pp. xlv–xlvi), paleobotanist Birbal Sahni noted: "Quite recently, an alternative explanation has been offered by Mr. Gee. *The suggestion is that the angiosperms, gymnosperms and insects of the Saline Series may represent a highly evolved Cambrian or Precambrian flora and fauna!* In other words, it is suggested that these plants and animals made their appearance in the Salt Range area several hundred million years earlier than they did anywhere else in the world. One would scarcely have believed that such an idea would be seriously put forward by any geologist today." The controversy was left unresolved.

In the 1990s, petroleum geologists, unaware of the earlier controversy, restudied the area. They determined that the salt deposits below the Cambrian deposits containing trilobites were early Cambrian or Precambrian. In other words, they found no evidence of an overthrust. The salt deposits were in a natural position below the Cambrian deposits. This supports Gee's suggestion that the plant and insect remains in the salt deposits were evidence of an advanced fauna and flora existing in the early Cambrian. This evidence contradicts not only the Darwinian concept of the evolution of humans but of other species as well.

Aside from fossil evidence, from genetics and developmental biology also contradicts the Darwinian theory of human evolution. Although the origin of life from chemicals is technically not part of the evolution theory, it has in practice become inseparably connected with it. Darwinists routinely assert that life arose from chemicals. But after decades of theorizing and experimenting, they are unable to say exactly which chemicals combined in exactly which way to form exactly which first living thing. As far as evolution itself is concerned, it has not been demonstrated in any truly scientific way. It remains an article of faith. The modern evolutionary synthesis is based on genetics. Evolutionists posit a relationship between the genotype (genetic structure) of an organism and its phenotype (physical structure). They say that changes in the genotype result in changes in the phenotype, and by natural selection the changes in phenotype conferring better fitness in a particular environment accumulate in organisms. Evolutionists claim that this process can account for the appearance of new structural features in organisms. But on the level of microbiology, these structures appear to be irreducibly complex. Scientists have not been able to specify exactly how they have come about in step by step fashion. They have not been able to tell us exactly what genetic changes resulted in what phenotypic changes to produce particular complex features of organisms. This would require the specification of intermediate stages leading up to the complex structures we observe today. In his book *Darwin's Black Box* (1996, p. 183), biochemist Michael Behe says, "In the past ten years, *Journal of Molecular Evolution* has published more than a thousand papers…There were zero papers discussing detailed models for intermediates in the development of complex biomolecular structures. This is not a peculiarity of *JME.* No papers are to be found that discuss detailed models for intermediates in the development of complex biomolecular structures, whether in the *Proceedings of the National Academy of Science, Nature, Science,* the *Journal of Molecular Biology* or, to my knowledge, any science journal."

Attempts by scientists to use genetic evidence to demonstrate the time and place that anatomically modern humans have come into existence have resulted in embarrassing mistakes and contradictions. The first widely publicized reports that genetic evidence allowed scientists to say that all living humans arose from an African Eve who lived 200,000 years ago in Africa turned out to be fatally flawed. Researchers have attempted to correct the mistakes, but the results remain confused. Considering the complexities surrounding genetic data, some scientists have suggested that fossils remain the most reliable evidence for questions about human origins and antiquity. In an article in *American Anthropologist* (1993 v. 95, no. 11), David W. Frayer and his coauthors said (p. 19): "Unlike genetic data derived from living humans, fossils can be used to test predictions of theories about the past without relying on a long list of assumptions about the neutrality of genetic markers, mutational rates, or other requirements necessary to retrodict the past from current genetic variation…genetic information, at best, provides a theory of how modern human origins *might have happened* if the assumptions used in interpreting the genetic data are correct." This means that the archeological evidence for extreme human antiquity documented in *Forbidden Archeology* provides a much needed check on the rampant speculations of genetic researchers. This evidence contradicts current Darwinian accounts of human origins.

Although there is much evidence from archeology, genetics, and developmental biology that contradicts the current Darwinian theory of human evolution, it does not tell us anything about the actual origin of human beings. This contradictory evidence simply tells us that we need a new explanation for human origins. But that is also important. Why offer a new explanation, unless one is really required? In my new book *Human Devolution*, I set forth such a new explanation, an explanation based on information found in the *Puranas* and other Vedic literatures.

Before we ask the question, "Where did human beings come from?" we should first of all ask the question, "What is a human being?" Today most scientists believe that a human being is simply a combination of matter, the ordinary chemical elements. This assumption limits the kinds of explanations that can be offered for human origins. Inspired by my studies in the Vedic literature, I have proposed that it is more reasonable, based on available scientific evidence, to start with the assumption that a human being is composed of three separately existing substances: matter, mind, and consciousness (or spirit). This assumption widens the circle of possible explanations.

Any scientific chain of reasoning begins with some initial assumptions that are not rigorously proved. Otherwise, one would get caught in an endless regression of proofs of assumptions, and proofs of proofs of assumptions. Initial assumptions must simply be reasonable on the basis of available evidence. And it is reasonable, on the basis of available evidence, to posit the existence of mind and consciousness, in addition to ordinary matter, as separate elements composing the human being.

For the purpose of scientific discussion, I define mind as a subtle material substance associated with the human organism and capable of acting on ordinary matter in ways we cannot explain by our current laws of physics. Evidence for this mind element comes from scientific research into the phenomena called by some "paranormal" or "psychical." Here we are led into the hidden history of physics (the knowledge filtering process also operates in this field of knowledge).

For example, every physics student learns about the work of Pierre and Marie Curie, the husband and wife team who both received Nobel Prizes for their work in discovering radium. The account is found in practically every introductory physics textbook. What we do not read in the textbooks is that the Curies were heavily involved in psychical research. They were part of a large group of prominent European scientists, including other Nobel Prize winners, who were jointly conducting research into the paranormal in Paris early in the twentieth century. For two years, the group studied the Italian medium Eusapia Palladino. Historian Anna Hurwic notes in her biography of Pierre Curie (1995, p. 247), "He saw the séances as scientific experiments, tried to monitor the different parameters, took detailed notes of every observation. He was really intrigued by Eusapia Palladino." About some séances with Eusapia, Pierre Curie wrote to physicist Georges Gouy in a letter dated July 24, 1905: "We had at the Psychology Society a few séances with the medium Eusapia Palladino. It was very interesting, and truly those phenomena that we have witnessed seemed to us to not be some magical tricks—a table lifted four feet above the floor...All this in a room arranged by us, with a small number of spectators all well known and without the presence of a possible accomplice." Pierre Curie reported that on such occasions, the medium was carefully physically controlled by the scientists present. On April 14, 1906, Pierre wrote to Gouy about some further investigations he and Marie had carried out: "We had a few new 'séances' with Eusapia Paladina (We already had séances with her last summer). The result is that those phenomena exist for real, and I can't doubt it any more. It is unbelievable, but it is thus, and it is impossible to negate it after the séances that we had in conditions of perfect monitoring." He concluded, "There is, according to me a completely new domain of facts and physical states of space of which we have no idea."

Such results, and many more like them from the hidden history of physics, suggest there is associated with the human organism a mind element that can act on ordinary matter in ways we cannot easily explain by our current physical laws. Such research continues today, although most scientists doing it are concentrating on microeffects rather than the macroeffects reported by Pierre Curie. For example, Robert Jahn, head of the engineering department at Princeton University, started to research the effects of mental attention on random number generators. A random number generator will normally generate a sequence of ones and zeros, with equal numbers of each. But Jahn, and his associates who have continued the research, found that subjects can mentally influence the random number generators to produce a statistically significant greater number of ones than zeros (or vice versa).

Evidence for a conscious self that can exist apart from mind (subtle matter) and ordinary matter comes from medical reports of Out of body experiences (OBEs). During traumatic events such as heart attacks, blood stops flowing to the brain, and the subjects become unconscious. But some subjects report separating from their bodies at such times. They report consciously observing their own bodies. The reality of such experiences has been confirmed by medical researchers. For example, in February 2001, a team from the University of Southampton, in the United Kingdom, published a favorable study on OBEs in cardiac arrest patients in the journal *Resuscitation* (v. 48, pp. 149–156). The team was headed by Dr. Sam Parnia, a senior research fellow at the university. On February 16, 2001, a report published on the university's web site said that the work of Dr. Parnia "suggests consciousness and the mind may continue to exist after the brain has ceased to function and the body is clinically dead." This is exactly the Vedic conception. At death the conscious self leaves the body, accompanied by the subtle material covering of the mind, and then enters another body of gross matter. Memories from past lives are recorded in the mind, and may be accessed by the conscious self in its new body made of gross matter, as shown by psychiatrist Ian Stevenson's extensive studies verifying past life memories of children.

If the human organism is composed of gross matter, mind, and consciousness (or spirit), it is natural to suppose that these elements come from reservoirs of such elements. This suggests that the cosmos is divided into regions, or levels, of gross matter, mind, and consciousness, each inhabited by beings adapted to life there. First, there is a region of pure consciousness. Consciousness, as we experience it, is individual and personal. This suggests that the original source of conscious selves is also individual and personal. So in addition to the individual units of consciousness existing in the realm of pure consciousness, there is also an original conscious being who is their source. When the fractional conscious selves give up their connection with their source, they are placed in lower regions of the cosmos predominated by either subtle material substance (mind) or gross material substance. There is thus a cosmic hierarchy of conscious beings. Accounts of this cosmic hierarchy of beings can be found not only in the *Puranas* but in the cosmologies of many other cultures. The cosmologies share many features. They generally include an original God inhabiting a realm of pure consciousness, a subordinate creator god inhabiting a subtle material region of the cosmos along with many kinds of demigods and demigoddesses, an earthly realm, dominated by gross matter, inhabited by humans like us.

This suggests that the universe of our experience should show signs that it was designed by a higher intelligence for accommodating human life and other forms of life. Modern cosmology does provide evidence for this. Scientists have discovered that numbers representing fundamental physical constants and ratios of natural forces appear to be finely tuned for life to exist in our universe. Astronomer Sir Martin Rees considers six of these numbers to be especially significant. In his book *Just Six Numbers* (2000, pp. 3–4), he says, "These six numbers constitute a 'recipe' for a universe. Moreover, the outcome is sensitive to their values: if any one of them were to be 'untuned', there would be no stars and no life." There are three main explanations for the apparent fine tuning of the physical constants and laws of nature: simple chance, many worlds, and some intelligent providential creator. Many cosmologists admit that the odds against the fine tuning are too extreme for a simple chance to be offered as a credible scientific explanation. To avoid the conclusion of a providential designer, they have posited the existence of a practically unlimited number of universes, each with the values of fundamental constants and laws of nature adjusted in a different way. And we just happen to live in the one universe with everything adjusted correctly for the existence of human life. But for modern science these other universes have only a theoretical existence, and even if their existence could be physically demonstrated, one would further have to show that in these other universes the values of the fundamental constants and laws of nature are in fact different than those in our universe.

The Vedic cosmology also speaks of many universes, but all of them are designed for life, and beyond all of these material universes, with their levels of gross and subtle matter, is the level of pure consciousness, or spirit. Originally, we exist there as units of pure consciousness in harmonious connection with the supreme conscious being, known by the Sanskrit name Krishna (and by other names in other religious traditions). When we give up our willing connection with that supreme conscious being, we descend to regions of the cosmos dominated by the subtle and gross material elements, mind and matter. Forgetful of our original position, we attempt to dominate and enjoy the subtle and gross material elements. For this purpose, we are provided with bodies made of the subtle and gross material elements. The subtle material body is made up not only of mind, but of the even finer material elements, intelligence and false ego (for the sake of simplicity, I have in this discussion collapsed them into mind). The gross material body is made of earth, water, fire, air, and ether. Bodies made of these gross and subtle material elements are vehicles for conscious selves. They are designed for existence within the realms of the subtle and gross material elements. According to their degree of forgetfulness of their original nature, conscious selves receive appropriate bodily coverings. Those who are more forgetful receive bodies that cover their original consciousness to a greater degree. The original conscious being in the Vedic universe (aside from God) is Brahma, the first demigod. His body, manifested directly from Vishnu (the expansion of Krishna who controls the material universe), is made primarily of the subtle material elements. He is tasked with manifesting bodies for the other conscious selves existing at various levels of the cosmic hierarchy. From the body of Brahma come great sages, sometimes known as his mental sons, and also the first sexually reproducing pair, Svayambhuva Manu and his consort Shatarupa. The daughters of Manu become the wives of some of the sages, and they produce generations of demigods and demigoddesses, with bodies composed primarily of the subtle material energy. These demigods and demigoddesses, by their reproductive processes, through a kind of intelligently guided genetic engineering, produce the forms of living things, including humans, who reside on our earth planet.

In the devolution process, our original pure spiritual consciousness is covered by layers of subtle and gross material elements. But the process can be reversed. There is a kind of re-evolution by which we can free consciousness from its coverings, and restore it to its original pure state. Every great spiritual tradition has some means for accomplishing this—some form of prayer, or meditation, or yoga. In my own practice of bhakti yoga, I rely on the process of vibrating the transcendental sound of the Hare Krishna mantra to restore consciousness to its pure state. However, I will simply advise each person to look deeply within the spiritual tradition of his or her choice, and find the form or prayer, or meditation, or yoga that is there to help one make progress toward the ultimate goal of life.

Ayurveda:
The Living Tradition of Vedic Medicine

Pratichi Mathur

सुखसंज्ञकमारोग्यम
sukhasaïjïakamärogyama

"What is called Happiness is Health."
Charak Samhita Sutra 9, 4

Ayurveda, you come across this word often enough—your friends who swear by it's miraculous effect on their health, the word 'Ayurveda' printed in bright colors on labels of cosmetics, skin care products, shampoos and elixirs that are flooding the natural healthcare stores. Model Christy Turlington sells with a sweet insistence her rejuvenation line of Ayurvedic beauty and skin and body care. Time magazine wonders if it is India's home spun Ayurveda and it's tradition of insistence on total well being—mind—body—spirit that is responsible for the rapid turn over of Beauty Queens?

Holistic health gurus Andrew Weil and Deepak Chopra write bestsellers incorporating the Ayurvedic wisdom. Ayurvedic café's, teas and cuisine, designer foods, personal-care products, cough syrups, mineral supplements, books, audiocassettes, and CDs on Ayurvedic wisdom are flooding our awareness, variously promising to 'nourish,' 'cleanse,' 'balance,' 'protect,' 'energize,' 'vitalize,' 'invigorate,' or 'regulate' the mind, the body, and the spirit, none other, but the Ayurvedic way.

The classic time tested Ayurvedic rejuvenation and detox program *'Panchakarma'* has become a catch all word (so much so that it found a place in the Webster's dictionary), and has become a dizzying trend at destination and day spas all over the world. From the studios of a humble massage therapist (passionately offering Ayurvedic lifestyle and food guidance as a complimentary therapy to massage);

to the crumbling old walls of acclaimed Ayurvedic hospitals in India—people are lining up, taking appointment years in advance, and are happy enough to be waitlisted for several months to a year in advance, all this, merely to avail an acclaimed Ayurvedic doctor's services or undergo a month to two month long *Panchakarma*.

I can never forget my mother's simple home spun Ayurvedic remedies. Little beautiful jars full of the softness of milk, the curing power of turmeric, the aroma of sweet sandalwood and the earthy nourishment of ground lentil *Urad* or *Chana daal* (Chick Peas) blended into a magic paste; applied with loving hands of my mother on my child body immersed in growth. Milk was cooked with presoaked and grinded fine almonds, pecans and walnuts, along with strands of pure saffron (which made interesting red streaks in the bubbling hot milk) and raw sugar boiled and cooled to perfection—first offered to Gods and then to me. Not a single part of my growing body was left not loved, or not massaged by my mother who cooked massaging oils to perfection, warming oils in winter and cooling coconut based oils in summer. One sneeze and the food was different, one fever and fasting was the ritual. My mother was my first healer and Ayurveda teacher, and her kitchen was her pharmacy and when she ran out of ideas, neighbors, grannies and visitors always had the right Ayurveda tip handy.

Last but not the least our grannies, mothers and aunts constantly reminding us never to drink cold water after coming home from the hot summer sun; to not eat mango's without first soaking them in water first, and insisted upon rubbing hot *ghee* and *heeng* (Asafetida) on our bellies when we had a stomach ache or were faking one to avoid going to school. Unfortunately these Ayurvedic remedies always worked! Who does not remember the warm blessing of a ginger and black pepper *Chai* bought to us during a cold and cough, the soothing relief of Rose and *Khus sherbats* in summer, and the '*khichri*' or '*pongal*' when we had fever or diarrhea? I vividly recall my grandfather's account of being struck by the deadly Tuberculosis epidemic thrice, and each time he came through stronger with the aid of Ayurvedically crafted diets, lifestyle changes, time tested Ayurveda herbs '*aushadhi*' and a will power sharpened through the practice of *Tapas* and *Yoga*. He lived healthy as a horse for his remaining life (about 50 more years) to the ripe old age of ninety.

The spirit of Ayurveda lives on in each one of us, in our families, in our choices, and in our collective memory. Ayurveda is the ancient and traditional system of natural healing from India. Ayurveda is based upon remembering, reconnecting and celebrating the eternal harmony and sacred connection between man and nature. The followers of Ayurveda begin to discover deep nurturance ever available in nature, and gradually become one with the great cycle and rhythm of nature. Ayurvedic thoughts and practices have a deep impact on the lifestyle of the Indian people. Almost every household is aware of Ayurvedic remedies for common ailments. Certain plants of medicinal value are nurtured in many homes. Ayurvedic principles are incorporated into daily living, often in the form of religious rituals, and in the use of healing and therapeutic spices in traditional Indian cuisine. The wisdom of Ayurveda has entered the very ethos and mentality of the Indian people. Over time, the goal of balancing the five elements within and without has entered into the national psyche. Therefore herbs and foods that work with the body's natural mechanisms and help the body heal itself, have evolved in importance for the Indian people.

Ayurveda is sometimes dismissed, even in India as herbal tradition, under the mistaken impression that it is little else. A careful study reveals that Ayurveda is an all encompassing, highly scientific, healing art that celebrates cause and effect; and it is the comprehensive application of the great Indian philosophies. India's folk medicine is also closely related to Ayurveda. Many old villagers think and speak the Ayurvedic language and prescribe Ayurvedic home remedies, even if what they practice goes by the name of folk medicine. Ayurveda is a rational system of medicine, whereas folk medicine has developed out of community experience and individual intuition. For example, in the earliest of Ayurvedic texts there is counsel for proper and adequate examination not only of the disease, but also of the patient, before treatment is undertaken. Diagnosis (*Nidana*) is an important and indispensable aspect of Ayurveda. The Materia Medica of Ayurveda is rich and diverse due to an uninterrupted contact with the people of India and due to an intermingling with folk medicine. The Ayurvedic pharmacopoeia contains medicinal uses of over 600 plants and over 8,000 recipes of drug combinations. Even today, people of India use extensively herbal drugs and extracts. The market for herbal remedies in India is almost twice that for modern drugs.

Western medicine grew and flourished in India due to exclusive state patronage; Ayurveda withstood the ravages of history and time. When Ayurveda was banished from the city and royal courts, it found a place in common man's home. When books on Ayurveda were being burnt and destroyed by the British, its knowledge lived in seed form in the speech of our elders and our collective minds. When the Muslim invaders destroyed universities like Takshashila and Nalanda, which were seats of Ayurveda studies, research and learning, Ayurveda flourished in mothers lap inside homes, and manifested in her knowledge of foods, spices and seasons. The fact that Ayurveda is still alive in hearts and minds of people not just in India but all over the world; the fact that it is somewhat of a peoples movement towards reasserting their right to heal themselves; the fact that Ayurveda is no longer a secret in archaic Sanskrit, but translated into almost every major language of the world; the fact that people all over the world are choosing Ayurveda more and more—stands witness to the intrinsic power of Ayurveda.

Today, as more and more people seek Ayurveda, governments the world over are not only taking notice but promoting it as well. Research projects in Ayurvedic pharmaceuticals are being heavily funded. The government of India has signed a memorandum of understanding with the Russian Government on collaboration in the field of Ayurveda teaching, treatment and research as part of the country's efforts at propagating India's traditional systems of medicine abroad. *Panchakarma* and *Kshar Sutra* are also in the process of being recognized by Russia. Hungary had recognized 40 Ayurvedic drugs. Indian teaching institutions like Benares Hindu University (BHU) and Gujarat Ayurveda University (GAU) are also partnering in the field of education and research with institutions in Japan, Australia, the Netherlands, Argentina, Italy and USA. A faculty of Ayurveda Medicine is being set up in Nelson Mandela School of Medicine in South Africa. England too is introducing an herbal medicine course to be regulated by an act of Parliament. India has also proposed an Ayurvedic Core Program of 1700 hours to England that has already upgraded Ayurveda to category-1 for single formulation. Today Ayurveda is taught and practiced in many European countries, USA, and even in South American countries such as Argentina, etc. The National Institute of Health (NIH) in Bethesda, USA is involved in researching the efficacy of Ayurveda in diseases such as Parkinson, Alzheimer's, and Rheumatoid Arthritis.

So what is Ayurveda exactly? Literally translated from Sanskrit it is composed of two words '*Ayus*' which means life and '*Veda*' which denotes knowledge. So Ayurveda is the knowledge of healthy living and is confined not only to the treatment of diseases. Life is a vast and an all encompassing phenomena, which includes death. On one end, life is a celebration of birth, growth, child bearing, youth and sexuality; on the other end, life also brings forth disease, decay, aging, and loss of vigor. Ayurveda is that ancient art and science that helps us understand this very 'life' with all its different shades and colors; understand how best we can undertake this journey; and how we transition through its different phases, example from teenage, to adulthood, to maturity, etc. Following the principles of Ayurveda brings about a profound understanding of the inner ability to have sound body, mind and spirit. From this point of view, Ayurveda is a compendium of life and not disease. This is a major agenda indeed for any system of medicine, but can it be any less—especially if true healing has to take place. Perhaps, this is exactly why Ayurveda manages to get to the root of the disease that distresses the mind or the emotion that ails the body.

Ayurveda has twin objectives—maintaining the health of the healthy, and cure illnesses of the diseased. Ayurveda, which is not just a system of disease and its management, but literally a living dynamic philosophy and manual on the art of living, is well fitted to meet its objectives. On one hand Ayurveda offers treatments like *Panchakarma* or even Surgery for the diseased; and on the other hand Ayurveda offers preventative medicine for the healthy. These include elaborate details for following ideal daily and seasonal routines, specialized diets for optimizing health and immunity (Ojas), *Rasayana Chikitsa* (promotive therapy), *Vajikarna Chikitsa* (aphrodisiac therapy), *Swasthavritta* (regimen to stay healthy furnishing details on topics such as exercise, smoking for health), *Sadachar* (social hygiene), etc.

Ayurveda advocates a complete promotive, preventive and curative system of medicine and includes eight major clinical specialties of medicine namely, (1) Medicine (*Kayachikitsa*), (2) Surgery (*Salya Tantra)*, (3) ENT (*Salakya Tantra)*, (4) Pediatrics (*Kaumatabhritya)*, (5) Psychiatry (*Bhutvidya*), (6) Toxicology (*Agad Tantra*), (7) Nutrition, rejuvenation and geriatrics (*Rasayan tantra*), and (8) Sexology and virilization (*Vajikarana)*. This shows what a developed science Ayurveda was in ancient times.

The exact origin of Ayurveda is lost in the mists of antiquity. Since Panini is placed at 7th century BC and Ayurveda depicts non-Paninian Sanskrit grammar, it is logical to place Ayurveda between 6th–10th Century BC. Tracing the continuity of Ayurveda, it is natural to look for the continuing thread in India's ancient Vedic tradition. Although the term Ayurveda, does not seem to appear in the *Vedas*, and it appears first in Panini's *Ashtadhayayi*, however, there are positive evidences to show that in the Vedic period, medicine as a profession was prevalent. The *Rig Veda* and the *Atharva Veda* both mention that there were thousands of medical practitioners and thousands of medicines. References to Ayurveda are found as early as the *Rig Veda*. The three Rig Vedic gods Indra, Agni and Soma relate to the three biological humors: Vata, Pitta and Kapha. References are made of organ transplants as in the case of the artificial limb of queen Vishpala, daughter of King Khela. The functions of physicians are also described in the *Rig Veda*.

Rishi Sushruta, famous Ayurvedic Surgeon, also holds that Ayurveda is a supplement (*upanga*) of the *Atharva Veda*. While several other sources including the famous Hindu epic *Mahabharata* speak of Ayurveda as an *upanga* of *Atharva Veda*; several other schools of thought hold Ayurveda as a fifth Veda (*Panchamveda*). Perhaps Ayurveda grew from *Atharva Veda* first as a branch and then as a comprehensive vast system deserving it's own status, or it developed parallel to the four *Vedas* as an independent knowledge (with close resembalance to the *Atharva Veda*).

Both *Atharva Veda* and Ayurveda deal with the curing of disease and attainment of long life, *Atharva Veda* by incantations and charms and Ayurveda with (divine) herbs. Such is the healing goal of *Atharva Veda* that it is often called *Bhaisajya Veda* and the word *Atharva* is synonymous with *Bheshaja*. The sages (*rishis*) described in Ayurveda are none other than Vedic rishis who formed the *Charan-Shakha* (mobile doctors, on the move from village to village) of the Vedic period and probably formed the early Atreya-Charka School of Ayurveda. The term *Charka* also literally means a wanderer. *Atharva Veda* is also known as *Atharvavani* or *Angirasa* which indicate its engagement with magic and charm. The *rishis* (sages) of *Atharva Veda* are occupied with removing the ills of darkness, disease, magic, ghosts, etc. Diseases are treated by '*mantra*' and '*tantra*'. Later in Charaka's work also, we see mention of several magic spells and other methods as recommended in the *Atharva Veda*. Dr. Das Gupta comments that Ayurveda practices were to cure those diseases that are produced by unwholesome diet, while the Atharvan practices to cure those ailments produced by sins and transgressions. *Atharva Veda* has references to anatomical and physiological factors, the diseases and other systematic knowledge of Ayurveda. Eight branches of Ayurveda are mentioned and about 100 hymns intended as cures of different diseases are mentioned.[10]

It is important to know that Ayurveda, as a separate science was not documented during this period, but was developed in the later Arsha period, when the magico-religious aspect of medicine in the *Vedas* was gradually supplemented during the Arsha period by observations based on scientific thinking. The material scattered in the *Vedas* was collected, subjected to rigid tests of efficacy and systematically arranged in Samhitas (text books or compendiums). Many of these compilations no longer exist. There is evidence which suggests that in ancient India Ayurveda had spread to several other parts of the world in some form or the other.

Ayurveda evolved over time. The Hindu *rishis* were never in a rush to define and develop a system with rigid principles of classifications that in time would limit the growth of the very science being developed. Instead, they engaged in detailed and deep study of the universe, painstakingly compiled one fact after another, and after a body of consistent knowledge had grown—established certain fundamental and immutable principles. The *rishis* developed a wide and valuable repertory on a variety of subjects of the utmost importance to man. Ayurveda is based on these fundamental principles that pertain to life (of man, plants and animals) on this earth. All this was made possible by the atmosphere of liberal thinking and rich development in the field of philosophy, chemistry, particle physics, etc., in ancient India. These fundamental principles of Ayurveda have not changed since the beginning of time itself.

We talk of Ayurveda's beginning perhaps referring to the time when its eternal principles were first cognized or comprehended by visionary thinkers, or when some gifted teachers first began teaching the eternal principles of Ayurveda. Perhaps, there never was a time when Ayurveda was not present in this universe in some form or the other. Maybe not in a tangible form like books and clinics (*Shabdarupa Ayurveda*), but present in the collective consciousness of this universe

10 Satya Pal Gupta, "Psychopathology in Indian medicine," pages 8-9

as eternal principles of unity between all things of the universe, of unity between man and nature, of the changeable but rhythmic nature of the universe, and of the unity between body and mind and as the truth that both are vehicles or tools for the one that is eternal—the spirit (*Artharupa Ayurveda*). Thus, Ayurveda originates from the creative intelligence behind this universe; the same intelligence that makes a flower bloom, a baby smile and planets oscillate around the sun. No wonder Sushruta comments that Ayurveda is Sanatana or eternal, perpetual, primeval, everlasting, and permanent.

It all began with Brahma, the Creator, who revealed the secrets of Ayurveda to the Vedic *rishis*. Several myths describe the passing down of information through a chain of consciousness beginning with the creator of all—Brahma on the top and Vedic *rishis* such as Bharadwaja, Atreya and Dhanvantari, at the receiving end. The *rishis* shared their knowledge with other *rishis*. Rishi Punarvasu Atreya further instructed his six disciples—Agnivesha, Bhela, Jatukarna, Parashara, Harita, and Ksharapani. All six disciples taught more disciples and wrote their own commentaries (Samhitas). The tradition of teaching 'worthy' students in Ayurveda continued until *rishi* Charaka (perhaps a single person or an entire school) revised the original text *Agnivesha Samhita* and Charakacharya became the head of the Atreya School of Physicians. This new revised version came to be known as *Charaka Samhita*. *Charaka Samhita* forms the core curriculum of Ayurveda universities and other education centers around the world till today. Dhanwantari, after learning Ayurveda, started a School (*sampradaya*) which concentrated on surgery under the name Dhanwantari *Sampradaya* (9-6 B.C.). He had six disciples namely Aupadenava, Vaitharana, Aurabra, Poushkalavata, Gopura Rakshitha and Sushruta. Among them Sushruta became more popular and composed a great treatise called *Sushruta Samhita* on surgery. Sushruta later came to be known as the Father of Surgery. Later, Vagbhatacharya (5th century A.D.) compiled the third set of major texts called *Ashtanga Hridayam* and *Ashtanga Samgraha*, which were really a synthesis of the work of Charaka and Sushruta.

The dates of the authors are still very controversial. Ayurveda's origin can be dated back to the 10th century B.C. However, its current form took shape between the 5th century B.C. and the 5th century A.D. Some historians place the lifetimes of Atreya, Charaka and Sushruta in the Vedic period, around 600 B.C. Atreya's School of Physicians and Dhanvantari's School of Surgeons became the basis of Ayurveda and helped organize and systematically classify it into branches of medicine and surgery. Sixteen major supplements (*Nighantus*) were written in the ensuing years—Dhanvantari, Bhava Prakasha, Raja and Shaligrama, to name a few—that helped refine the practice of Ayurveda. New drugs were added and ineffective ones were discarded. Expansion of application, identification of new illnesses and finding substitute treatments seemed to have been an evolving process.

Close to 2000 plants that were used in healing diseases and abating symptoms were identified in these supplements. *Sushruta Samhita, Charaka Samhita*, and *Ashtanga Samgraha* represent the *Brihat-trayi* or systemization of Ayurveda.

The growth and expansion of Ayurveda continued till about the end of the Buddhist era. Then onwards the Muslim invaders with their anti-Hindu and anti-Buddhist crusade weakened Ayurveda. The Muslim invaders destroyed many universities where Ayurveda flourished, including Takshashila, Nalanda and Mithila. Where as the Muslim *Hakims* (medicine men) flourished under state patronage, the Hindu Vaidya held only the lowly offices of spell makers to the poor. The British came down heavy on the imparting of Ayurvedic knowledge and promoted British owned pharmaceutical companies and modern medicine; and soon, Ayurveda, the mainstream medicine of the Hindus, like every thing else associated with the Hindus, was systematically crushed, and prevented from developing.

Ayurveda's importance diminished and it gradually faded away from center stage, as generations of Indians were beguiled and misinformed with the quick fixes and rapid cures of modern medicine, requiring no dietary restrictions or internal discipline whatsoever. Allopathy gave instant results and rapid cures. Antipyretics and analgesics started working very well on people. Allopathic pharmacological industry developed rapidly. During the British rule, the British not only invaded the Indian territory but also created a major impact on the Indian culture and the Indian mentality, which caused the Indians to turn towards the Allopathic system of medicine.

A national brain-washing by modern "rational Macaulay education" was underway and medicine based upon the Cartesian model of man as machine— soulless and stripped of choices—treating the 'liver' or the 'gall bladder' and not the person as a whole came to stay. Medicine was no longer about preventing disease, optimizing life, to bring about balance, or to rejuvenate, and, if death was inevitable, preparing for the final journey with dignity. Modern medicine was all about a world full of hostile allergens, bacteria, and microbes out to get us. Ayurveda's premise, that unless and until the hosts inner immunity caves in no allergy or infection will manifest, was quickly forgotten and so were the accompanying behaviors which ensure optimum immunity, strong metabolism (*agni*), and ability to resist and adapt to change of season and different living and environmental conditions, etc. Plants and animals are constantly altering and adapting their inner balance to be in equilibrium with the changing outer environment. The common man in British India now had a pill, an antidote, an inoculation, a guarantee! The message was loud and clear: Live as you want, eat as your tongue dictates, sexually indulge per fantasy and generally believe (and support) that the anti-death/anti-aging pill is only a matter of research and time.

Ayurveda has Indian *Darshan* (philosophy) at its root and is often called 'applied' Indian *Darshan*. What the ancient Indian sages envisioned and expanded in beautiful and complex epistemologies, Ayurvedic scholars and scientists put to test in the hard reality of day to day life. The fact that Ayurveda could derive so much practical benefit from Indian philosophy is a salute to the Indian minds where they developed philosophies, which were not merely dry intellectual theories but carried the warmth and passion of day-to-day life, and stood to test in the applied science of Ayurveda. Ayurveda aims at deliverance from the three types of pain (intrinsic, extrinsic, and superhuman); it's goal is none other than *Moksha;* and just as all the Indian philosophies consider integral to their thought a basic similarity between the universe (*Loka)* and the individual (*Purusha),* Ayurveda too comprehends the human being as not merely a conglomerate of matter and energy but a spiritual phenomena in interaction with the universe.

The *Samkhya* system, like most of the other *darshanika* schools, had been popularly confined to a metaphysical speculation. But the expounders of Ayurveda like Charaka and Sushruta put the *darshanika* principles on the applied footing of the science of medicine. Concepts of matter (*Prakriti)* being composed of qualities (*Gunas)* known as *Sattva, Rajas* and *Tamas,* is the foundation of Ayurvedic thinking and comes from the *Samkhya Darshana.* Even the *Panchamahabhuta* (five gross elements) and the *Tanmatras* (five subtle states of matter) were well-developed concepts in Indian *Darshans. Trigunas* (*Sattva, Rajas,* and *Tamas)* are the basic matter for the constitution of *Panchamahabhutas* and each *Mahabhuta* has got its own specific *Trigunatmak* constitution. It is, therefore, quite evident that *Panchamahabhutas* cannot be explained without understanding its upper cosmological link i.e. *Trigunas.* The scientific methodology (*Pramana Vijnana)* for elucidating correct knowledge as laid down in Ayurveda is very similar to the *Nyaya Darshana* (School of Logic) and the *Samkhya* school of evolution.

The *Vaisheshika* school of Indian physics and categorization of the world of things in atoms (*anus)* is so relevant that Ayurveda can even be called applied *Vaisheshika.* Ayurveda's recognition of *Vaisheshika* nine categories of substances and of the 24 *Samkhya* elements (*Tatvas)* in Ayurvedic texts reflects their applicability in the field of medicine. The concept and realty of soul and of the transmigratory nature of 'Self' were well developed in the Indian *Darshans.* One can say that the fundamental principles of Ayurveda are mostly derived from the *Samkhya-Yoga Darshana* and the applied Ayurveda is largely based upon *Vaisheshika* and *Nyaya* schools of *Darshans.*

One is over awed at the wisdom of the ancient Hindu scientists who unfolded the secrets of nature after astute observation and re-examination of evidence for centuries. So rest assured, Ayurveda made no declarations in a hurry or even based its studies on a 20 year controlled study on mice or men. The entire universe is a laboratory for Ayurveda, its ingredients are simply the basic building blocks of this universe itself: the five great elements (*Panchmahabhutas*)—Space (*Akasha*), Air (*Vayu*), Fire (*Tejas*), Water (*Aap*) and Earth (*Prithvi*). Shake up the five elements and you have the recipe for creating this universe in all its entirety and variety.

Man is a part and parcel of this universe and can hardly be considered in isolation. The *Panchamahabhautik sharira* (body made up of five elements) along with *Manas* (mind) and *Atman* (soul or Self) constitutes you and I—the *Purusha* (the living, breathing, feeling self) in constant interaction with the outer universe (*Loka*). The *Panchamahabhautik* body will one day become exactly that: reduced to ashes and the *Atman* in its eternal quest to unite with the *Paramatman* (universal spirit/principle) will move up and down in the Karmic wheel taking on new bodies, discarding old ones; as per its evolutionary agenda and consciousness.

The 'Self' of the person (*Purusha*) is a continuum of the universal Self while the physical body composed of *Panchamahabhutas* (five great elements) originates from the *Panchamahabhautik* seed and derives nourishment from food and drinks of the similar composition. Hence equilibrium and non-antagonism between the internal and external milieu of man is essential for the maintenance of the living body. Since the individual human being is the miniature replica of the universe; the individual (*Purusha*) or microcosm, and the universe (*Loka*) or macrocosm stay in constant interaction with each other and also derive and draw materials from each other in order to maintain their normalcy and homeostasis. This interaction and exchange continues in a normal way such as by breathing the air, eating foods available in nature, etc. So long as this interaction is wholesome and optimum, the individual is in optimum health. When this harmonious process breaks down, a disease state starts.

Hence, the guiding principle of treatment in Ayurveda is restoring the harmonious exchange between *Purusha* and *Loka* and to restore to normal the *Panchmahabhutas* (five elements) composing the *Purusha* and usher in a state of balance with due processes. Atreya, an Ayurvedic sage, comments that the one who contemplates the whole world as being in himself and himself in the whole world with equanimity, to such a person is born a true understanding leading to final emancipation. (*Charaka Samhita.* V, 5, 30). This point of view helped Ayurveda understand the human being as not merely a conglomerate of matter and energy, but deeply appreciate the physical, psychological, and spiritual levels of human existence; and what it means in interaction with the universe. It is unique to Ayurveda that the subject of study is human plus universe and not the human alone as an isolated unit. In fact this Law of Uniformity of Nature (*Loka-Purusha Samanya*) was a fundamental and ground breaking discovery of this age. This law "paved the way for observing intimate relationship between microcosm and macrocosm and for applying the physical laws governing gravitation, hydraulics, thermodynamics, electricity, magnetism, motion, etc. to the biological field...minute observation of nature and its phenomena led to postulation of many concepts."[11]

In a living being, the five elements (*Panchamahabhutas*) combine to form forces that are instrumental in helping a living being 'live'. These forces are known as *doshas*. Air and ether elements combine to form the force of *Vata*, responsible for all movement in the body, and it governs mainly all nervous functions. All motions, transportation and electro magnetic activities are controlled by *Vata*. There are 80 kinds of possible disturbances due to *Vata*. Pain, stiffness, paralysis, and hypertension, heart diseases—all these are caused by *Vata*. Fire and water elements combine to form the force of *Pitta*. *Pitta* governs the process of conversion, consumption and other chemical changes in the body including the work of enzymes and hormones. *Pitta* is responsible for digestion, pigmentation, body temperature, hunger, thirst, sight, courage, etc. There are 40 kinds of possible disturbances due to *Pitta*. Burning sensations, excessive body temperature, blue moles, jaundice, and pharyngitis are examples of disorders caused by *Pitta*. The elements of water and earth combine to form the force of *Kapha*. *Kapha* regulates the other two *doshas*. *Kapha* maintains the body-fluid and controls growth and strength of the body. *Kapha* is responsible for the connections of joints, the solid nature of the body and its sustenance, sexual power, strength, patience, etc. Among the 20 possible disturbances due to *Kapha* are anorexia nervosa, laziness, mucus expectoration, hardening of vessels, obesity, suppression of digestive power, etc.

विसर्गादानविक्षेपैः सोमसूर्यानिलाः यथा धारयन्ति जगद्देहं कफपित्तनिलास्तथा ।

visargādānaviksaipaih somasūryānilāh yathā dhārayanti jagaddeham KaphaPittanilāstathā ।

Just as the moon, the sun, and the wind sustain the world by the act of giving, taking, and distorting, so do Kapha, Pita and Vata sustain the body. (Sushruta, *Sushruta Samhita* 1, 6)

According to *Rishi* Charaka, wherever there is life, there are *tridoshas*; and as such, every living cell is permeated with the three *doshas* enabling them to perform their function. Dead cells do not have the *tridoshas*. Ayurveda not only recognizes these forces (the *tridoshas*) but also explains how to harness them and develop an optimum food and lifestyle program that balances the three *doshas*. When *doshas* are in balance the individual is disease free and an imbalance causes disease

---

11 Sharma, P.V, "Essentials of Ayurveda," Page xliv

to grow. Ayurveda explains how right from birth to death, *doshas* influence the health status and physical constitution of a man, either positively or negatively. The concentration levels and preponderance of each dosha in an individual is believed to be genetically determined. Therefore, *doshas* in different permutations and combinations constitute the very nature/disposition of an individual. This is known as *Prakruti* or *Sharira Prakruti*.

Ayurveda is deeply concerned with the concept of true balance. This balance entails not only a correct functioning of systems and organs, psyche and spirit but also a balanced and creative relationship with our fellow creatures, nature as a whole, between family members, our climate, the civilization we live in, between our ideals and customs, between truth and our selves, and with God. Ayurvedic texts flourish with details on right behavior, right thinking, right action, right response, right eating, right lifestyle, etc. A healthy individual makes for a healthy society and a body that is balanced holds a spirit that is free—free for spiritual advancement.

"Healthy" is termed as "*Swastha*" in Ayurveda—one who stays in his "*sva*" (self). This "*sva*" involves the total personality of man comprising of consciousness (*atman*), body (*sharira*) and mind (*manas*). *Sva* also denotes *Prakriti* or constitutional normalcy which makes the concept of *sva* different from person to person. This is quite different from the world of ideal blood counts, ideal height to weight ratios, ideal heart rate, etc. Ayurveda regards each individual as unique, a brand new painting with its own set of colors. So what may be normal to one may be quite abnormal to another. Ayurveda realizes that people do not come from a cookie cutter—so Ayurveda provides the encouragement and tools for self analysis, understanding one's native nature (*Prakruti*) and departure from one's native nature (*Vikruti*). Ayurveda recommends a return to nature, to what is simple and intrinsic to man's life, and provides information towards making responsible choices that promote good physical, mental, and social health.

Glance below at the definition of health by Maharishi Sushruta:

समदोषः समाग्निश्च समधातुमलक्रियः
प्रसन्नात्मेन्द्रयमनाः स्वस्थ इत्यभिधीयते

samadoṣaḥ samāgniśca samadhatumalakriyaḥ
prasannātmeieeindrayamanāḥ svastha ityabhidhīyate

Our body consists of three doshas (forces or energies), seven dhatus (bodily tissues), and three malas (waste products) and metabolism agni. The person who has all three

doshas, agni, seven dhatus and the three malas in a state of equilibrium, and who possesses a sound soul, senses and mind, is healthy. When there is a disturbance in their state, the body becomes diseased.
(Sushruta, *Sushruta Samhita* 15, 45)

As evidenced in the above *shloka*, Ayurveda was the first ever medical system to deliver such a comprehensive and unifying definition of health in one giant sweep. The physical body is in balance when its constituents—biological forces (*dosha*), bodily tissues (*dhatus*) and waste products (*malas*) and power of metabolism *(agni)*—are in a balanced (*sama*) state. Is this healthy? Perhaps as per modern medicine, yes.

What better health can one have than a perfectly controlled autonomous nervous system controlling the body's automatic functions (*doshas*), a perfect digestion (*agni*) ensuring good energy and growth, excellent excretion *(mala)* function preventing toxin build up, and lastly as a consequence of such beautifully balanced function one enjoys strong vital body tissues (*dhatu*). This description of a person's condition of body leaves nothing to desire. What a beautiful picture indeed; what a lofty goal to aspire for. But to Sushruta, this is but a small part of the whole picture.

If the individual does not possess a healthy mind which is the abode of healthy emotions and thoughts, and also the master of the five senses (it controls), then the picture of health is lacking and wanting. Not content with the necessity of both body and mind to be healthy and in sync, Sushruta also adds the third dimension, that of the Spirit. To what use is the body bristling with vitality and a mind poised with strength to a soul that is not deeply established in 'Self' as opposed to ignorant of 'Self' and happy in its journey through life. From this last addition, Ayurveda becomes literally an enfoldment of the journey of the spirit (Purusha), whereby the attainment of the four *Purusharthas—Dharma, Artha, Kama* and *Moksha*—become the paramount goals of the individual.

सत्वामत्माशारिरंच जयमेतत् त्रिदंडवत् ।
satvämatmäçäréraïca ïayametat tridaëòavat |

The mind, soul and the body—these three form the tripod of life. (*Charaka Samhita*, 30, 26)

Ayurveda does not recognize life as a collection of cells exhibiting biological and nervous activity. Life covers a transcendental sweep, and becomes an essential prerequisite for the full development of human potential and spiritual pursuit.

Life in Ayurveda is the all-important vehicle to achieving the highest harmony, balance, and happiness in life.

From this point of view, Ayurveda shines forth as a *Moksha Shastra* whereby health is not the goal for health sake. Consciousness is refined from gross to subtle, so that a healthy individual can successfully accomplish his four human goals of *Dharma, Artha, Kama*, and, last but not the least, *Moksha*. Ayurveda does not stop at mere physical and mental health. It prescribes spiritual health and a spiritual journey that ends in *Moksha*, or liberation from material existence. This lofty goal is unique to Ayurveda in comparison to other world medical systems and it is a goal it shares in common with the six *darshans* of India. Charaka, ancient Ayurvedic physician and scholar, considers diseases as 'obstacles' to the accomplishment of *Dharma, Artha, Kama*, and *Moksha*. According to Dr. Gupta, 'if dyspepsia and insanity are the physical and mental disorders, the cycle of birth and death is certainly a spiritual disorder, and Ayurveda is fully conscious of this disorder, and it directs everyone to overcome this disorder by attaining liberation (*Moksha*)."[12]

Vagbhata, ancient Ayurvedic scholar who defined *Dharma* as, घ्रियते लोकः अनेन इति धर्मः (*dhriyate lokaù anena iti Dharmaù*), meaning, *Dharma* is that which regulates and preserves the universe. He is here referring to the cosmic laws or eternal truths that regulate the universe. Vagbhata recognizes, *Artha* as that by which one achieves the society, अथ्यते याच्यते इति अर्थः (*arthyate yācyate iti Arthaù*), and he recognized *Kama* as pleasure, which is again of two kinds—instant or delayed. The concept of instant gratification, called ऐहिक सुःख (*aihika suùkha*), is that happiness which is changeable and is related to the material world. This is the kind of crazy instant happiness or pleasure that we achieve after a mind numbing sugar binge, a sensual one night stand, or a delicious indulgent meal.

The concept of accumulated happiness and pleasure called पारलौकिक सुःख (*paarlokik suùkha*) is attained through self control, *tapas,* self realization, spiritual gratification, transcendental happiness or, shall we say, harbingers of *Moksha*. Accumulated happiness (*paarlokik suùkha*) is eternal happiness as opposed to the momentary transient fleeting happiness of the day to day world and its basic instinctual happiness known as *aihika suùkha*. Eternal happiness is the Ayurvedic concept of *Moksha* which becomes available to the one who perseveres even in the face of three kinds of temptation and pain; overcomes sense gratification; and embraces a life of discipline, balance and moderation. Material welfare was never the goal of life and its science Ayurveda. Man and Universe are looked upon not as merely physical in essence. Ayurveda deals with a world of here and now, as well as with a world of hereafter.

---

12 Satya Pal Gupta, "Psychopathology in Indian medicine," page 21

Ayurveda's focus on *Moksha* points to the fact that Ayurveda did not grow purely as a medical science isolated from spiritual and cultural influences. Ancient India was a hot bed of intellectual activity and Ayurvedic philosophy is deeply concerned with the nature and mystery of life itself and it maintains that "there was no time when either the stream of life or the stream of intelligence or consciousness did not flow" (*Charaka Samhita* 30.27). From this it emanates that Ayurveda is as old as the instinctive urge to eliminate pain, and since pain is an innate character of life itself, then definitely Ayurveda is co-eval with life itself. Charaka describes Ayurveda as permanent or (*shashvat*) and eternal (*anadditva*). Since the experience called life is continuous, hence, Ayurveda is also as perennial as life itself.

In day to day life, the great science of Ayurveda is transmitted to the masses through the relationship between a skilled *Vaidya* and the patient, *Rogi*. The *Vaidya* is an honorable epithet describing a "student of the Veda, Ayurveda". Regarding the *Vaidya*, Maharishi Charaka comments, "He who practices not for money nor for caprice but out of compassion for living beings (*bhutadaya)* is the best among all physicians…the physician who regards compassion for living beings as his highest religion fulfills his mission (*siddharthah*) and obtains the highest happiness." (*Charaka Samhita*, 6, 1, 58-62).

The word *Vaidya* is derived from the Sanskrit word *Vidya* (knowledge), and hence means "knowledgeable" or "learned". Whatever be the calling, the physician is expected to be clever, brilliant, hard working, soft-spoken, devoted to truth and virtue (*satyadharmapara*). "The Physician who is ill-dressed, harsh in speech, arrogant, vulgar, or who visits uninvited, is to be avoided, even if he is as brilliant as Dhanwantari (a famous Ayurvedic doctor) himself." In ancient India, one could become a *Vaidya* by following any one of the following procedures—by learning the art and science of Ayurveda from a teacher, or by living and working with the teacher in his house; or the student could go to a *gurukula* where the students live together with the teacher or guru in the schools situated in the forests away from human habitation; or lastly, the student could join one of the medical centers located in the larger cities such as Takshashila, Kashi (Varanasi) and Nalanda. Today aspiring *Vaidyas* can go to colleges, gurukulas or apprentice with teachers located in India and other countries.

To the suffering patient, the *Vaidya* is not just a skilled and smart physician with excellent knowledge of drugs and pathology, but over time the *Vaidya* becomes a good friend, a guide, a parent figure, the wise one, the sage, and represents God himself. A beautiful relationship transpires between the healer (*Vaidya*) and the patient and the *Vaidya* understands subtle aspects of the patient's journey, mind, attitude, life circumstances and even astrological position of key planets (*Jyotisha* or vedic medical astrology is also applied in conjunction with Ayurveda since time immemorial).

The *Vaidya* is in an excellent position to provide council, to heal with words, look and touch, to empower the herbs with sacred intention and to gently through suggestion and medical expertise, put back on the path of balance the lost, the misguided, the uninformed and the unfortunate suffering one. Compare this scenario to the fifteen minute doctor's office visit, pressured by time and insurance company guidelines, the doctor quickly medicates the lung, liver or cancer; and looks up your name in the file while he or she is at it.

I am a *Vaidya*. A few days a week, I greet new faces who walk into my practice seeking solace from the afflictions of daily living, including but not limited to disease. Naturally people seek out someone like me only when they have exhausted all other resources. Sitting face to face with the person, all differences disappear. What comes alive in our Ayurvedic session are the common truths of human suffering and the dilemma of human existence. My clients cry and ask, "Why am I even alive?", "Why can't I loose weight?', "Why can't I feel happy in spite of taking antidepressants?"

Pain exists in different forms. We are sometimes spiritually pained and on several occasions, we are mentally perturbed and there are occasions when we are physically attacked by pain through various diseases. Often, all three types of pain come together to leave a person bewildered and hopeless. The multiple diagnostics and hard to read laboratory tests do not even begin to describe the pain. As a *Vaidya*, I take my time. I look deeply into my *rogis* eye. I see the pain. I listen to their speech, I hear the pain. I touch them, and I see them suffer with pain. I palpate their organs. I may feel their pulse, which indicates a *dosha* balance or imbalance. I check out their tongue which stands witness to their digestion. The excretions and secretions also tell their story. I also listen to their history, their life's account, their joys and sorrows, favorite foods good and bad habits. I slowly get to know them more and more. I know when they get up, when they go to bed. I know who they love and hate and how they love and hate.

Slowly a phenomenon so complex, so refined, and so subtle emerges. I see and honor the *purusha*, a unity indeed of spirit, mind and five elements (body). I see the influence of karma (we may also do an astrological chart), I see the role of choices the person has made under the influence of karma; and I see the potential this person has stepping into his or her *Purushartha* (will power).

According to Ayurveda the cause of disease is not any one factor, isolated in time and space, just waiting to be discovered under the microscope. The Ayurvedic *rishis* know this. Just as hundreds of factors become cooperative when a single flower blooms, in the same way hundreds of factors become co-operational in the development of disease as well as during the process of regaining of health. Rishi

Charaka gives a comprehensive account of the subjects of *Vada-Vidya* (art and science of discussions) and *pramanavadya* (science of perception) in two separate chapters, which reflects that a great importance has been laid to logical subjects in the medical field.

Ayurveda, as a medical science stresses on methodology of investigation, "those alone that act after investigation" (Charaka) are considered wise. In fact, scholars find that speculative, logic, and inductive tendencies in Ayurveda even predate the *Nyaya* doctrine of logic so we can infer that perhaps Indian medicine was one of the main practical areas in which logic and reasoning was brought in and utilized and later codified in the *Nyaya Sutras*.

Means and methods of systematic study are described in the *Charaka Samhita*. Charaka investigates the cause of disease in the chapter titled *Nidana Sthana*. According to Ayurveda, things either exist (*Sat*) or do not exist (*Asat*), and they can be investigated by the four *pramanas*, or valid means of knowledge. The first *pramana* is *Atopdesha*, scriptural knowledge or authoritative statements. The second is *Pratyaksha* or direct perception or cognition, definite and immediate, arises from the conjunction of soul, senses, the mind and the sense objects. Charaka accepts the limitations of this form of knowledge. The third is *Anumana* or derived logical inference, cause and effect reasoning, reason working on given premises. The final and the most unique *Pramana* is *Yukti* which we can call a 'compound inference'.

Yukti as a means of knowledge is an independent and original contribution of Rishi Charaka in the field of epistemology. It is a means of knowing past, present and future, by which *Buddhi* (mind) perceives results brought about by many and various factors and by means of which all three objectives of life can be achieved. (*Charaka Samhita*, I, II, 25). We may also describe it as a correlation of a set of causes or circumstances with an effect based on common sense. This may also be called the law of probability for one can foresee an effect under a given set of circumstances. Charaka gives the example that by the combination of the factors of water, soil, seed, agricultural labor, and effects of seasons, there results crops.

The application of *Yukti* has been useful in Ayurvedic therapeutic and pharmacological realms. In the investigation of the cause of disease, by application of *Yukti,* unlike western medicine which relies heavily on evidence from direct perception, Ayurveda can look into and investigate more factors than what are merely available for direct perception or even inference. A whole world of co-operative causes (*hetu*) opens up. Charaka comments, "because the scope of perception is very limited, while that of the imperceptible is large which is then known by scriptures, inference and reasoning (*Yukti*)."[13]

---

13 Sarma, P.V "Charaka Samhita" text with English translation, Sutrasthana, 6

According to a scholar Dr Das Gupta, Ayurveda's half mythical accounts of the divine origins of Ayurveda also point to the fact that Ayurveda was always occupied from the beginning with the investigation of the nature of causes (*hetu*) and the reason (*linga*) for legitimate inferences into the enquiry of the causes of diseases and the apprehension of signs and symptoms of the same.[14] This holistic and multidimensional Ayurvedic approach is significantly different from the 'reductionist' approach of modern medicine which seeks (and often fails) to isolate the cause of disease. Modern medicine is propounding theory after theory for explaining common diseases like asthma, diabetes, arthritis, eczema, stroke, etc. The often conflicting and often unfounded theories of modern medicine cropping up in large numbers often lead nowhere. Most theories are short lived and constant search for the very basic principle of disease is yet to be discovered.

Until date, no theory of the western pathology can satisfactorily explain the origin of all the diseases by uniform application. Ancient Ayurvedic scientists had also discovered germs and parasites (*Krumi* and *Krimi*) more than 2,000 years before modern science, yet they had the common sense not to call them as the universal "cause" of disease. The *Tridosha* theory of Ayurveda does not oppose germ theory, but comprehends it. "The scientific system is yet to find a natural law which pervades medicine" was a comment in Journal of Ayurveda (1925) and Dr Gupta comments on western medicine, "Yesterday, it was the Perfidious bacillus which was at the root of all diseases. Today, it is the disturbances in the endocrine system. Tomorrow it is just possible that changes in blood alkalinity will be alone responsible for all our troubles. We are not sure about our truths, and are constantly shifting ground even in such an important matter such as origin of the diseases."[15]

Sometimes, in Modern medicine, the truth discovered under the name of scientific medicine is so variable that the truth of today is rejected as false the next day. I explain my case with the help of the study that debunked the popular Hormone Replacement. According to Dr. Gary Farr, "Each year, doctors prescribe hormone replacement therapy (HRT) to millions of women entering menopause. During the period from 1982 to 1992, the use of hormone therapy in the U.S. more than doubled and today about a third of women aged 45 to 65 rely on it...Recently, the preliminary results of a trial by the NIH's National Heart, Lung, and Blood Institute showed that women on hormone therapy had experienced more heart attacks, strokes, deep venous thrombosis and pulmonary embolism, compared to those on a placebo...Such widespread promotion of this treatment implies that credible science has proven it safe and effective, but unfortunately this is not so. There are also credible studies that link synthetic hormones with

14 Das Gupta S.N, "A history of Indian Philosophy," page 395
15 Sharma Shiv, "The System of Ayurveda," Author is quoting Dr. Sen Gupta Page 277

breast cancer, showing increased risk with duration and dosage. What is striking is that the mounting evidence of heart attack risk associated with HRT. Why do they release statements to the media calling results 'inconclusive' and warning women against making decisions about interrupting treatment…?"[16]

Ayurveda's concept of origin of disease is quite unique and all compassing. In Ayurveda, the mind-body question is not even up for debate—it is a given that mind and body are one and the same. What affects the mind will affect the body and vice versa. So Ayurveda with its deep understanding of the cause of disease, the routes of disease and the manifestation of diseases is often always successful in areas where traditional medicine fails or only offers symptomatic management at best. Disease is defined by Sushruta as "*dukkha samayoga*" that is contact with *dukkha*—unhappiness of any kind (due to physical discomfort or mental anguish due to pangs of jealousy, grief, anger, passion, etc). Basically, all that is unpleasant to the body and mind creates *dukkha*. From this follows that if disease is sorrow; then health (physical and mental) is happiness सुखसंज्ञकमारोग्यम ॥

According to Ayurveda there are four kinds of diseases—*gantuka* (adventitious), *aharirika* (physical), *manasika* (mental) and *svabhavika* (natural). So the adventitious or exogenous disease which can occurr are caused by accidents, bites, organisms, spirits, stings, falls, etc. The physical (innate or internal) diseases occurr due to an internal imbalance of the *doshas* leading to metabolic imbalances, infections, edemas, degeneration, etc. Infections occur when the inner *doshic* balance of the individual caves in, while modern medicine considers infections externally sourced. As soon as the delicately held balance of *doshas* is compromised due to imbalanced eating and lifestyle (*mithya aharavihara),* infections set in and thrive and grow. The immunity factor (*ojas* and *vyadiksamata*) is an all important indicator of *sharirika* diseases and signify specifics such as who will develop the disease, what season will worsen or improve the disease, intensity, duration, and stregth of the disease, period of recovery, etc.

The *manasika*, psychic or mental disease manifests themselves in states of anger, pride, greed, hate, fear, cruelty, grief, etc. These unchecked states gradually lead to conditions such as insanity (*unmada*), etc. According to Charakacharya the psychic diseases are caused by non-fulfilment of desires and facing of the undesired. Natural disease is the natural decay to be expected with advancement of age, change of seasons, etc. Natural diseases cover old age, natural hunger and thirst, natural sleep, and natural death. Even though these experiences are natural in time and space, since they create unpleasant reactions (in body and mind), they are also considered as "disease".

---

16 Farr Gary, online article "Menopause/Menopause-Related Problems, One Therapy No Longer Fits All," posted on www.becomehealthynow.com

In Ayurvedic medicine, each disease type has its own unique approach and treatment. While the adventitious disease is treated surgically, the physical is treated medically, the mental psychologically, and the natural disease is treated spiritually. This wide range of treatment approach and modality is unique to Ayurveda. Ayurvedic four-fold treatment approach to the four-fold disease indicates maturity of thought in appreciating the unique "source" and nature of disease, and deliberation on appropriateness of disease intervention (when, how, degree) versus acceptance, "letting go" and helping man flow through the "natural" stages/diseases of life. Spiritual therapy involves recitation of mantra, wearing roots and gems, following religious precepts, atonements, fasting, invoking blessings, pilgrimage, etc. In case of vitiation of *doshas* (physical or internal disease), Rishi Charaka recommends three types of therapy which, "entering into the body inside, alleviates the disorders caused by diet. The therapy which by external contact through massage, fomentation, fasting, sprinkling, pressing, etc., removes the disorders. Surgical operation consists of excision, incision, puncturing, rupturing, scraping, extraction, sacrifying, probing and application of alkli and leeches." In case of psychic or mental disease, Rishi Charaka reccommends "restraint of mind from the unwholsome objects."[17]

Maharishi Charaka suggests a judicious use of drugs (*aushadha*), diets (*anna*), and lifestyle practices (*vihara),* prescribed jointly—contrary to the cause of disease; contrary to the disease itself; contrary to both the cause and the disease, or; similar to the cause of the disease; similar to the disease; similar to both the cause and disease. This constitutes treatment (*upashaya*) in Ayurveda. This ancient Ayurvedic approach has its echo in naturopathy, homeopathy, and even in modern day Allopathy. Ayurveda treatment is based on ten fundamental considerations—*ushyam* (the seven *dhatus* and *doshas*), *desham* (surrounding), *balam* (strength), *kaalam* (season), *analam* (fire of digestion, *agni*), *prakriti* (body), *vayaha* (age), *satvam* (mental state), *satmyam* (compatibility), and finally, *aharam* (dietary habits).

In reference to the case of Hormone Replacement Therapy (HRT) which I mentioned earlier, menopause would be considered in Ayurveda as a "natural" or *svabhavika* disease and while all efforts would be made to ease the transition of the menopausal woman from youth to old age, no "experiments" would be devised to pump estrogen back into the woman's body just when the intelligence of the body has made so much effort to expel and destroy estrogen at a timely age and appropriate manner. The natural change may be unpleasant but the Ayurvedic treatment will remain in this case more conservative than revolutionary. Ayurveda does not necessarily consider "intervention" in natural process as science. Instead

17 Sharma P.V, "Charaka Samhita," Text with English Translation, Volume I, Sutrasthana 54

of working against the tide, Ayurveda works to assist nature which is already pre-armed with intelligence and intention.

This brings us to an important fact about Ayurveda. Since Ayurveda recognizes the role of nature in the manifestation of both disease and health, Ayurvedic treatment emphasizes *kala* (the time factor). The role of the Vaidya is only to assist nature, not interrupt it. Ayurveda also holds that given time, the body (and its entities) will heal itself from *svabhavika* (natural) diseases with the aid of nature. This is known as the Theory of Natural Subsidence or *svabhavoparamvada*. An example is the natural subsiding of spring allergies (natural Kapha manifestation) in summer (Kapha pacified by heat of sun). The *Vaidya* is not at war with nature to deliver health, rather, the *Vaidya* works with nature, using nature's own laws, tool box, and abundant medicine chest filled with naturally available medicines and remedies to restore health and vitality in a short time with practically no side effects.

The definition of medicine itself is very wide in Ayurveda. "Nothing exists in the realm of thought or experience that cannot be used as a medicine."[18] This also explains the Ayurvedic view that all experiences, physical or mental, have an impact on the state of *doshas* thereby affecting the state of health or disease of the individual. "It merely means that all existing phenomena, physical or physiological, psychic or emotional, that is, anger and tranquility, joy and sorrow, fear and confidence. Love and hate, foods and drinks, drugs (of vegetable, mineral or animal origin), fasts, massages, postures and exercises, desirable or undesirable situations; social, climatic, or geographical conditions; laudatory or adverse comments, abuse and praise; good, bad, or indifferent thoughts—all have a bearing on body chemistry. There is nothing that can be experienced or conceived that does not influence the body or the mind of the individual to a lesser or a greater extent. Since anything that affects the constitution one way or the other can be utilized as a therapeutic agent—thereis nothing that is not medicine."[19]

Ayurvedic treatment consists of *shodhana* (purification of body by eliminating waste and excessive doshas), followed by *shamana* (pacification of vitiated doshas). *Shodhana* is accomplished through five actions (*karmas*)—*vamana* (emesis), *virechana* (purgation), *asthapana basti* (non-unctuous enema), *anuvasana basti* (unctuous enema) and *shirovirecahaan* or *nasya* (snuffing). Blood letting or *raktamokshana* has also been added to this list as an option. If *ama* or digestive toxins are present, then first the digestion of *ama* and restoration of digestive power is undertaken (*deepana-pachana*), before *shodhana* is administered. In this entire process Rishi Charaka cautions to maintain and stabalize strength of the patient. While pathology and strength of disease should reduce, the strength of patient

18 Sharma P.V, "Ayurvedic Medicine, Past and Present," page 160
19 Ibid.

(*bala*) should continue increasing. With mental diseases (*manasika*), Ayurveda recommends pacification in the mental *doshas* (*rajas* and *tamas*) and an increase of the pure and still quality of mind (*sattva*). *Sattvavajaya* is the therapy established to deal with the psychiatric disorders. Specific *rasayanas* (specialized herbs) known as *medhya rasayana* promote mental faculties and prevent psychic disorders.

Merely delivering *shodhana* or *shamana* therapy to arrest pathology and restore balance is not enough. The patients themselves play an important role in their own restoration of balance and health. The *Vaidya* furnishes a customized list of *pathyapathya* which are the wholesome or unwholesome foods and behaviors. It is now the patient's responsibility to make choices that are beneficial to his or her condition, that do not promote the pathology and in fact endow the body with strength, immunity, and longevity. Rishi Atreya commented in the *Charaka Samhita*, "The food, which maintains the balanced *dhatus* (*doshas*) in normalcy and restores the equilibrium in mal-balanced ones, should be taken as wholesome otherwise unwholesome." Rishi Charaka provides an extensive general list of both categories and the specific details of what is wholesome and what is unwholesome changes as per *prakriti* (natural constitution), *vikriti* (disturbed constitution), *agni* (metabolic capacity), *ritu* (season) and *vyadhi* (specific disease), *kala* (age), *bala* (strength), etc., of the patient. Further, Charaka comments, "wholesome and unwholesome foods produce good and bad effects respectively."

With the all important concept of *pathyapathya,* Ayurvedic medicine takes on a radically different approach from the contemporary western medicine where you are required to mostly pop a pill or undergo surgery. More often than not, disease management in western medicine incorporates minimal or no dietary modifications. I am personally aware of asthma and bronchitis patients walking into ER and being provided upon thirst with a glass full of ice and icy water to sip on. In Ayurveda this cold icy water is *apathya* or unwholesome as it increases the *vata* (cold) *kapha* (wet) pathology in the case of bronchial asthma. Instead, Ayurvedic medicine recommends sipping hot water to provide soothing relief and to counteract the cold and wet that the patient is experiencing in the lungs.

In my own practice I recommend hot water to people who suffer from chronic allergies, bronchitis, sinusitis, or other types of phlegm related conditions. My clients come back amazed as if I have provided them with some *guru mantra* or magic self heal "hot" potion. When they actively stop choosing cold foods and drinks, and protect themselves from cold exposure—that is just one level of therapy. Next, they actively seek out warm cooked foods and drinks, and resort to warm therapies (hot towels, hot water bottle, hot oil massage, steam bath, etc.) that is yet another level of therapy. The clients can now feel the difference. In Ayurvedic medicine, patients actively participate in their own healing; cooperate with the *Vaidyas* advice; understand how to work and flow with the natural laws; and cooperate with the rhythm of their own body and its entities.

The patients, thus informed of the knowledge of wholesome and unwholesome by the *Vaidya,* soon begin to grapple with the practical application of this knowledge in their day to day life. The choices that the patients ultimately make (and experience their immediate and long term consequences as a result) ultimately allow for the patients to get in touch with and consequently deal with perhaps an inner mental world of resistance, self sabotage, patterns of destructive behavior, habits of laziness, addiction to taste buds, etc. When patients begin to work at this level of awareness around their health—this is yet another and deepest level of therapy. The net result is a patient, no doubt suffering because of disease, but at the time cruising along happily; in charge of his body's state of health and disease more than ever before; actively sculpting a life around optimum lifestyle and optimum foods that would restore balance, vigor, and generate enthusiasm for living.

Along with the concept of wholesome and unwholesome, Ayurveda recommends following a diurnal routine (*dinacharya*), nocturnal routine (*ratricharya*), and seasonal regimen (*ritucharya*) along with living by the recommendations laid down under *sadvritta* (noble code of conduct incorporating health attitudes and behaviors). This health promotive and preventative aspect of Ayurvedic medicine is laid out under *swasthavritta*. Ayurvedic *sadvritta* is similar to the Yogic discipline of *yama* and *niyama* (basic activities to do and not to do). *Sadvritta* conceptualizes health gained and nurtured from a larger life that is lived in balance, with due respect to the immediate environment and natural laws, and ability to create a socially healthy society. Ayurvedic *rishis* were aware that abnormal interpersonal relationships produce psychological stress which in turn causes psychosomatic disorders. *Sadvritta* rules ensure proper socialization of the individual. Personal transgressions, sinful acts, avoidance of responsibilities and duties, etc., are all root causes of psychic self-afflicted misery—such as anxiety, worry, anger, regret, etc. Thus, for optimum health, good conduct and proper personal behavior in every sphere of life was advocated by the Ayurvedic *rishis*.

Thousands of years ago the Vedic *rishis* had a vision. They conceived of a healthy society made up of healthy individuals with sound mind, body, and spirit in sync with nature. Since Ayurveda and the universe share an intimate relationship, Ayurvedic principles are nature's own principles. Ayurveda as a medical science is always in compliance with the laws of nature. From this point of view, both the *Vaidya* and the *rogi* are subject to the laws of nature and have to work within the scope and rules of the ecosystem. *"yatha pinda tatha brahmanda"* meaning thereby, that whatever is found in the *pinda* (individual), the same is found in the *brahmanda* (cosmos). Ayurvedic scholars elucidate that just as we are concerned about the balanced state of our body, similarly, we should be aware and cautious about the balanced state of our environment and ecology. According to Ayurveda, the individual and environment around him share a deep and direct relationship; both of them are deeply and immediately affected by each other. Hence, Ayurveda is mankind's first environment friendly medical science which emphasizes that individuals live in harmony with nature and as a part of nature.

Ayurvedic medicine is humanistic, socially responsible, and deeply insightful. It is now a growing criticism that modern medicines approach, and its complex processes lack, medical ethics that take into consideration traditional values such as sympathy, charity, compassion, tolerance, and equity. Ayurveda's emphasis on ethics for the *Vaidya* include, "You shall not desert or injure your patient even for the sake of your life or your living. You shall not commit adultery even in thought. Even so, you shall not covet others' possessions. You should not be a drunkard, or a sinful man, nor should you associate with the abettors of crimes. You should speak words that are gentle, pure and righteous, pleasing, true, wholesome, and moderate. Your behavior must be in consideration of time and place and heedful of past experience. You shall act always with a view to acquisition of knowledge and the fullness of equipment"[20]

A system that has survived through the centuries; in spite of being crushed, ignored, and suppressed over the course of history, cannot be lightly dismissed as unscientific. In more recent times (last 30 years or so) Ayurveda is once again being revived from the traces of history and being put on the fast paced track of international issues such as preventive medicine, diseases like AIDS and cancer, and general health and healing. The modern man, distressed with several diseases, stress, and an incompetent medical system, is once again turning to Ayurveda for help and to restoring much needed sanity and dignity to human life on earth.

Medicine is a changing discipline. For medical science to evolve, scientific diversity and openness are necessary prerequisites. The value of the scientific nature of Ayurveda is for each to judge for themselves. "As for those who call it stagnant, I would remind them that an unstable modern science groping in the dark is not necessarily any more progressive, nor a stable science based on basic but true and unchanging principles stagnant. Progress means a move in the right direction and it ends when the destination is reached. The conflicting unfounded theories of the Western medicine cropping up in large numbers lead no where...(While) The principles of Ayurveda are founded on keen observation and solid facts...Those who may call Ayurveda unscientific may have done so in their ignorance."[21] In India alone, Ayurveda is treating more than 70% of the population and that

20 `Sharma, P.V, "Cahraka Samhita", Text with English translation, Vimanasthana, 13
21 Sharma, P.V, "The System of Ayurveda," page 276

too entirely by choice of the people, due to its greater efficiency in bringing real relief and not merely symptomatic relief with side effects. The Hindu system of medicine is a living science, and millions of people in India and all over the world are presently benefiting from it. Ayurveda is restoring confidence and hope of millions all over the world.

It is amazing that in spite of several developments and new discoveries within the fold of Ayurveda (such as use of mercurial drugs, etc.), Ayurveda never discarded its basic fundamental principles. Progress and experimentation is encouraged in the Ayurvedic tradition. Rishi Atreya spoke three thousand years ago that the science of life shall never attain finality. Therefore, humility and relentless industry should characterize your every endeavor and your approach to knowledge. The entire world consists of teachers for the wise and of enemies for the fool. Therefore, knowledge conducive to health, longevity, fame, and excellence, coming even from an unfamiliar source, should be received, assimilated and utilized with earnestness—as recorded by his senior disciple Agnivesha. But experimentation in Ayurveda is firmly rooted in the deep set immutable laws of nature. The Ayurvedic principles provide a stable base and backdrop for the experimenting scientist. Regarding researching and experimentation in modern medicine, Dr. Muthu complains, "We are not sure about our truths, and are constantly shifting grounds, even in such an important matter as the origin of diseases."[22]

Ayurveda views a synthesis between "eternality and progress and tradition and change."[23] Despite prolonged contact with foreign culture in both ancient, medieval, and modern India, influence of Muslim *hakims* and modern doctors, and the rise of new discoveries and trends within Ayurveda itself—Ayurveda never compromised with its basic concepts, which are the same today as they were in Rishi Charaka's time. This speaks volumes about a science that has already worked out its doubts and error and has come to certain mature immutable conclusions (truths). This is why Ayurveda tenets are known as 'wisdom' and not mere 'knowledge'. Ayurveda principles stand witness to the power of truth. I remember reading something to the effect, "What is philosophy but the love of truth, what is religion but the worship of truth, and what is science but the discovery of the same truth." Ayurveda intricately combines philosophy, spirituality and science of this universe in one 'test tube'. The Vedic scientists also known as *rishis, aptas,* or *siddhas* came forth in prose and verse (*shlokas*) ecstatically describing all the multiple facets of this universe and the essential inter connectivity of its multiple facets.

"An uncritical rejection of any science is as detrimental to it as its uncritical acceptance. Such rejection only means a denial of existence of reality outside

22 Sharma, P.V, "The System of Ayurveda," page 277
23 Sharma P.V, "Essentials of Ayurveda," Page lvii

the available scientific method."[24] In the era of global medicine, Ayurveda has now entered center stage. As western medicine gropes to thread together its fragmented research and compartmentalized knowledge base; as theory upon theory is discarded; as the trial and error approach becomes more and more costly to the human experience; as the commonly prescribed antibiotics, steroids and other chemical and synthetic drugs and hormones continue to give side effects; as people feel more and more exasperated by being ignored in a 'monolithic' over-burdened, hugely expensive health care system where insurance companies, pharmaceutical companies, government bureaucrats and other interest groups call the shots; as mere symptom management with hosts of side effects and no real relief becomes another burden in the already stressed day to day life; as costs of surgeries, drug regimens and hospitalization becomes prohibitive; more and more people turn to the warm refuge of Ayurveda. The autonomy and dignity of the individual must be preserved in any medical system. Fortunately, Ayurvedic medicine caters to the individual's unique needs.

Sometimes, because in its own country of birth, India, Ayurveda lacks the patronage, funding and status that western medicine receives in India; because its critics claim that Ayurveda does not provide scientific proof as per the methodology in vogue today; because authentic Ayurvedic information is written in Sanskrit language which only few understand, it is criticized as being a closed, and esoteric subject; because unlike modern medicine Ayurvedic theories cannot be subjected to the peculiar process of experimental verification and statistical validation, without a distortion of the very premise of Ayurveda (which includes but is not limited to direct perception and logical inference); because today's modern physicians and scholars reject all that is not validated by set scientific methods, Ayurveda is rejected as a relic from the hoary past. It is often dismissed as mumbo jumbo ancient philosophy by both Indian and western scholars and doctors; its recent revival and un-diminishing popularity amongst the masses in the world is construed as a "new age" trend.

However, what was described as lacking "scientific validity" and predicted to have collapsed (or collapsing) decades ago is still alive and serving the bulk of Indians who live in villages and trust the local Vaidya with their life. Not contained within the borders of the Indian subcontinent, more and more Ayurvedic centers and hospitals are being opened in remote corners of the world. The initiative for the latter is being undertaken not only by enterprising Indians, but by their enthusiastic western counterparts.

It may be pointed out that in spite of the poverty in India (another gift of the colonial westerners) Indians on the whole are healthier, both physically and mentally than their western counterparts. Ayurveda and its contribution on the

24 Dahanukar and Thatte, "Ayurveda revisisted,"1989, page 7

basic day to day life of all Indians have a major part to play in this basic fact. For example, the poorest of the poor in India uses Turmeric (*haridra* or *haldi*) in their cooking. Turmeric contains the flavanoid curcumin, which is known to have anti-inflammatory properties. This all-around wonder spice helps detoxify the liver, balance cholesterol levels, fight allergies, stimulate digestion, boost immunity, and enhance the complexion. It is also an antioxidant. Ayurveda recognizes it as a heating spice, contributing bitter, pungent and astringent tastes. For centuries Ayurveda prescribed the benefits of spices such as Turmeric (*haridra*), Asafetida (*heeng*), Cardamom (*ela*), etc., and prescribed their daily use to optimize metabolism.

Ayurveda is alive in Indian homes in the form of turmeric and literally hundreds of other medicinal spices that Indians use in daily cooking; foods cooked with season fresh vegetables only (and not frozen, canned and vacuum packed); food cooked, eaten and shared in the midst of family circle (and not through a quick drive through or on microwavable plastic TV trays); an inner understanding and acceptance of the laws of nature exhibited in the reverence to the seasonal rhythm marked by seasonal festivals, change of season fasts, special adherence to winter and summer foods such as heating sesame candy or *ladoos* in winter, drying corn in humid rainy season, and cooling *lassi*, and moist cooling vegetables like cucumber and *kakari* are eaten as a snack in summer.

An average Indian who has not been overly exposed to western medicine's tight compartmentalized view of health and disease will not panic at the sight of phlegm in spring (and run to get a flu or allergy shot) and will work with it to cleanse their system (*Kapha darshan*) by additionally taking honey which acts like an expectorant, adding *Yoga kriyas* like *kunjjal* and *neti*, etc. In summer, if the hot mangos cause diarrhea Indians do not run for anti-diarrhea tablets. Instead, they are happy their body is releasing built up heat and toxins and cooperate with the body's natural processes by either fasting or going on an exclusive *khichadi* (rice and *mung* lentil gruel) diet. In summer, if people notice skin boils, etc., they immediately realize heat or *pitta* has built up and they automatically stop consuming heating foods and begin cooling therapy like drinking coconut water, etc.

If somebody suddenly twists an ankle or their limbs and joints hurt, a quick hot oil massage (to alleviate *vata*) is the first choice of most Indians. For acute or chronic pain, Indians resort to *Yoga asanas* and other herbs. They hunt for and expect a cure, not merely symptomatic relief. Pain killers and steroidal injections are not the natural choice in an average Indian household. They will ask, "why should we numb the pain? Why not heal it?" If due to a fall or accident bones have been damaged, milk cooked with turmeric is a no fail solution to restoration of bone health in Indian households from time immemorial. Visits to the local

MD for day-to-day ailments (cough, cold, fever, sinus, diarrhea, constipation, bloating, and flu) is rare and most seasonal and day to day ailments are handled competently through home practice of Ayurveda.

If somebody gets a mild burn in the kitchen, they immediately apply cooling heat absorbing *ghee* to the area and minimum damage is seen on the skin. Teenage acne, pimples and other skin disorders like dry skin, etc., are purely treated by the Ayurvedic home remedies (*ubtan, mukhalepa,* etc.) with never even a thought to resort to harsh antibiotics, pimple "frying" creams, and so on. Massaging women after child birth, and specific diet and regimen that most women (even in urban areas) follow after child birth, such as eating jaggery and ginger sweets (*ladoos*), drinking boiled water mixed with spices, resting for certain number of days, eating a certain diet for healthy lactation, etc., ensures normal health of both mother and infant with minimal post delivery complications. Many diseases are in this way nipped in the bud and Ayurvedic home remedies are used freely and frequently to restore balance to the organism throughout India.

Home remedies are not the only way Ayurveda delivers results. In fact, to present Ayurveda only as "kitchen remedies" is an over simplified description of the grand medical science of Ayurveda. The ancient Hindu sages elaborated with amazing and mind boggling details on disease and their cure. Diseases are grouped in several classifications for the *Vaidyas* to specialize in. The most usual classification of disease is into the following seven categories: 1) hereditary diseases (*adibala prabritta*), 2) diseases of the embryo (*janmabalprabritta*), 3) diseases of the doshas (*doshabalprabritta*), 4) accidental or caused by wounds, poison, etc. (*sanghabalprabritta*), 5) diseases caused by seasons or passage of time (*kalabalprabritta*), 6) diseases caused due to improper, unethical, actions or contact (*daibabalprabritta*), and 7) natural diseases (*svabhabalaprabritta*).

Diseases have been further classified as curable, curable with effort, not curable but can be maintained with effort, and incurable (*asadhya*). Ayurveda addresses all forms of disease from the common cold to extensive memory loss and tumors. As a sweeping example you will find in the *Charaka Samhita*, descriptions on seven types of leprosy, six types of diarrhea, five types of abdominal tumors, five types of anemia, twenty groups of *Krimis* (micro organisms), two types of sciatica, two types of jaundice, five disorders of the spleen, pathogenesis of diabetes, and twenty types of diabetes, boils and their complications, varied types of external and internal swellings, four types of epilepsy, leucoderma, gout, insomnia, anxiety, etc.

In India sometimes even the modern physicians, while writing up a prescription of antibiotics or cough syrup, also provide *pathyapathy* or guidance of what is wholesome and what is unwholesome in terms of food, such as do not eat banana and yoghurt during a cough; eat *khichadi* (rice and lentil gruel) during fever or diarrhea. The physician has not acquired this Ayurveda based knowledge during the course of their western medicine training, but they have acquired it from their mothers and practiced it in their own homes. They know it works. So they prescribe Ayurvedic dietary information in conjunction with western drugs for better results. Sometimes these physicians also prescribe popular Ayurvedic formulations for common conditions such as cough syrups, constipation remedies and even energy and strength boosting tonics like the ever popular *Chywanprasha*. This energy boosting jam made with Indian gooseberry (*amalaki*) and other goodies was formulated at the time of Agnivesha (5-6 BC), and has maintained its reputation through the ages. The western medicine trained doctors have themselves grown up with the Ayurvedic formulations and know of their benefit personally. These MD's have no qualms in prescribing them to their patients as they come with no side effects.

The highly popular Ayurvedic formulation LIV 52 (Himalayan Drugs Company) is used freely as the liver therapy for all ages, etiologies, and prescribed by all types of doctors (and not just the *Vaidya*). Maharishi Ayurveda's Amrit Kalash is another internationally prescribed formulation known for its anti-cancer and immunity enhancing properties. Ayurvedic laxative Trifala and Ayurvedic antacid Amalaki are two plant-based herbs that every child knows about in India and are now gaining popularity all over the world.

Ayurveda has for long emphasized the use of Turmeric in cooking as well as in preparation of medicines. "In March 1993, researchers at Harvard Medical School published results of laboratory tests of a new method of screening for potential AIDS drugs. The new test found three inhibitors; one of them is curcumin, a chemical found in the food spice turmeric. It was effective against HIV in both acutely and chronically infected cells. Several years ago, studies of AIDS in Trinidad found that persons of African descent were more than 10 times as likely to have the disease as persons of Indian descent. One reader of AIDS Treatment news started using a turmeric extract with a very high concentration of curcumin—about 100 times the concentration in ordinary turmeric—which he obtained from a San Francisco health food store. A week after he started using it his regularly scheduled blood tests showed a substantial drop in p24 antigen (a measure of viral activity)."[25]

"Turmeric is an Indian discovery and cannot be patented: So decreed the US Patent and Trademark Office before sweeping six claims on the matter off the table. The claims were challenged by the Indian Council of Scientific and Industrial Research in March 1995. Earlier attempts to challenge the patenting of the medicinal properties of Neem had failed, leading to suspicion of US laws and

25 Internet source,—http://www.diet-and-health.net

the US policy on intellectual property rights."[26] More and more health products in the west are now touting the using of Turmeric. Indians, as we saw, eat turmeric daily.

For thousands of years the beneficial properties of Neem (*Azadirachta indica* A. Juss) have been recognized in the Indian tradition. Each part of the Neem tree has some medicinal property. Neem has been extensively used in Ayurveda. The Sanskrit name of the Neem tree is *Arishtha* meaning "reliever of sickness" and hence is considered as *Sarbaroganibarini*. The tree is still regarded as a "village dispensary" in India. The importance of the Neem tree has been recognized by US National Academy of Sciences, which published a report in 1992 entitled "Neem—a tree for solving global problems". More than 135 compounds have been isolated from different parts of Neem and several reviews have also been published on the chemistry and structural diversity of these compounds. These compounds are anti-inflammatory; anti-arthritic; antipyretic; hypoglycemic; anti gastric ulcer; antifungal; antibacterial; diuretic; anti malarial; antitumour; immunomodulatory, etc. Various parts of the Neem tree have been used as traditional Ayurvedic medicine in India for several of the properties mentioned above.

Neem oil and the bark and leaf extracts have been therapeutically used as folk medicine to control leprosy, intestinal helminthiasis, respiratory disorders, and also as a general health promoter. Its use for the treatment of rheumatism, chronic syphilitic sores and indolent ulcer in Ayurveda has also been evident. Neem oil finds use to control various skin infections. Bark, leaf, root, flower and fruit together cure blood morbidity, biliary afflictions, itching, skin ulcers, burning sensations, and pthysis. The tremendous international interest in Neem can be gauged by the number of patents filed on the various properties, active principles and their extraction and stabilizing processes in US and Japan. Over 30 patents have already been granted.[27] As the western world comes to know of plants and herbs long known to Ayurvedic medicine there is going to be a mad rush for patents.

We own the success of Ayurveda to visionary doctor sages like Charaka and Sushruta. Charaka re-edited the text of Ayurveda from the teaching of Atreya and Agnivesha. The *Charaka Samhita* is the most complete text on health care and longevity. A Charaka Club was established in New York in 1898, to honor the great Indian physician. Persian and Arabic translations of the *Charaka Samhita* had appeared in the 8-10th century A.D., and a first English translation appeared in the 19th century. Charaka's name appears as 'Sharaka Indianus' in the Latin

---

26 Internet source,—http://www.rediff.com/news/aug/23tur.htm
27 Internet source,—http://www.helloindya.com/neem/patent.htm
    and "Medicinal properties of Neem: New Findings" by D.P. Agrawal on
    http://www.infinityfoundation.com/mandala/t_es/t_es_agraw_neem.htm

translations of Avicena, Razes and Serapion. The *Charaka Samhita* consists of 120 chapters distributed in 8 sections: (i) General principles of Ayurveda, (ii) Diagnosis of disease, (iii) Specific determination of taste, etc,. (iv) Anatomy, physiology, including embryology, (v) Prognosis of disease, (vi) Treatment of disease, (viii) Pharmaceutics, and (viii) Pancha Karma therapy.

Charaka mentions in the *Charaka Samhita* that the individual is a replica of the universe and is composed of innumerable cells, which are in turn made up of five great elements (Panchamahabhutas). Charaka describes that the sperm and ovum are made up of parts and each part can be subdivided and different organs of the being are represented in these subparts. He also describes how certain hereditary diseases are conveyed from parent to child through the working of genes (*bija, bijabhaga, bijabhagavayava*).[28] Twenty types of disease-causing germs that cannot be seen by the naked eye, and parasites such as worms, are described (*krimi, krumi*), some residing outside and some within the body. So the germ theory which is the backbone of Allopathic modern medicine was already known to Charaka but he clearly rejected the idea that germs were the only or important cause of disease. According to Charaka it is the imbalance in the energies that compose us and vitiate our tissues that causes disease, and germs thrive in such a congenial environment. Concept of immunity and resistance to disease (acquired and inherent) are well developed by Charaka.

While the *Charaka Samhita* lists 1500 plants with descriptions, only 350 are pronounced medicinal. The medicinal plants are categorized in 50 groups, based on the medicinal value to be derived from them. There is a clear warning that the improper collection and use of the plants can have unfortunate results. Certain plants can prove poisonous, and this aspect too has been classified by Charaka. 149 important diseases are discussed at length including their etiology, pathogenesis, signs, symptoms, and treatment. 340 plants and plant products, 64 mineral rejuvenation therapies, longevity inducing drugs (*rasayanam*), aphrodisiac drugs, and proper diets and lifestyle on a daily and seasonal regimen has been advocated and laid down in great details.

Charaka has mentioned the ethics of the medical profession, the do's and don'ts of medical practice, and even calls for regulation by the State to protect genuine physicians and ban pseudo-physicians and quacks since they can endanger the life and property of the people. Charaka's ideal for the *Vaidya* was: "Not for self, not for the fulfillment of any earthly desire of gain, but solely for the good of suffering humanity should you treat your patients and so excel all. Those who sell the treatment of disease as merchandise gather the dust and neglect the gold." Kashiraj Divodasa Dhanvantari, a surgeon/scholar who lived in the third millennium BC, has in his works described the stages of the human embryo from the

---

28 Charaka Samhita, 3.6-7

time of fertilization until full term so well that one is amazed at their observation. The logical inference one can draw is that they must have had some sort of aid of optical instruments to be able to describe microscopic changes in the zygote.

Obstetrical surgery too seems highly developed. This is evidenced in the detailed descriptions provided in ancient Indian texts regarding the induction of abortion in cases where the pregnancy could endanger the health or the life of the mother; curetting in case of incomplete abortion; the induction of labor in cases of delayed delivery or uterine inertia; versions of various kinds in cases of mal-positions and mal-presentations; the removal of the fetus in cases of difficult labor or defects in the maternal passage, by an abdominal section (reminiscent of the modern C-section); and the delivery of retained placenta by manual method especially massage (reminiscent of the Credas method).

Ayurveda has a well-developed school of surgery. Sushruta was the first surgeon in the world to deal systematically, exhaustively, and elaborately with the entire subject of surgery, including gynecology, obstetrics, and diseases of the eye including details in the development and anatomical structure of the eye. His ophthalmologic work describes diseases of the eyelids, conjunctiva, sclera, cornea, uveal tract, lens, retina, and vitreous. His description of pterygium (*arman*) is most elaborate. Sushruta's surgical treatment of trichinas (*pakshama-kopa*) may well be compared with Jaesche-Arill operation. His views regarding the prognosis of the various ocular diseases e.g. uveitis (*adhimantha*) and glaucoma (*gambhirika*) stand fundamentally unaltered today. Sushruta was the first surgeon to have developed the technique for Rhinoplasty for which he is acclaimed as the pioneer plastic surgeon in the world.

Dr. Hirschberg, a German surgeon, declares, "the whole plastic surgery in Europe had taken its new flight when the cunning devices of Indian workmen became known to us. The transplanting of sensible skin flaps is also an entirely Indian method." In fact, according to Melissa Stewart in "Science in Ancient India", Sushruta's attached flap method is still used to reattach fingers, limbs, ears and noses even to this day.

In May of 1959, Parke Davis and Co., in their series "Great Moments in Medicine" published a color picture depicting a surgical operation by Sushruta. Of course, Sushruta's wise beard in the painting shows that the western artist was unaware that was Sushruta (1000 BC), himself laid down the rule that a surgeon was to enter the room close shaven, with clean cut nails and dressed in spotless white garments.

Operations to fit artificial limbs made of iron, cranial surgery to remove tumors, simple procedures to remove foreign bodies, blood transfusions (using a silver tube), etc., are recorded in Vedic literature even earlier to Ayurvedic literature.

Sushruta has vividly described surgical instruments in details, including 101 kinds of blunt instruments, and 21 kinds of sharp instruments. The 101 blunt are further divided into cruciform, pincer-like, picklock-like, tubular, pricker like and accessories. In fact, Sushruta's lion faced forceps (*Simhamukha Swastika*) is an ancestor of the modern Lion Forceps, the latter having lost the face of the Lion which characterized its prehistoric prototype, but retaining the sturdy grip of its "jaws". Sushruta has also described 14 types of bandages. Blunt instruments include historic but exact copies of modern day catheters, syringes, dilators, pincers, tubular appliances for inhalation, etc. Sharp instruments included knives, scalpels, hooks and sharp probes, and so on. These instruments were generally made of very high quality steel, as the ancient Hindus were proficient in the art of metallurgy. Other substances used were copper, tin, lead, gold, and silver, and ivory.

Sushruta recommended mastery over 32 moves such as extraction by moving to and fro (*nirghatna*); raising up and incising a part bringing together the lips of the wound (*vyuhana*); contracting or curling up (*vartana*); moving a foreign body (*chalana*); puncturing (*vyadhana*); etc.

Operations for hydrocele, cataract, reducing of hernia and ruptures, and setting of bones have not materially changed since Sushruta first performed them in 1000 BC. Lapratomy (opening of the abdomen), including the Caesarean section, crushing and extracting of the fetus, amputation of limbs, extraction of foreign body, plastic and rhino plastic operations, lithotomic (removal of stone), removal of fistula and piles were commonly practiced.

Sushruta described two types of diabetes mellitus, one of genetic origin and other due to dietary indiscretion. On genetically transmitted diabetes Sushruta says, "A person would be diabetic if his father and grandfather are diabetic". In fact, he mentions that such type of person is sub-clinically diabetic. The genetically transmitted entity of insulin dependent diabetes mellitus is well known today. What is striking is his description of such an insulin dependent diabetic whom he describes as a thin, restless individual. The characteristic of diabetes of dietary origin are described to be exactly opposite, which also fit in with the future of non-insulin dependent diabetics mentioned in modern medicine. The factors that predispose one to diabetes mellitus are the one's that stand confirmed today, namely, lack of exercise, sedentary habits, sleeping during day time, and excessive eating of particularly sweet and fatty substances. These individuals lack enthusiasm, are over weight, obese, and have excessive appetite.[29]

The short but triumphant history of western medicine began in 16 AD with rapid accumulation of knowledge in field of anatomy and physiology, advanced in 19 AD with discovery of germs and the theories of antisepsis and use of anesthesia.

29 Sharma, P.V, "Sushruta Samhita," Text with English Translation

And now in this century we witness the use of antibiotics and advanced diagnostic procedures, including microsurgery. Naturally, to the western trained pragmatic mind, the idea of a healing modality like Ayurveda is worth ignoring. Even the case of Ayurvedic herb Rauwolfia Serpentina (traditionally used for hypertension and stress), and its sudden explosion on the western medical scene in early 1900, was dismissed as adventitious, and not more than mere trial and error on the part of an eastern "pragmatic" mind. That a whole system of reasoning and thought, and thousands of years of research and applied work, could be behind this herb's efficacy was not a thought that crossed too many minds.

The hard bound logical empiricism of western medicine is perhaps no more closer to realize Ayurveda's "culturally configured knowledge". But the western mind's superior, almost privileged positioning and exclusive ownership of the manual and processes of "science" may be questioned, and the source of their remarkable presumptions must be challenged. Yes, Ayurveda is not free of its cultural context but by merely universalizing the medical concepts, are we any closer to the truth is the question. Germ theory, infection theory, use of anesthesia, and surgery (including brain and plastic surgery) were already old accomplishments of Ayurveda by the time the theory of "logical empiricism" was cognized by the western world. Ayurveda offers its deep understanding and decoding of laws of nature as "scientific" and western medicine offers its logical empiricism (reality exists prior to and independent of people's attempts to understand and control it) as a representation of realty.

What was perhaps hoped was that the "intrinsic superiority" of western medicine and its sure shot "pragmatic" approach will gradually "kill off" all such "half baked", non-scientific medicines. But this has not been the case. Instead of "dying off", eastern modalities of healing, including Ayurveda, are becoming more and more popular. Yes, Ayurveda has a highly culturalized and abstract theoretical system, but it is at the same time grounded in practices and well recognized procedures that can, if future generations require, be experimented upon and validated. Ayurveda is the ultimate "sustainable" medical system that puts back, or replenishes, what we take out of the system, with minimal damage to the environment or to the creatures that depend on it. Ayurveda's naturalism reveals a true line of continuity between humans and nature.

After years of practicing, teaching, and living Ayurveda, I believe that Ayurveda in spite of being so ancient (that its history cannot be traced in any linear form), is intellectually coherent in itself, with its basic ideas and concepts supporting its assumptions about physiology, pathology, treatment methodology, etc. The underlying logic has stood the test of time and is a living practice today as always. Also, I believe that to understand and appreciate Ayurveda, one has to pause long enough to understand Vedic India, its thought, and the interconnected universe of the Hindu mind set.

Any hurried, fragmented, compartmentalized approach towards understanding Ayurveda will not deliver the goods and will lead to uninformed skepticism. An understanding of the history of India and how it influenced Ayurveda is also an all important factor. The western medical community, in a hurry to classify all eastern medicine as "alternative" and western minded Indians, in a hurry to adapt and identify with the technologically advancing west, may in the rush completely miss out on an all inclusive, deeply insightful, logical, scientific, psychosomatic medical system—Ayurveda.

Ayurveda remains as its *rishis* predicted "eternal". As an original universal medicine in the new world, it is slowly gaining validation and acceptance all over the world. We have to remember that Ayurveda is not merely a practice or a therapy but a well developed scientific medical system that can be employed for physical, mental, social, and spiritual health. The world community is now progressively realizing the need for proper documentation of Ayurveda and to protect and preserve this knowledge so that it can be used in generations to come for the benefit of mankind.

Ayurvedic medicine represents healing which is internalized, and consciousness or *Atman* based versus externalized or treatment based. The Vedic goal of deliverance from all misery through correct application of true knowledge about the "Self" and consequent gaining of enlightenment is the Ayurvedic path of gaining health—perfect, permanent, eternal health; and not merely a temporary calming of symptoms. Health, that is established in awareness of "Self" (*Atmachetna*) is not merely body dominant as body is merely an expression of the "Self".

The *Vedas* inspired Ayurveda, making it an infinite organization and celebration of natural laws. In the light of limitations of western medicine and its obvious inability to heal the multi-dimensional human being, the Vedic model of healing represented by Ayurveda becomes more and more relevant today. Ayurveda upholds the fabric of Vedic intelligence by first understanding, then respecting all the laws of nature which combine to create the human experience with its unique outer "material" and inner "divine" make up. The tradition of Ayurveda healing—alive, dynamic, growing, and expanding—is a salute to the Vedic minds and their vision of truth.

Pratichi Mathur
President,
Ganesha Institute For
Ayurveda and Vedic Studies L.L.V

How Vedic Astrology Can Assist Us

Chakrapani Ullal

Vedic culture is very mysterious, mystical and philosophical, as well as scientific. It is so filled with deep knowledge that I'm sure modern science is unable to grasp its concepts. But over the years, science has begun to recognize some of the philosophical truths indicated in the Vedic scriptures. For an objective mind, it is universal in its appeal and suggests a way of life filled with harmonious living in body, mind, spirit and nature, bringing creative inspiration.

Vedic knowledge is a vast science with its many branches of knowledge including Vastu (architecture), Ayurveda (science of longevity), etc., which are complimentary to one another and integrate with one another harmoniously. It is impossible for any one person to even begin to fathom but a small part in one lifetime. It is much more than a science. It is a science of the sciences, the key to knowledge. It is the knowledge that links man to nature, which demonstrates the universal interconnectedness and interdependence of all phenomena.

We turn our attention now to the subject of a branch of the *Vedas* called Vedic astrology or Jyotish, which is called the "eye of the *Vedas*". It has a cognizing influence of the truth of life and self-knowledge. It acts as a mirror to an individual without which one may not know how to approach life most effectively. It is also called the "Science of Time". Time is the source power that rules the universe. All things originate through the procession of time. Hence, Vedic Astrology constitutes the science that maps the structure of time. Astrology is considered divine knowledge that is pure, supreme, secret, and exalted.

Astrology can be defined as the science of correlations of astronomical facts with terrestrial events, and demonstrates the Vedic understanding of the universal interconnectedness and interdependence of all phenomenon, that microcosm and macrocosm are but reflections of one another. Just as mathematics is the organizing principle of science when dealing with inanimate matter, so also astrology is the organizing principle which deals with life and its significance in relation to

197

all living bodies. The planets are seen as reflectors or transmitters of light and solar energy. The solar and planetary rays, like radio waves, affect biological and psychological processes. The rays of influence are unseen vibrations that are not perceptible to the physical eye.

Astrology gives insight and guidance to the fortunes and misfortunes of men, issues of empires and republics, floods and earthquakes, volcanic eruptions, plagues, pestilence and other incidents concerning terrestrial phenomena in relation to the regular movements of the planets.

Over 10,000 years ago the ancient sages, in their super-conscious state, cognized that there is energy in planets, and that they send out different rays at different angles which bear influence on everything animate and inanimate on other planets. Through their sensitized intuition and repeated observations these highly evolved souls were able to find out the different characteristics inborn in the planets and also discovered that each rules a distinctive part of the human mind/body. It was also found that particular groups of stars known as constellations have different characteristics, and that they modulate the influence of the planets.

On a personal note, in my own life as a young boy of five or six years I engaged in a search of the mysteries of life and was initiated into meditation at the age of 7 by my maternal uncle who devoted his entire life to spirituality (except for taking a job to meet life's minimum needs). This initial introduction not only made me fascinated with spirituality, sages and saints, but also made me seek some answers as to why people are the way they are. Why person "A" is not like person "B" or "C", why those differences exist even though "A", "B" and "C" have common interests. These and similar questions led me to my home environment and my father who was a professional astrologer.

I was living in a village and my father, being the village astrologer, would see many of the people of the town on a regular basis. Whenever they had any questions relating to their health or problems within their families or worship of the family deities they would first come to the astrologer to see how the planets were influencing their lives. They would also come for counsel as to how to deal with not only the problems relating to the planets, but also how to deal with the personal issues within the family. In a way, the astrologer would act as a family guide and advisor in all matters.

As I was a curious young person, I would participate in all these consultations by watching and listening to my father. Many times, even when the client would be approaching my father he would tell the client what they were coming for and what would be the outcome of the client's question. He would do that easily because from the early morning, even before a client would arrive, he would have already made the calculations about the planetary dispositions during the day and how they would be changing during the course of the day. Most of the time, the birth chart of the client would be a secondary consideration, the main challenges of the client's were dealt with through Prasna or horary astrology where a chart is cast for the moment a question is asked.

By watching this process it not only intrigued me but inspired me. Thus, the process of learning astrology began at an early age and continued to grow, watching the mysteries of life unfold in front of my eyes. As this process continued, my interest grew further and as I became older I began to not only actively study but started seeking astrologers who were visiting the village from different towns. When a well-known astrologer would come to the town I would take some of my friends who were interested in knowing their future and discuss their charts with the astrologer. This gave me an opportunity not only to understand the charts of other people, but also see the modes and styles of different astrologers. In fact, my major learning process began when I would take groups of interested seekers to the famous visiting astrologer and discuss their charts.

For many, many years I must have visited hundreds of astrologers to discuss others' charts. Since my services were always free it was easy for me to have people seek my guidance to discuss their charts with these astrologers. As I attained a certain degree of proficiency, I myself became a student of some of the very well known astrologers in my area and learned directly from them. It was only many years later, in the late 1960's that I decided to become a professional astrologer. In fact, for many years, even though I was making a living doing other work, I started visiting clients who wanted to consult me as a hobby and many times it would surprise me that many predictions would come true. In fact, I would like to mention one such incident.

I was studying in college in Bombay when one of my classmates (not a very close friend) came to my room to invite me to his wedding on a particular date. He had never consulted me astrologically. When he gave me the invitation I looked at him and asked him whether he had already distributed the invitations. He said "yes" and that he had invited 5000 people for a reception and dinner at the Bombay race track. At that moment, I told him that the marriage would not take place on that day. Mentally I calculated the position of the planets (as a future astrologer) and came to the conclusion that their were obstacles to the marriage on that day. Low and behold, the marriage was postponed on the day before the wedding because his grandmother died. That one incident made me famous with more than 5000 people. Thus, my popularity began as an astrologer even though I did not start becoming a professional astrologer until much later. I continued my work in a management position at a company as I continued doing astrological readings as a hobby.

During the period of my astrological studies the simultaneous interest that I had, due to the influence of my uncle who was a spiritual seeker, was to pursue saints and sages. Perhaps this very important hobby changed the direction of my path in life and brought soberness and contentment to my nature. In my pursuit of sages, I met one of the greatest sages of India at that time, Bhagwan Nityananda. I have never seen a man as great as him since then. I spent all my weekends and holidays for seven years visiting him and being in his presence until his *mahasamadhi* in 1961. During this period I met not only Swami Muktananda with whom I developed a deep connection and association, but many great sages who since have entered *mahasamadhi*. In 1958, I met Swami Muktananda who became my chief mentor and who persuaded me to come to America in 1979. I was closely associated with him in America until he took *samadhi* in 1982.

My connection with the gurus inspired me further to take deeper interest in astrology so that I could help people. It is because of this inspiration that I pursued astrology with a passion.

For me, astrology explained the meaning of all the philosophical truths. It brought a deep connection to the spiritual principles and how they work in the world. By studying my own chart I was able to learn about myself more intimately which led me to try to better myself by constant reminder of the tendencies of the planets. The search for answers to the questions about the mysteries of the cosmos, and about people in general, led me to the regular practice of meditation and the study of astrology which continues to this day.

It is only through repeated study and observation that we come to absorb any knowledge to a deep extent. It is wise, therefore, to maintain a proper respect and an attitude of humility when approaching any serious study while at the same time keeping in mind that at each step along the continuum of one's expanding understanding it is its own reward in the way of valuable insight.

While philosophy and meditation are the main ingredients necessary for the inner search, astrology explains a lot of things about the universe and the living beings within it. Astrology tries to explain one of the most complex subjects, the theory of karma and reincarnation.

The theory of karma says that every action has an equal and opposite reaction, or "as you sow, so shall you reap." Karma is due to our actions and our actions are due to our thoughts. Man reflects his inner ideas onto the outer world and perceives things as he wants them to be, not as they are.

Karma is what we have already created by our actions in the past which will bear result in the future. Therefore, the future is based on the past. There is no favoritism in the determination of the law of karma as everyone is treated equally, and equal opportunity for growth is given to everyone as well. We have to experience our karma of the past. The astrologer only reads the planetary influences that simply indicate the results of the previous karmas. Therefore there is nothing like fate in the absolute sense, controlling our lives. It is only the law of karma which impels human beings to live a right kind of living, for failure to do so may create bad karma which will make us suffer. Having this knowledge helps regulate our actions, thus making the individual wiser and better.

This theory explains why we see suffering and abundance, joy and misery in the world of a compassionate God. We as responsible human beings make choices according to our likes and dislikes which will naturally carry the rewards or punishment according to the law of karma. The compassionate almighty while dispensing these challenging karmic principles will also respond sympathetically to our recognition of our own follies and to the remedial measures we may take by way of prayer, chanting, meditation and other devotional activities as well as service to others. Vedic philosophy has always denied the existence of a merciless fate which would play with human beings as it pleases. On the contrary, the sages have undeniably declared that human beings have control over their actions, but their actions have no control over their results.

The more we understand about the theory of karma the more we are able to accept the challenges we face in day-to-day life. The more we understand the influence of the planets and their intense magnetic energy which they throw out in a subtle way, the more we are able to understand the nature of human beings. Each human being is totally different in physical, mental, psychological and emotional aspects, even if two people are born on the same day in the same hospital within the same hour. That is why a great sage described this as follows: "A child is born on that day and at that hour when the celestial rays are in mathematical harmony with his individual karma. His horoscope is a challenging portrait, revealing his unalterable past and its probable future result…the chart shows what we are now because of what we have thought and done in the past…Astrology, by providing us with a blueprint of our attachments, problems, talents, and mental tendencies, offers us a way of not only realizing in a specific sense exactly what our karma is, and helping us work with these confrontations within and without, but also a way of beginning to rise above and gain a perspective on this karma."

This brings us to the question of free will, and how it operates. Our ability to exercise will without the interference or influence of any factor outside of ourselves, gives the impression that we have the freedom to act at will. But Professor Einstein is stated to have observed, "Honestly, I cannot understand what people mean when they talk about freedom of the human will." Similarly, Professor Schoperhauer has stated that "Man can do what he wills but he cannot will what he wills." These statements from scientists also indicate that they seem to think a kind of determinism that exists in the nature of human beings.

The real situation regarding karma and free will, as explained by astrology, is that we human beings are partly free and partly determined. The circumstances of the major events of our life such as birth, death or initiation into spiritual life may be due to the uncanny operation of destiny. In other words, one's physical nature, heredity, and the social position of one's family or position in the cosmos are determined. Thus, one cannot change one's parentage, one's nationality, one's place geographically in his country, and even one's innate temperament, or the fund of one's life-energy, which are all natural endowments. These are, in the main, determined. But nature has endowed human beings with sufficient freedom to make or mar their own self. Astrology never disputes the fact that, since the spark of divinity is present in all of us, sincere efforts to perform actions in the right way will be rewarded.

However, in another sense, our life is predetermined to the extent that each one of us enters the world with impressions (which in Sanskrit are called "samskaras"), which are the primitive emotions and tendencies that motivate our lives. They are impressions carried over from our past lives in our sub-conscious minds that motivate desires, and in turn produce our thoughts and actions. Thus, human beings reflect their inner ideas on the outside world and their perceptions are colored by their past experiences.

Alan Leo, an eminent astrologer of the West, views karma and free will thusly: "The idea seems to be prevalent that astrology teaches fatalism. Those, however, who have studied the subject knows that it does not teach absolute fatalism. We are not utterly bound: neither, on the other hand, are we entirely free. We are limited and restrained by ignorance. All our misfortunes are the result of our imperfect knowledge. Had we even but a little more knowledge, there would be much less suffering."

Our actions follow the avenues of our own karma, but our will at each moment is free to fashion our future karma. It is determinism to the extent that it is shadowed by the unchangeable past.

Astrologers say that there are two forces, Daiva and Purushakara, fate and individual energy. The individual energy can modify and even frustrate fate. Moreover, the stars often indicate several fate possibilities; for example, that one may die in mid-age, but that if, through determination, one gives attention in that area it can be overcome, one can live to a predictable old age. Thus, astrology does not say that events must and should happen, but gives the benefic and malefic tendencies which can be directed or modified through conscious effort. The horoscope shows a man's character and temperament. Though it may show that he could become a criminal, it does not mean he is fated to become so. What it means is that he is just the sort of person who will have criminal tendencies, but they can be checked by proper care and training. Additionally, if emotional and financial challenges are indicated in any particular year, one can certainly meet the crisis better if one knows that it might occur.

Then, how would one define astrology? It is the philosophy of discovering and analyzing past impulses and future actions of both individuals and nations in the light of planetary configurations. Astrology explains life's reactions to planetary vibrations.

Astrology has been called the science of indications, but it does not follow that the stars rule our destiny. The stars merely record a destiny that has already been formed. They are then a symbol, not a force, or if their actions constitute a force, it is a transmitting energy, not an originating power. The planets do not dictate, but indicate the energies that are influencing a situation in a given time.

As stated, astrology is the science of time. The timing of events becomes the most important element in bringing benefits to people. Many people have decisions to make and astrology helps people to make decisions in every branch of life. No matter what the area of concern; health, finance, relationship, type of profession, type of education suitable for oneself, all of these can be addressed by looking at the astrological tendencies and strengths indicated now and for the future. So, therefore, it has definitely benefited enormously many, many clients by bringing proper guidance to their lives in making decisions for themselves and their families.

The birth horoscope reveals the general path of destiny by way of the disposition of the planets. The timing of events is indicated by the planetary cycles, called Dasha and Bhukti periods, because they show when a planet will come into its relative strength or weakness. The exact timing is further determined by the transiting planets that are influencing the Dasha or Bhukti lords. The Dasha and Bhukti cycles are unique to Vedic Astrology and are an essential component to the astrologer's accuracy of predictions.

The relationship between Karma and astrology can be likened to that of a thermometer and body temperature. The thermometer does not bring about a fever, just as the planets do not cause events to happen. Rather, they indicate the challenges one has to face in life's pilgrimage due to causes generated by the individual's past actions.

Of course, there are persons to whom astrology does not apply, in which case such persons are masters of their own destiny. Such people are sages who control their own senses and also the five elements of the Universe. They control the time and the creation; in other words, they control the planetary effects. Such great beings' free will prevails over the tendencies of the planets. They can do and undo things. This is why the great sage Parashara says: "Oh! The Best among Brahmins! I tell you the maximum longevity for various beings: for gods and sages it is limitless."

So astrology has been given to humanity to help guide them by making them conscious of their patterns and tendencies in this life. Vedic philosophy is therefore a way of life incorporating basic principles and guidelines to follow to live in this world in peace and harmony with the environment and one's self. These guidelines for conscious living are called the four *Parusharthas* and they are:

Dharma (right conduct)
Artha (wealth and finances)
Kama (pleasure and entertainment in the earthly domain)
Moksha (ultimate liberation)

That is why when astrology is practiced with right knowledge and understanding and the client has the right spirit, it helps them rise above the challenges, thereby enabling one to reach higher goals and evolution of life towards God consciousness.

The Use of Gems in Vedic Astrology (Jyotish) and Ayurveda

Howard Beckman

From my earliest days as a youth gems fascinated me. My great uncle was an importer of high-end precious gems and was well known in his day worldwide, at least by those in the highest echelon of the international gem trade. He was always traveling to India and had a long history with Bharata, as he was actually born there. I remember as a young boy traveling with him to India beginning at about age 12. His clients included many different Maharaja's families living in Rajasthan as well as many different types of people stretching from Delhi in the north to Trivundrum and Chennai in the south. India was like walking into a storybook for an American boy who had only read stories of this incredible land and its people.

Once when we were visiting one of my uncle's royal clients the men were admiring a very large ruby of incredible deep red color and brilliance. As it filled the inner palm of my hand, I assume now the gem must have weighed at least 50 to 75 carats. (Such a prize is to be found nowhere today and if it were the cost would be astronomical.) The maharaja smiled at my fascination with the fiery gem and exclaimed, "It holds the power of the Sun"! A little confused by his statement I looked toward the young prince, who was about the same age as I was. In my mind I thought he meant it had some power that had to do with his young son. Realizing my mistake everyone had a good laugh at my expense. The maharaja then said "no, the luminary in the sky, the SUN"!!!

This started my keen interest in the so called "esoteric" properties of gems, which were little known outside of India and certainly not known to more than 95% of the world's gem traders. I was taken to see an astrologer (at the suggestion of the maharaja), although my uncle admittedly was not all that convinced of the science of using gems for these reasons, and the astrologer recommended several gems that would be helpful for me to wear throughout life. Within 5 years I had my first book on Hindu (Vedic) astrology and my interest in Vedic science grew from a small spark to an all-consuming flame. I began to study yoga, then meditation and by the time I reached university was already starting to learn the basics of Vedic astrology and Ayurveda.

A year after university I obtained a degree as a Graduate Gemologist from the Gemological Institute of America and was later given the title of "Senior Member, NGJA" by the National Association of Jewelry Appraisers. After university my studies continued in Jyotish and the use of gems and still do to this day as we are constantly researching the effects of gems on patients in our Ayurvedic clinic as well as prescribing through diagnosis of the Vedic astrological horoscope.

As one of only five Planetary Gemologists certified by the Planetary Gemologists Association in Bangkok, Thailand I am called upon constantly to help with analysis of horoscopes for gems and have many other astrologers and Ayurvedic doctors consulting with us in this regard due to our research and experience in this field. It is a field that is making great strides medically by using gems for illness and disease both of the physical body and the mind. It is a noninvasive therapy that has produced definite repeatable results medically. (It should be noted that only natural gems, not synthetic, have this inherent energy and also that certain gem treatments commonly used for color or clarity enhancement will render the gem "dead" and ineffective.) Our research and record keeping of case histories of gem use in jewelry for astrological reasons has also allowed us to not only prove the efficacy of gems, but in "debunking" commonly held incorrect notions as far as how to recommend them, as well as baseless superstitions.

GEMS TRANSMIT VIBRATIONAL ENERGY

It is the energy force of the cosmos that sustains all living organisms. This energy is called "*prana*". It energizes our bodies throughout life until it leaves at the time of death, leaving the gross material body to decay and return to the elements from which it arose. The Vedic scriptures calculate our life spans in the number of breaths we are allotted during our lives. If we use this energy more quickly, then the life span will be shorter. (Long distance runners are renowned for dying in their 50's.) If we conserve our energy, especially through systems such as the yoga system, then the life span may be extended. The Ayurvedic system of healing first evaluates the intake and distribution of *prana* within both the physical and subtle (ethereal) bodies of an individual.

Gem therapy has been used by many ancient cultures and especially the wearing of gemstones on the body had great significance for the Vedic culture, other than the purely cosmetic or ornamental value that gems are mostly used for today. The science of Ayurveda when combined with Vedic astrology gives a wealth of knowledge in the correct application of gemstones to amplify planetary rays, which can have a dynamic effect on one's physical and emotional health, one's ability to prosper materially, and the general well-being of individual persons here on earth.

To promote healing within the body, cells, organs and glands that are overstressed must have their present vibrational frequency reduced. When too slow-moving the vibrational frequency needs to be increased. The brain's activity (which can be read with biofeedback equipment) will show the state of health via the brain waves' vibrations. In severe anxiety-ridden states of mind such as in "panic attacks" the brain's frequency will be a high Beta state above 25 HZ, or cycles per second. Muscles will be stiff and the adrenal glands will be on overload. Often the eyes are seen as excessively dilated and shaking or tremors may occur. To counteract this, the brain's vibrational frequency must be reduced to an Alpha state, which is 8.5 HZ. The symptoms of stress and anxiety will then automatically dissipate as endorphins are released into the blood system. Daily meditation encourages such relaxation and also helps one to focus on the inner self, rather than our incessant mental reactions to the material stimuli all around us.

There are five basic rhythms, or frequencies, of the brain. High Beta we have described as 25 HZ causing extreme anxiety and stress. Beta is the state of stimulation that is required for paying attention to our work, responsibilities, and daily affairs of life. This frequency vibrates at 14-30 HZ, or cycles per second. The Alpha state of brain wave vibration, which we mentioned is utilized in meditation, is between 7.8 and 14 HZ. The Theta state of brain activity, which can be seen in a hypnotic state, meditative trance, or in dreaming, vibrates between 3.2 to 7.8 HZ. The Delta state of brain vibration is that of deep sleep, where there is absolutely no awareness of the external environment. This rate is between 0.1 to 3.2 HZ.

Inducing different vibratory rates to the brain is used to induce healing within the body. For great physical pain the Delta state is used, or to avoid it, such as anesthesia when having major surgery on the body. The Theta or dreaming state can be induced to calm a person who is suffering from a trauma of one sort or another. The Alpha state allows one to regain equilibrium from great anxieties and having a regular Beta brain wavelength is essential to have the capacity to make any headway or successes in this world.

As gems have such vibratory qualities, we may utilize them to not only affect the brain, but also the higher vibrations in the physical body necessary for healthy functioning of all our internal and external organs. Dr. Young and Bruce Tainio of Cheny University in Washington have made the following statements from their research in this regard. "The average frequency of the human body during the daytime is between 62 and 68 cycles per second. If it drops below this rate the immune defense system will start to shut down. Cold symptoms appear at 58 cycles, flu at 57, candida at 55, glandular fever at 52, and cancer at 42 cycles per second".

Natural (meaning from the earth, which does not include synthetic, man-made material), untreated gemstones, which are repositories of cosmic colors, can restore the pranic energy to the cells of the body, so that its natural vibratory rate and normal health may be regained when it is in a diseased condition. Blue sapphire can tranquilize or have a sedative effect. Emerald can be used as an analgesic. Yellow sapphire has antiseptic properties, and diamond's ability to stimulate cell growth are just a few examples of how gems can affect the healing process in the body.

THE SEVEN RAYS

The seven rays are seen by all of us at some time or another in the magnificence of a rainbow. In some locales this phenomenon is seen more often than in others, but wherever it is seen, it is always composed of the same seven visible colors of the color spectrum, and two additional colors that are invisible to our naked eye. The colors violet, indigo, blue, green, yellow, orange, and red are visible to the eye, whereas ultraviolet and infrared are not. In fact everything has a predominant color that may actually be quite different from the way the eye may view it. In the *Vedas* there are many references to the individual planets in our solar system each carrying and vibrating a particular ray of color. The seven visible rays correspond to the major planets Sun, Moon, Mars, Mercury, Jupiter, Venus, and Saturn, and the two invisible rays ultraviolet and infrared are attributed to the invisible 'shadow planets' Rahu and Ketu. These planets, also known as the north and south nodes of the Moon (or Dragon's Head and Dragon's Tail), emit high-frequency rays of violet and red respectively, and so are not usually counted amongst the primary rays.

The rays are said to be the components of the universe's complete manifestation in all that it encompasses, seen and unseen, and are therefore unlimited and omnipotent. In the *Kurma Purana*, Chapter 43, verses 1-2, it is stated, "The rays that compose His (God's) body are omnipresent and illumine the limitless worlds of the universe. Among them, seven are the best as they form the original cores of the seven planets." From this we can ascertain that these seven rays are topmost among all the rays that form the universe. These rays emanating from the Supreme carry out the functions of creation, maintenance, and destruction in accordance with Divine Will and the movements of eternal time. Therefore all things are comprised of the rays and their inherent radiating energies. All sound and forms in this material universe can be said to originate within the seven rays.

The major planets of our solar system radiate and are virtually composed of the condensations of colors of the seven rays. The Sun is of red color, the Moon of orange, Mars of yellow, Mercury of green, Jupiter of blue, Venus of indigo, and Saturn of violet color. Rahu (also known as 'the Dragons's Head') reflects the ultraviolet, and Ketu (also known as 'the Dragon's Tail') reflects the infrared. Therefore the gemstones of these planets are also undiminishing repositories of these same cosmic rays, or seven colors. Ruby is the concentration of red color, pearl of orange, red coral of yellow, emerald of green, yellow sapphire of blue, diamond of indigo, and blue sapphire of violet. Viewed through a prism the true colors of these gems are revealed to the eye. The only two that also appear exactly as their cosmic color to the unaided eye are ruby (red) and emerald (green). Even with the aid of a prism the vibrational wavelengths of gomed (hessonite garnet)—the ultraviolet of Rahu—and cat's eye (chrysoberyl)—the infrared of Ketu—are invisible. These gems can release their storehouses of colors to the physical and ethereal bodies when utilized to heal in various ways, the most common way being when they are worn upon the body in rings and pendants. Less commonly known are the practices of vibrational therapies using high-frequency wavelengths of light and energy transmitted through the gems by therapists.

The five elements of earth, water, fire, air, and ether are also condensations of these same cosmic colors. Earth is the concentration of the green cosmic color, water is the concentration of both orange and indigo, fire is made of red and yellow color, air is violet, and ether is blue. The five senses have their individual colors as well: sight is due to the vibration of the red cosmic ray, smell is due to green, the sense of touch is within the violet color, sound vibration is blue, and taste sensation is orange. These same individual rays also color the sense organs of our bodies, which we use to experience our five senses. Therefore, if one looks at them through a prism, the eyes will predominantly show the red color, the nose (especially within the nostrils) will show the green color, the tongue will appear mostly orange, the skin appears predominantly violet, and the ear-holes will exhibit blue color. These cosmic rays are what give the specific sense-capabilities to the organs. The human organism is composed of cells that form groups and are the building blocks of our bodies. The cells themselves are composed of the seven rays, and these rays must be in balance to maintain cells in a healthy condition. This done, then the body itself remains in a healthy condition.

Because of actions and reactions both internally and externally, the rays constantly go through change. When these changes are due to either external pollution of the environment in which we live or internal pollution due to improper diet, habits, or lifestyle, the result is that cells become extremely adversely affected. This disrupts the balance and equilibrium of the rays within the cells. When it gets to the point where three or more rays are disturbed and are not quickly restored to balance, then disease enters the body and creates illness. This illness may be physical or emotional, but generally both are affected since one is connected to the other. Therefore disease begins from disruption of the astral body and its subtle balancing system, and it seems that a more diseased physical condition is caused by a greater disruption of the natural balance of the cosmic rays. When all seven rays come into complete 'disarray,' then the illnesses become for the most part incurable or are soon fatal.

Cancers are an example of all the rays becoming unbalanced, and unless a person becomes completely disciplined to take drastic—say, ascetic—measures to instigate the healing process, it is generally incurable. Even surgery to remove cancerous tumors cannot be permanently successful unless a person takes such health-balancing measures to heart, for serious disease will crop up elsewhere if the lesson is not learned. Ultimately the cells of the body will disintegrate and Spirit will 'depart' from the physical form at the time of death anyway, but to hasten this unnecessarily is not the optimal set of circumstances. The rays also comprise the subtle astral bodies that we inhabit, so even when leaving our physical forms, our 'subtle bodies' are still comprised of the cosmic rays. By taking advantage of color therapy—gem therapy being its most potent form of application—we can restore the balance of the cosmic rays within the physical and astral bodies, allowing for a full span of life.

The *Tridosha* (three humors) of *Ayurveda* also find their source in the seven rays. The Ayurvedic *vata* (air) comprised of air and ether is born of cosmic blue and violet. *Pitta* is fire, thus being of the cosmic red and yellow colors, and *kapha*, being combined water and earth, is of the indigo, green, and orange colors.

Colors are also either hot or cold. The male planets are Sun, Mars, and Jupiter, and thus their colors red, yellow, and blue are hot cosmic energies. The female planets Moon and Venus, and the sexless planets Mercury and Saturn, along with their cosmic colors orange, indigo, green, and violet, are the cold cosmic rays. Coldest of all is the green, also the color of Earth.

To heal using these vibrations it is necessary to determine the color lacking within the make-up of a person at the present time. For disorders where there is too much heat, cold colors must be applied, and for imbalances caused by cold, the opposite must be applied. When there is a disorder of all three *doshas*, then all the cosmic colors must be applied simultaneously. This will counteract the imbalance and begin the healing process on all levels, be they exhibited in the physical, mental, emotional, or ethereal dimensions of the body. Unity of mind, body, and Spirit will promote health on all levels, particularly through the chakras, where there is an interlinking with our mental and psychological energies.

Those readers familiar with the etheric or vital body of a person know that there are seven major vortexes of etheric energy. They are in specific places within the body called chakras. Atop these centers are the physical endocrine glands that produce hormones in the physical body to enable specific bodily functions. The healthy function of these glands is dependent upon the health of the 'etheric body' surrounding the physical, which vitalizes them and continues proper nervous system functions through etheric processes involving the *nadis*. These also utilize specific cosmic colors and indeed are composed of the individual colors for each chakra.

When there are imbalances within bodily organs, it is generally the result of planetary forces by the planetary ray (color) of the planet ruling the particular organ. Paracelsus (1493-1541) stated that if a man has an elemental deficiency whose essence radiates from Mars (and as a consequence suffers from weak blood), he should be given iron. "If a man gets angry, it is not because he has too much bile, but because the Mars correlative element within the body is too powerful." Johannes Kepler (1571-1630), whose theories became laws of physics still holding true today, practiced astrology, and in his lifetime cast many horoscopes for kings and queens in Europe. He said: "Man is made from the elements and absorbs them as much as food or drink—from which it follows that man must also, like the elements, be subjected to the influence of the planets." It is the work of great thinkers such as these that also linked the color and gem healing therapies in the West to the science of astrology.

We have found three basic tissues strongly affected by particular colors. Ectodermal tissue (skin, nerves, and brain) is powerfully affected by the red cosmic color. Mesodermal tissue (muscle, blood, and bone) is affected by blue, yellow, and indigo cosmic rays. Endodermal tissue (the linings of intestines and organs) reacts significantly to violet and green color. Particular problems in these tissues will often have a positive response to infusion with these colors, but these are only the physical tissues. Only about 10% of disease is caused solely by physical body imbalances; the great majority of illness has its root in the subtle bodies of mind and emotions. Therefore the auric field (ethereal bodies) must be carefully examined in order to prescribe the correct remedy of color therapy. Dr. Kilner's work in this field showed that the human aura was blocked and darkened in places where the disease was seated, and clairvoyants have mentioned seeing this same phenomenon. Using vibrational healing methods treats the subtle, ethereal bodies, and as a result can stop the onslaught of disease to the physical body.

This process can only be affected in its maximum potency through the use of gem therapy, as no other elements contain such concentrated and inexhaustible stores of the cosmic colors. Astrologers and Ayurvedic physicians have for ages recommended the wearing of gemstones on the body, as have Tantrics and mystics of many cultures around the world. Ayurveda also has a method of crushing, burning to ashes, and treating the gems to make medicines called *bhasmas* or *pisthis* that are crushed and purified gems, but not burned to ash. Gem elixirs, made by placing potent gems into water for an extended period, or directing high vibrations through the gems to the water can also be made. The process of placing gems in water for this reason is an ancient medicinal process used not only by the Vedic culture, but also by ancient cultures from every corner of the globe.

These cosmic rays can also be transmitted to a person through the use of distant healing. The late Dr. Benoytosh Bhattacharya of Calcutta, India used a color wheel or a disc set with gemstones attached to an electric motor turned at 1300 to 1400 rpm. He would place a photograph of the ill person in front of this spinning wheel, and the person would instantly receive the vibrations. Modern technology has allowed even far greater vibrations to be transmitted through the gems and has been used very effectively in distant healing. Although the skeptics may scoff at this, enough experiments have been performed to prove that it is not merely a figment of anyone's imagination. The cosmic rays will travel and envelop anyone or anything, wherever they may be. We do not suggest that this is equal to the direct healing method for one and all persons or ailments, but it is also a valid phenomenon utilizing gemstone therapy.

Even supposedly 'incurable' diseases have been reversed by the use of the seven gems together, adding the powerful invisible rays of ultraviolet and infrared. It is the deficiency of cosmic colors within our bodies, and not the germs, bacteria, and viruses that are the ultimate factors in causing disease. When this is understood and proper remedial measures taken, then one is well on the way to being cured and maintaining a better state of health from then on. Imbalance of the rays causes the disease, and balancing through diffusion of these rays to the body is the most effective cure. A more powerful science of healing has not been discovered to compare with the science of healing through color, and the stocks of these cosmic colors are best transmitted with the vibratory properties of natural gemstones.

PLANETARY GEMOLOGY

The science of planetary gemology is one that has been used in accordance with astrology for thousands of years. It is the science of understanding how gemstones transmit and reflect planetary rays, and how they will increase planetary influences in a person's life. Gems never 'decrease' a planet's energy or its cosmic rays. There is a school of thought wherein some astrologers posit that wearing a gem for a planet which causes suffering due to unfortunate positioning at the time of a person's birth will 'propitiate' that planet, or cause it to give less trouble. Extensive practice and experience in this field, however, has proven this idea to be a great misconception. Therefore the recommendation of any gem must be given a great deal of concentrated thought by the astrologer or planetary gemologist in order to determine whether a gemstone will truly have a positive effect on someone. Mistakes can be costly if malefic cosmic rays are unintentionally increased. Therefore it is only sensible that a conscientious astrologer who recommends gems to his or her clients will carefully study the science of planetary gemology in order to correctly prescribe gems.

This is not a science that can be used only by Vedic astrologers. Western astrologers can also learn planetary gemology in order to give viable remedial measures to their clients for mitigating or lessening malefic influences and increasing benefic influences. This is achieved by strengthening planets that can counteract certain rays that are causing problems, or by strengthening planets that rule positive areas of life but are simply weakened due to their placement in the horoscope.

One essential point is that the tropical zodiac may not be employed to recommend gems, nor can the divided house system commonly used by western astrologers. To do so will cause the astrologer to make grave errors that can possibly end up intensifying the very difficulties that one is trying to help mitigate in the client's life. Otherwise, if the astrological practitioner has very diligently studied this method of increasing planetary rays, then either system may be used, Vedic or Western. Both have been used throughout the history of astrology in the world to recommend wearing of gems.

The first consideration is the inherent 'strength' of a planet. There are a number of methods used to determine this, and Vedic astrologers have a very exacting system of assigning planetary strengths. First, it is determined how the planet fares in the zodiac sign and house that it occupies. If it is already very strong, then there may be no need for the gemstone to be worn. This can be seen by the strength of personality attributes, emotional attributes, and intellectual attributes, and by the physical constitution of the body.

One of the first factors that an astrologer considers is the 'houses' that a planet owns in the horoscope. According to the ascendant or rising sign, houses are considered benefic or malefic. Basically this has to do with whether these houses rule positive or negative attributes, or more plainly, the areas of suffering or enjoyment in life.

When a planet is so weak that it cannot adequately distribute its rays, remedial measures are called for, yet the therapist must be especially careful when recommending gemstones for naturally malefic planets or for rulers of the 6th, 8th, and 12th houses, as these have the greatest ability to cause adverse effects.

The Sun, Mars, Saturn, Rahu, and Ketu are considered natural malefic planets. Great care must be exercised in recommending their gemstones due to the ability of those planets to cause stress within the body and mind, to increase the chances of accidents, and to expand their power to cause suffering. The natural benefic planets are the Moon, Mercury, Jupiter, and Venus, and their gemstones are less likely to cause malefic effects, but there are other considerations to take into account.

The gemstone for a particular planet may be highly recommended during its major (*maha-dasha*) or minor (*bhukti*) planetary periods. More often than not this is helpful, but again, if a certain period is meant to bring trial and tribulation without a lot of material progress, then the gem may possibly have some adverse effect. Therefore the optimal approach is to look at all the pros and cons of wearing each gem (in accordance with the horoscope of the person), and then make a decision based on his or her specific needs and desires. There is no blanket rule like "Jupiter is ineffective so wear a yellow sapphire." Just as the astrological science is so complicated that as one finds that certain rules may be overshadowed by other considerations, the same is true in utilizing planetary gemology.

One important and very practical piece of advice that could be offered to any person desiring to take advantage of gem therapy is that he or she wear gemstones they can wear throughout most of their lives. Precious gemstones have the most power and represent a significant purchase for the majority of persons. Although some of us have the means to wear gems for shorter periods of time without financial burden, this makes the benefits available through planetary gemology more accessible to a wider range of persons.

Another good rule of thumb is that you purchase the best possible quality gemstone that you can reasonably afford, even though it may seem like a fairly large sum of money. The gem will never lose its beauty, potency, or monetary value, and will be beneficial for as long as the person wears it. If it is determined that the gem will indeed be beneficial for the major portion of one's life, then the actual monetary cost becomes less of a consideration in relationship to the benefit derived. It should be noted that the wearing of gemstones is unlike using electro-gem therapy or taking elixirs: positive effects on health are unquestionably gained through short-term treatment with the latter methods, but in order to truly reap the benefits of enhancing planetary rays for gains in wealth, reputation, marriage, children, career, communications, etc., the gemstone must be worn on the body constantly. If it is worn only periodically, the effects will be far less.

MEDICINE FOR THE NEW MILLENNIUM

In our own work and through sharing with the many health practitioners and Vedic astrologers using the science of gem therapy, we have seen that the use of electronic gem therapy can be considered almost miraculous to many patients who have recovered from various ailments after being treated with it. Many people have seen the symptoms of their illnesses or chronic difficulties removed, and thus began living a more healthy and fulfilling life.

This science has been used for thousands of years not only in India, but also by a number of other cultures from around the globe. Yet now more than ever, the marriage of the further-advanced science of electronics with the sciences of light, color, and gemstone therapy has allowed a much larger quantity of people the world over to take advantage of this most effective form of healing. Electronic gem therapy allows the practitioner to treat patients with the healing potencies of gemstones without great expense, and with no discomfort whatsoever.

The science of Vedic astrology has become more and more popular in the west due to the fact that in the hands of a knowledgeable and experienced practitioner the predictive abilities are "uncanny" in the minds of many. Yet this science has been practiced for thousands of years in India and still today in Indian society astrologers are usually consulted at all important junctures of life for advice as to correct action for the greatest possible successful result. In this vein planetary gemology allows us to strengthen positive planetary rays that can increase benefits in health, career, relationships and all material categories of our lives. Certain gems may also increase our spiritual proclivities enabling us to focus better on meditation and contemplation of higher realities beyond the physical world.

For some in the world precious gems are simply a means of displaying one's wealth or as concentrated wealth that is easily transported anywhere. For most, though, gems are known only as decorative items for adorning one's body. As more and more persons world wide become introduced to this very effective means of healing, the use of gems will become more widespread in healing and ultimately find their way into the world of allopathic medicine (some allopathic doctors in Europe and the UK and a very few in North America are already using gems combined with electronic frequency instruments), which is mainly geared to treatment with drugs.

As more people find qualified Vedic astrologers and consult with them the science of planetary gemology will also become better known. Whether for medical reasons or for influencing other more "subtle" energies that affect our lives (as can be determined through astrological analysis) the usage of natural, untreated gems will become increasingly utilized as people look for more natural means of healing.

Vāstu Shāstra:
The Divine School of Architecture

Arun Naik

While recalling my past, some memories are etched forever. I too remember when, as a first born, I was made to offer Lotus flowers and Vilva leaves made in gold at Sri Vishwanath Temple in Varanasi, India. I was an infant, and was so attracted towards the Vishwanath Shivling that I nearly fell into the little pool around the Shivlingam.

My childhood memories are full of reminiscences of the visits to Shri Vishwanath temple, Ganga *ghats*, religious festivals, rituals, holy men, worship, stories from mythology, a Hindu religious milieu, and doting uncles. As I grew up, my leaning towards spiritualism and philosophy, and later into occultism, began to develop. By the time I was eight, Shiva had become my friend, god, brother, protector, tutor, playmate. The "existence" of this world intrigued and baffled me; I used to wonder who I was, why I lived and why did the world exist. These questions gave me sleepless afternoons and perhaps my first attempt was to look at the walls of our house and try to understand the magical way in which they held our living space and us. Little did my innocent mind realize that it was trying to unravel the world's most complex mystery.

My father had revolted in the family, had moved away from our native land and had purposely unlinked himself with the family tradition and family members. He had studied to be an engineer and wanted his children to be like him. But strangely enough and without my knowing, my ancestral tradition pulled me. At appropriate times in life I came across different masters who initiated and guided me. When I was initiated in the Shakta tradition of Tantra, I hid the news from my father. The world of Tantra suited my rational temperament, and I was immediately drawn to it. Later I realized that there is a close and a definite relationship between the *Vedas* and the origin and theory of Vāstu Shāstra, as between the Tantras and the full grandeur and practice of Vāstu Shāstra. Vāstu roots are in the *Vedas*, but it blossoms in the world of tantra. Vāstu Shāstra is the Vedic counterpart of the Chinese Feng Shui.

To me the practice of Vāstu Shāstra is an expression of my deep undenying faith in the Divine, a way of life where each act is an offering to Him, an action which translates as a prayer to the gods, and a practical application in real life of the principles derived from the *Vedas* and Tantra.

We are living in a period of great transition. In the times to come this period will be remembered as being a witness to a Big Bang at the level of Matter and Spirit. At the level of Matter the lifestyles, gadgets and gizmos, car and bike designs, sports, our attitudes towards morality-relationships-sex, general levels of incomes, and so much else has changed. At the level of Spirit we have entered the era of knowledge where the IQ levels are shooting towards the moon, there is an unprecedented growth in the scientific and technical advancement, the Net has become the world artery as also its life support and a source of information which deluges us with information on almost all subjects.

This generation is also a witness to the restoration of respect to performing arts and various crafts, introduction of TV, graduation from duplicating machines to electronic photocopiers, calculating machines to modern computers, from discreet kisses in the school bylanes to bold acts on home TV, mobile phones, SMS, and everywhere else. Parallel to this eruption, there is another eruption of new religions and faiths, and a renaissance of old sciences, classical and occult knowledge and practices.

Vāstu holds a rather critical position. It relates to Form which is Matter, and to Space which is Spirit. We who live in this transitional period need its benefits at both the levels of Matter and Spirit.

The world is changing, evolving, I feel. In my view most of the changes are positive and should be welcomed, the negative changes would die in any case with time. But it is also crucial that the traditional knowledge and traditional sciences be understood in their correct perspective to get the optimum benefit from them, and this article is a little effort in this direction.

I am thankful to Stephen Knapp who has been striving to explain to us the importance of Vedic religion. He inspired me to write this article on Vāstu Shāstra and gave me a free hand. I sincerely wish him well.

VĀSTU SHĀSTRA:
THE DIVINE SCHOOL OF ARCHITECTURE

Several scholars have attempted to describe Vāstu Shāstra as an Indian system of architecture. *Monier-Williams Sanskrit-English Dictionary* describes Vaastu as follows:

> Vaástu: the site or foundation of a house, site, ground, building or dwelling place, habitation, homestead, house RV. &c. &c.; an apartment, chamber VarBRS.; m. N. of one of the 8 Vasus BhP.; of a Râkshasa Cat.; (prob.) f. N. of a river MBh.; n. the pot-herb Chenopodium Album L.; a kind of grain ÂpShr. Sch. (cf.—maya).

The literal meaning as described above may be upheld by some, but it does not so much as touch the tip of the glory of this sacred Vidya.

The world is witnessing a renaissance of Vāstu Shāstra, and it is important that its deeper meaning and philosophy is understood in correct perspective.

THE DEFINITION AND PURPOSE
OF VĀSTU SHĀSTRA

The Vedic and the Agamic traditions of ancient India always held that the microcosm is a reflection of the macrocosm. A dwelling is an ecological unit, a microcosm which reflects the Cosmos, the macrocosm. Vāstu Shāstra is the applied aspect of this philosophy, a highly refined method of creating a living space which is a miniature replica of the cosmos as perceived by the *Vedas*. Vāstu Shāstra is about emulating the attributes of the Cosmic Space, about bringing the divine sentinels of Cosmic Directions into our homes, about creating Harmony by creating a living environment where the forces of nature are balanced and at peace with each other.

Sri Aurobindo has said…"Indian sacred architecture of whatever date, style or dedication goes back to something timelessly ancient and now outside India almost wholly lost, something which belongs to the past, and yet it goes forward too, though this the rationalistic mind will not easily admit, to something which will return upon us and is already beginning to return, something which belongs to the future." (SA, *The Renaissance in India*)

There is a prayer in the *Sama Veda*:

ॐ द्यौः शान्तिरन्तरिक्षꣳ शान्तिः पृथिवी शान्तिरापः शान्तिरोषधयः शान्तिर्वनस्पतयः
शान्तिर्विश्वेदेवाः शान्तिर्ब्रह्म शान्तिः सर्वꣳशान्तिः शान्तिरेव शान्तिः सामा शान्तिरेधि ।
सुशान्तिर्भवतु ॥

*May there be peace in the sky, may there be peace in mid region, may there be peace
on earth, may there be peace in the waters, may the medicinal plants be peaceful, may
the forest be peaceful, may there be peace in gods, may Brahma be peaceful, may all the
creation be peaceful, may there be peace and peace only, may such peace come to us.*

Vāstu is about creating an Inner Space, the *chidakash*, where this divine peace
can park itself. And it achieves it by creating a harmonious external environment — the *bahyakash*.

At a more earthly level, Vāstu Shāstra aims at establishing a dynamic balance
between Form and Energy so that harmonious conditions are created for the
inhabitants. Vāstu buildings have harmonious energies and they promote stabil-
ity, prosperity, happiness, and mental peace for the occupants and owners.

The sages have emphasized that the ultimate aim of a human being is to move
towards a higher state of consciousness, to change its mortal imperfection into a
divine perfection. This movement results in the realization of Truth, or Self. This
knowledge of Self is termed Para Vidya or Higher Knowledge, and the means to
acquire it is called Apara Vidya, or Lower Knowledge. Apara Vidya has been categorized as ten: the Four *Vedas*, four *Upavedas*, and six *Vedangas*. The *Mundaka
Upanishad* clarifies it (1.1.4-5):

द्वे विद्ये वेदितव्ये इति ह स्म यद्ब्रह्मविदो वदन्ति परा चैवापरा च ॥ ४ ॥
तत्रापरा ऋग्वेदो यजुर्वेदः सामवेदोऽथर्ववेदः शिक्षा कल्पो व्याकरणं निरुक्तं छन्दो ज्योतिषमिति ।
अथ परा यया तदक्षरमधिगम्यते ॥ ५ ॥

*Two kinds of knowledge must be known, this is what all who know Brahman tell us,
the higher and the lower knowledge. (4) The lower knowledge is the Rgveda, Yajurveda,
Samaveda, Atharvaveda, Siksha (phonetics), Kalpa (ceremonial), Vyakarana (grammar), Nirukta (etymology), Khandas (metre), Jyotish (astronomy); but the higher
knowledge is that by which the Indestructible (Brahman) is apprehended.*

Thus all the *Vedas*, *Upavedas* and *Vedangas* are Apara Vidya. We examine here
the role of Vāstu as Aparavidya.

To a spiritual aspirant Krishna in *Bhagavad-Gita* has unveiled the three-fold
path of union with the Divine: through the Yoga of Works, the Yoga of Knowledge
and the Yoga of Devotion. In the presence of Devotion and Knowledge, Works
become a sublimed offering to the Divine. In works or actions man closely follows

nature, trying to emulate its forces and various processes as nearly as possible. In return, Nature rewards him with further growth, success and social recognition.

Thus a process is initiated where the aspirant works, offers his work to the Divine, and spiritually evolves towards perfection.

Vāstu supports this process. It contributes by creating a space which is in harmony with nature, which supports the positive growth of ideas, interpersonal relationships, flow, movement and action; a space where the Yoga of Works finds adequate expression. Vāstu, therefore, is a school of architecture inspired by the divine spark in the hearts and minds of great sages for whom nothing was beyond the purview of divine thought, सर्वं खल्विदं ब्रह्म । and with principles which are steeped deeply into spiritual principles of life itself.

The principle of Vastu is that the Cosmic World with its order and stern discipline has been built by the gods who occupy all the spaces, from the celestial Space within the Cosmic World to the little spaces in our homes, and even our mental space, *chidambaram*. Man's existence in the Cosmic World has a purpose: it must ascend to immortality and godhood; and the gods, having occupied man's inner Space, strive to create different states in man's consciousness for his ascension from mortality and low nature to Truth, godhood and immortality. Vāstu Shāstra helps the effort of the gods by creating an external space—a dwelling, a place to worship and meditate, or a place to work by applying the same laws which the gods have used to create the Cosmic World. This, indeed, is the ultimate function and the highest objective of Vāstu Shāstra.

VĀSTU SHĀSTRA AND VEDAS

The Supreme Being is a Cosmic Architect who has shaped the Universe within a framework of certain natural laws, the laws of Cosmic Vāstu Shāstra as contained within the *Vedas*. The *Vedas* are *anadi*—timeless, and *apaurusheya*—not the work of any man. They were never created nor would they ever get destroyed. The *Brihadaranyaka Upanishad* says that the *Vedas* are the very breath of Ishwara.

स यथाऽऽर्द्रैधाग्नेरभ्याहितात्पृथग्धूमा विनिश्चरन्त्येवं वा अरेऽस्य महतो भूतस्य निःश्वसितमेतद्यद्ऋग्वेदो यजुर्वेदः सामवेदोऽथर्वाङ्गिरस इतिहासः पुराणं विद्या उपनिषदः श्लोकाः सूत्राण्यनुव्याख्यानानि व्याख्यानान्यस्यैवैतानि निःश्वसितानि ॥२॥४॥१०॥

As clouds of smoke proceed by themselves out of a lighted fire kindled with damp fuel, thus, verily, O Maitreyi, has been breathed forth from this great Being what we have as Rig-veda, Yajur-veda, Sama-veda, Atharvângirasas, Itihâsa (legends), Purâna (cosmogonies), Vidyâ (knowledge), the Upanishads, Slokas (verses), Sûtras (prose rules),

Anuvyâkhyânas (glosses), Vyâkhyânas (commentaries). From him alone all these were breathed forth. (Translation by Max Mueller)

The *Vedas* contain the genetic code of Creation. Each time God wants a Creation, he appoints a Brahma to do the job. Brahma's age is of 100 Cosmic Years, after which he and the Creation are dissolved, there is a lull, a state of no-matter for another 100 cosmic years, and then God appoints a new Brahma to manifest a new Creation, and this cycle continues.

To understand the duration of 100 cosmic years needs a bit of calculation. One cycle of the four Ages—*Satya, Treta, Dvapara,* and *Kali*—is of 4,320,000 years on earth. Two thousand such cycles—8640000000 years on earth make one day and one night of Brahma. So 100 cosmic years are a whopping 311040000000000 years on earth, after which the universe is dissolved and absorbed into the Supreme Being. During the dissolution and the 100 cosmic years of no-Creation, the *Vedas* stay with the Supreme Being. When God appoints the next Brahma, he uses the knowledge of the *Vedas* to manifest the next Creation.

The *Vedas* are thus seen to contain the grammar of Cosmic Space, the syntax of Creation, and in a true sense the principles of Cosmic Vāstu. These principles were used to create the present Creation too. The *Nasadiya Suktam* describes the situation when neither was there Existence, nor non-Existence.

नासदासीन्नो सदासीत् तदानीं नासीद्रजो नो व्योमा परो यत् ।किमावरीवः कुह कस्य शर्मन्नम्भः किमासीद् गहनं गभीरम् ॥ १०१२९०१

Then was not non-existence nor existence: there was no realm of air, no sky beyond it. What covered in, and where? and what gave shelter? Was water there, unfathomed depth of water?

न मृत्युरासीदमृतं न तर्हि न रात्र्या अह्न आसीत् प्रकेतः ।आनीदवातं स्वधया तदेकं तस्माद्धान्यन्न परः किं चनास ॥ १०१२९०२

Death was not then, nor was there aught immortal: no sign was there, the day's and night's divider. That One Thing, breathless, breathed by its own nature: apart from it was nothing whatsoever.

तम आसीत् तमसा गूळ्हमग्रेऽप्रकेतं सलिलं सर्वमा इदम् । तुच्छ्येनाभ्वपिहितं यदासीत् तपसस्तन्महिनाजायतैकम् ॥ १०१२९०३

Darkness there was: at first concealed in darkness this All was indiscriminated chaos. All that existed then was void and formless: by the great power of Warmth was born that Unit.

And then evolved Space, Air, Fire, Water and Earth.

तस्मा॑द्वा ए॒ तस्मादा॒त्मन॒ आका॒शः॑ संभू॒तः। आ॒का॒शाद्वा॒युः।वा॒योर॒ग्निः। अ॒ग्नेराप॑ः।
अ॒द्भ्यः॑ पृथि॒वी। तैत्तिरीयोपनिषद् २।१।१।

From Brahman evolved Space, From Space evolved Air, From Air evolved Fire, From Fire evolved Water, From Water evolved Earth. (Taittariyopanishad 2.1.1)

Poetic as it may seem, it reflects a beautiful process of the manifestation of Creation, a process which is at the same time gradual and steady, encompassing the past, supporting the present, and paving way for the future. This is an evolution where the Formless acquires Form. It is the process of the Divine Consciousness metamorphosing the elements; it is the phenomenon of subtle turning into gross.

According to the *Tantras* when the Divine Consciousness chose to create, it first gave rise to primordeal *Anhat Naad*: the Cosmic Sound and the Eternal Vibration. No physical thing could have caused it to vibrate, because Form had yet to evolve. When the *Naad* vibrated, it created a Beat and a Rhythm, both of which depend upon Time. Thus was born Time. The *Naad* needed space to vibrate to express itself, and so evolved *Akash*, the Space. With Space was born *Roop* (*rupa*) or the Form. This is the theory of the Creation of the universe, its elements and forms. Each subsequent development gave rise to a complete system of governing rules and attributes, and one may refer to them as the grammar of these elements.

The earliest reference to Vāstu is found in *Rigveda* where the sage offers a prayer to 'Vastoshpati', the Lord of Vāstu, for protection, happiness and prosperity.

ॐ वास्तो॑ष्पते॒ प्रति॑ जानीह्यस्मान्त्स्वावे॒शो अ॑नमी॒वोभ॑वानः।
यत्त्वेमहे॒प्रतित॑न्नोजुषस्व॒शन्नो॑ भवद्विपदे॒ शं चतु॑ष्पदे॥ ७-५४-१
वास्तो॑ष्पते॒ प्रत॑रणो न॒ एधि॑ गयस्फा॒नो गो॒भिरश्वे॑भिरिन्दो।
अ॒ज॒रास॑स्ते स॒ख्ये॒ स्याम॒पितेव॑ पु॒त्रान्प्रति॑ नो॒ जुषस्व॥ ७-५४-२
वास्तो॑ष्पते॒ शग्म॑या सं॒सदा॑ ते स॒क्षीमहि॒रण्वया गातु॑मत्या।
पा॒हि क्षेम॑उ॒त योगे॒वर॒न्नोयू॒यम् पा॑त॒ स्वस्ति॑भिः॒ सदा॑ नः॥ ७-५४-३
अ॒मी॒व॒हावास्तो॑ष्पते॒ विश्वा॑ रू॒पाण्या॑विशन्।
सखा॑ सु॒शेव॑ एधि नः॥ ७-५५-१

1. *O Guardian of the Homestead: bring no disease, and give us happy entrance. Whate'er we ask of thee, be pleased to grant it, and prosper thou quadrupeds and bipeds.*

2. *Protector of the Home, be our promoter: increase our wealth in kind and steeds, O Indu. May we be ever-youthful in thy friendship: be pleased in us as in his sons a father.*

3. *Through thy dear fellowship that bringeth welfare, may we be victors, Guardian of the Dwelling! Protect our happiness in rest and labour. Preserve us evermore, ye Gods, with blessings.*

4. *VASTOSPATI, who killest all disease and wearest every form, Be an auspicious Friend to us.* (Translations courtesy Ralph T.H. Griffith)

The earliest application of Vāstu Shāstra may be said to be in the construction of ceremonial alters for Vedic rituals. The *Shulbhasutra*, the Vedic geometry, was used to calculate and design these alters. Numerous passages of *Katyayan, Baudhayana* and *Apastambha Shulbha* deal with the size of sacrificial altars and their method of construction. The *Shrautasutras, Grihyasutras* and *Dharmasutras* contain detailed instructions for performing the Vedic rites and the associated architectural aspects, like the construction of the *vedi* and selection of the place for performing the rites.

In a step away from the *Shulbhasutra*, in the *Rigveda* Agni declares himself to be the measurer of the Celestial Space. Agni is one of the most important of all of the Vedic deities, the priest of the gods and god of the priests, and his declaration reflects the relationship between Space, measuement, *Veda* and the Vedic deities.

अ॒ग्निर॑स्मि॒ ज॒न्मना॑ जा॒तवे॑दा॒ घृ॒तं मे॒ चक्षु॑र॒मृतं॑ म आ॒सन्। अ॒र्कस् त्रि॒धातू॒ रज॑सो वि॒मानो॒ ऽज॑स्रो घ॒र्मो ह॒विर॑स्मि॒ नाम॑ ॥ ऋ॰ ३०२६०७

Agni am I who know, by birth, all creatures. Mine eye is butter, in my mouth is nectar. I am light threefold, measurer of the region, exhaustless heat am I, named burnt-oblation. (Rigveda 3.026.07)

The antiquity of Vāstu Shāstra is reflected in its direct link with the English word Geometry and its Latin root. In Vāstu, measurement of land is an integral part of its work and it is called *Jyamiti*. In Sanskrit *Jya* means the earth and *miti* is the method of measurement. Therefore, Geometry actually means "measuring the Earth".

THE VĀSTU LITERATURE

It is believed that when Krishna Dwaipayana had categorized the *Vedas*, there were as many as 1,180 branches of the *Vedas*: *Rigveda* had 21 branches or *shakhas, Yajurveda* had 109, *Samaveda* had 1000, and *Atharvaveda* had 50. Today out of 1180 *shakhas* barely 6 or 7 survive. These existing 6 or 7 *shakhas* cover the entire gamut of Vedic thought as it exists today, and also contain within them the seeds of Vāstu principles. Though a major part of the Vedic literature is lost, a good number of Vāstu texts survive. Some of the more important and established Vāstu texts are listed below.

1. *Vishwakarma Vāstu Shāstra*
2. *Samarangana Sutradhar*
3. *Mandana Sutradhar*
4. *Rajasimha Vāstu*
5. *Deeparnava*
6. *Shilparatna*
7. *Mayamata*
8. *Manasara*
9. *Manushyalaya Chandrika*
10. *Kashyapa Shilpa*
11. *Aparajita Priccha*
12. *Vishwakarma PrakashSanatkumara Vāstu Shāstra*

Vāstu is also related to the construction of the forms of various Agamic deities and their temples, and so several references to Vāstu principles are also found in the following Agamic and Puranic literature:

1. *Karnikagama*
2. *Suprabhedagama*
3. *Vaikhanasagama*
4. *Hayasirsha Tantra*
5. *Agni Purana*
6. *Matsya Purana*
7. *Vishnudharmottar Purana*
8. *Brahmanda Purana*
9. *Bhavishya Purana*

This list is by no means the exhaustive list. In addition to these texts, Vāstu principles are also scattered in various other books.

THE VĀSTU MANDALA: A SYMBOL OF COSMOS

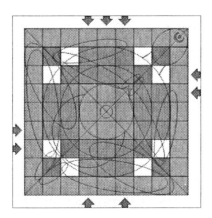

The Vāstu mandalas are drawn to denote the subtle effect of various forces on the land. It forms the basis of all Vāstu planning and represents the highest level of Design Philosophy from concept to theory to the actual process of construction.

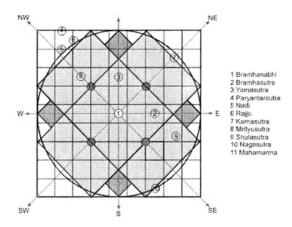

1 Bramhanabhi
2 Bramhasutra
3 Yamasutra
4 Paryantarsutra
5 Nadi
6 Rajju
7 Karnasutra
8 Mrityusutra
9 Shulasutra
10 Nagasutra
11 Mahamarma

Reference Lines of a Mandal

By character, space has no shape. But when a bit of space is isolated and confined within boundaries, then it acquires a shape and character and vibrates accordingly. The Mandalas show the nature of this shape.

A square is taken to be a perfect shape and a fundamental form. Vāstu rejects the use of circular shapes in dwellings. A square is also the shape of the earth element. The earth element contains within it the elements of space, air, fire and water. The earth element also contains the elements of speech, touch, shape, taste and smell. It has poise, balance and makes a practical basis for designing a building. Vāstu Shāstra draws a square, crisscrosses it with grids and diagonal lines to identify zones of different cosmic energies and their flow within the area, and calls it a Vāstu mandala.

Each side of the Vāstu mandala is divided into several different parts called *pada*. The smallest Vāstu mandala is of 1 x 1 *pada* for designing alters and shelves, to 32 x 32 for designing townships. The most common mandala is of 9 x 9 *pada* which is generally accepted for all building designs.

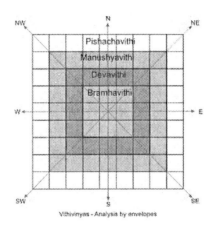

Vithivinyas - Analysis by envelopes

Though the Vāstu mandala is a convenient designing base, it is also seen as a symbolic form of the cosmos. The space is divided into four different areas around the center.

The central region of 9 squares is where the energy is most intense. It is called Brahmavithi. This has the highest concentration of energy and no construction should be allowed here.

Surrounding it is Devavithi, the region of light and gods, and Manushyavithi, the region of man. Construction is allowed in these two areas.

The outermost area is called Pishachvithi, the region of darkness where again no construction is allowed.

The outer region also indicates 32 cosmic energies. Their placement determines the positioning of the main door and other directional attributes of the mandala.

MARMA

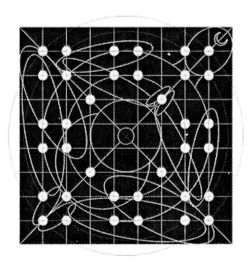

The horizontal, vertical and diagonal lines drawn inside the mandala are the meridians through which the cosmic energy flows and the plot becomes a living entity. The points or nodes where all the three directional meridians cross each other is called a *marma*.

These are similar to sensitive acupuncture points in the human body, and should be left unhurt. No pillar, wall, door, window should be placed upon these nodes.

Marma faults are avoided by shifting the centre line of the pillar, door, etc., by half the dimension of the node.

THEORY OF SHAPES

Energy follows form and Vāstu shapes are no exception. Vāstu has attributed different and distinct characters to the energies that reside inside various geometric forms. Some are considered Divine in nature and therefore beyond use, while some are considered useful and others are considered bizarre and useless.

A circle is a primary shape, the shape of the Sun and Moon. The circle has unique properties, almost mystical and magical. The sages have attributed the circle to be representing Rudra or Shiva, and apart from being used in temples and some sacrificial alters, is not used in the design of a house.

The triangle is verily used in Tantra to represent Shiva if it is pointing upwards, or Shakti if it is pointing downward. Owing to its occult significance, and also perhaps due to its acute angles, triangular shapes are also avoided in Vāstu design of homes.

The square is called a Brahma mandala because its four sides represent Brahma, the Creator. The Vāstu mandala is a square, and it represents a high level of design philosophy. The square and its derivative, the rectangle, are the basis for evolution of Vāstu designs.

THE DEITIES OF THE VĀSTU MANDALA

Various deities occupy different areas in the Vastu mandala, most of whom are Vedic deities. These include: 1. Ish, 2. Parjanya, 3. Jayant, 4. Indra, 5. Surya, 6. Satya, 7. Bhrisa, 8. Akash, 9. Agni, 10. Pusha, 11. Vitath, 12. Grihakshat, 13. Yama, 14. Gandharva, 15. Bhringraja, 16. Mriga, 17 Pitra, 18. Dwarpal, 19. Sugreeva, 20. Pushpadanta, 21. Varuna, 22. Asura, 23. Shesh, 24. Paap, 25. Rog, 26. Naag, 27. Mukhya, 28. Bhallat, 29. Kuber, 30. Rishi, 31. Aditi, 32. Diti, 33. Aap, 34. Aapvats, 35. Marichi, 35. Savita, 36. Prithvidhar, 37. Brahma, 38. Vivasvan, 39. Rudradas, 40. Rudra, 41. Mitra, 42. Vishnu, and 43. Indrajaya.

Each deity of the Vāstu mandala represents a cosmic force which translates on Earth as a physical attribute which are understood and recorded by Vāstu Shāstra.

Each direction also has its guardian, called the Eight Dikpals:

Indra, the Lord of East,
Agni, the Lord of South-East,
Yama, the Lord of South,
Nirruti, the Presiding deity of South-West,
Varun, the Lord of West,
Vayu, Lord of North-West,
Kuber, Lord of North,
Ish, Lord of North-East.

Sri Aurobindo says…"Cosmos cannot be governed by a Power that does not transcend Cosmos". Divine is the only power which can transcend Cosmos, and when it manifests as Krishna the Avatar, He declares himself to be all of them. He says, "I am…Sun among all the shining bodies…Indra among the gods…Kuber, the guardian of wealth and friend of Shankar, among the Yakshas and demons…

Agni among the eight Vasus…I am Varuna the master of the West, Yama is my principal manifestation among the controllers who take note of all the good and bad deeds of creatures, examines their conscience and gives reward or retribution according to their karma." (*Bhagavad-gita*, Chapter Ten)

ज्योतिषां रविरंशुमान् Among Lights and Splendour I am the Radiant Sun
रुद्राणां शङ्करश्चास्मि I am Shiva among the Rudras (Ish)
वित्तेशो यक्षरक्षसाम् Lord of Wealth among the Yakshas and Rakshas (Kuber)
वसूनां पावकः I am the Agni among the Vasus
वरुणो यादसामहम् I am Varuna among the people of the sea
यमः संयमतामहम् I am Yama, Lord of the Law, among those who maintain rule and law
पवनः पवताम् I am Wind among Purifiers (Vayu)

These gods are guardians, not guards, of the Cosmic Directions. Most of them are discussed in *Rigveda*. Sri Aurobindo refers to them as "a parable of human life emerging, mounting, lifting itself towards the Godhead". He says: When the Rishis speak of Indra or Agni or Soma in men, they are speaking of the god in his cosmic presence, power or function. This is evident from the very language when they speak of Agni as the immortal in mortals, the immortal Light in men, the inner Warrior, the Guest in human beings.

Furthermore, let us discuss the various powers and significance of each of the directions. This will provide insight in how to use our various actions or purposes in accordance with the directions in particular areas of our house or dwelling, and how it may amplify the intent of what we do. This will help us determine what actions should be done and where so that we have the least amount of resistance to peace and the attainment of our goals in life.

East denotes deities of Light
West denotes deities of Darkness
North denotes gods of Birth
South denotes gods of Death

The North East is the source of all energies, and
South West is where they travel and disappear.

East

In Vāstu Shāstra Indra is the ruler of the East. In the *Vedas* he is the King of Antariksha (space) with all its mighty heroes:

त्वम् भुवः प्रति॑ मान॒म् पृथि॒व्या ऋ॒ष्ववी॑रस्य॒ बृह॒॑तः॒ पति॒र् भूः ।
विश्व॒॑म् आ॒प्रा अ॒॑न्तरि॑क्षम् महि॒ त्वा स॒॑त्यम् अ॒द्धा नकि॒र् अ॒॑न्यस्॑ त्वावा॑न् ॥ १०५२१३

Thou art the counterpart of earth, the Master of lofty heaven with all its mighty Heroes: Thou hast filled all the region with thy greatness: yea, of a truth there is none other like thee.

He is often referred to as the maker of rains, "he fights the stayer of rains":

न यस्य॑ द्यावा॑पृथि॒वी अनु॒ व्यचो॒ न सि॒न्धवो॒ रज॒सो॒ अन्त॑म् आन॒शुः ।
नोत स्ववृ॒ष्टि॑म् मदे॑ अस्य॑ युध्य॑त॒ एको॑ अ॒न्यच् चकृषे॒ विश्व॑म् आ॒नु॒षक् ॥ १०५२१४

Whose amplitude the heaven and earth have not attained, whose bounds the waters of mid-air have never reached. Not when in joy he fights the stayer of the rain: thou, and none else, hast made all things in order due.

Indra is the Lord of the luminous Mind, who fought Vritra, the demon who symbolizes the negative forces of ignorance and evil:

इन्द्रा या॑हि॒ चित्रभानो सु॒ता इ॒मे त्वा॒॑यवः॑ ।अ॒ण्वीभि॒स् त॒ना पू॒॑तासः॑ ॥ १००३०४

O Indra marvelously bright, come, these libations long for thee, Thus by fine fingers purified.

इन्द्रा या॑हि॒ धि॒येषि॒तो विप्रजू॑तः सु॒तावतः॑ ।उप॒ ब्रह्मा॑णि वा॒घतः॑ ॥ १००३०५

Urged by the holy singer, sped by song, come, Indra, to the prayers, of the libation-pouring priest.

आर्च॒न् न॒ अत्र॑ म॒रुतः॑ स॒स्मिन्न॒ आ॒जौ विश्वे॑ दे॒वासो॑ अमद॒न् न॒ अनु॑ त्वा ।वृ॒त्रस्य॑ यद् भृ॒ष्टि॒मता॑ व॒धेन॒ नि त्वम् इन्द्र॒ प्रत्य् आ॒॑नं ज॒॑घन्थ ॥ १०५२१५

The Maruts sang thy praise in this encounter, and in thee all the Deities delighted. What time thou, Indra, with thy spiky weapon, thy deadly bolt, smotest the face of Vritra.

The planet of the East is Surya, the Sun, the Lord of Light and Truth, the illuminator of the Universe, and also the illuminator of the spiritual space within us. The Sun is the god of the intuitive or higher mind. The visible world would cease to exist without Light, and therefore Surya is also Savitri the Creator and the manifesting power of the Divine.

He is the Divine Sun, the visible god. Ceaselessly he carries on his divine work through his rays, which are carriers of light and heat, which represent Knowledge and Truth.

उद् उ॑ त्यं जा॒तवे॑दसं दे॒वं व॑हन्ति के॒तवः॑ ।दृ॒शे विश्वा॑य॒ सूर्य॑म् ॥ १०५००१

His bright rays bear him up aloft, the God who knoweth all that lives, Surya, that all may look on him.

त॒रणि॒र् वि॒श्वद॑र्शतो ज्योति॒ष्कृद॑सि सूर्य ।विश्व॒म् आ भा॑सि रोच॒नम् ॥ १०५००४

Swift and all beautiful art thou, O Surya, maker of the light, Illuming all the radiant realm.

स॒त्येनोत्त॑भिता॒ भूमिः॒ सूर्ये॒णोत्त॑भिता॒ द्यौः ।ऋ॒तेनादि॒त्यास् तिष्ठन्ति दि॒वि सोमो॒ अधि॑ श्रि॒तः ॥ १००८५०१

Truth is the base that bears the earth; by Surya are the heavens sustained. By law the Adityas stand secure, and Soma holds his place in heaven.

सूर्यो॑ नो दि॒वस् पातु॒ वातो॑ अ॒न्तरि॑क्षात् ।अ॒ग्निर् नः॒ पार्थि॑वेभ्यः ॥ १०१५८०१

May Surya guard us out of heaven, and Vata from the firmament, and Agni from terrestrial spots.

जोषा॑ सवित॒र् यस्य॑ ते॒ हरः॑ श॒तं स॒वाँ अ॑र्हति ।पा॒हि नो॑ दि॒द्युतः॒ पत॑न्त्याः ॥ १०१५८०२

Thou Savitar whose flame deserves hundred libations, be thou pleased: from failing lightning keep us safe.

चक्षु॑र् नो दे॒वः स॑वि॒ता चक्षु॑र् न उ॒त पर्व॑तः ।चक्षु॑र् धा॒ता द॑धातु नः ॥ १०१५८०३

May Savitar the God, and may Parvata also give us sight; may the Creator give us sight.

चक्षु॑र् नो धेहि॒ चक्षु॑षे॒ चक्षु॑र् वि॒ख्यै त॒नूभ्यः॑ ।सं चे॒दं वि च॑ पश्येम ॥ १०१५८०४

Give sight unto our eye, give thou our bodies sight that they may see: may we survey, discern this world.

सु॒सं॒दृशं॑ त्वा व॒यम् प्रति॑ पश्येम सूर्य ।वि प॑श्येम नृ॒चक्ष॑सः ॥ १०१५८०५

Thus, Surya, may we look on thee, on thee most lovely to behold, see clearly with the eyes of men.

His chariot traverses the sky ceaselessly, and symbolically all the gods follow in his march. The gods represent the divine faculties which find expansion in the human intellect with association of Light and Truth. This is revealed in the Surya-Savitri known as the Gayatri Mantra of Vishwamitra which continues to be held in highest respect, a mantra which improves our thinking and judgment, gives better control over our anxieties and emotions, cultivates determination and self-esteem, and inner peace and prosperity:

तत् सवितुर् वरेण्यम् भर्गो देवस्य धीमहि ।धियो यो नः प्रचोदयात् ॥ ३०६२१०

May we attain that excellent glory of Savitar the God: So May he stimulate our prayers.

From this we can understand that the East is the best direction to conduct all things to do with light and truth, or the seeking of it, such as meditation, worship, reading the sacred texts, chanting mantras, etc.

South-East

The South-Eastern direction is governed by Agni who is represented as a young man with golden hair, riding on a blue ram. The two flaming heads of Agni belong to the sacrificial fire and the domestic one. Agni is one of the three supreme deities of the *Rig Veda*, viz., Agni, Vayu and Surya.

The Vāstu texts have ascribed this direction as the best place for the kitchen, hearth, heat generating equipments, electric panel and so on.

However, Agni is neither the physical fire, nor is he the deity behind the physical fire. The most important, the most universal of the Vedic gods, Agni is the purifier, devourer and enjoyer, the fire that prepares and perfects; he is the fire of Life, referred to in *Rig Veda* as *Vaishvanar*, the Universal Person who is present in all, and as *Jataveda*, Knower of all. Agni is the Light, the Knowledge which assumes the form of force. Agni is the spiritual Fire, a force that compels human beings higher and higher towards spiritual progress, and also the Cosmic fire which maintains the Universe.

He is the priest of the gods and god of the priests. The gods cannot accept *havi*, the offering, directly from humans. It is Agni who accepts it on their behalf and processes it on to the gods. These three gods preside over earth, air and sky respectively. As a friend of the householder, the guardian of the house and its people, Agni plays the role of a witness present during all religious rituals.

A water source in the South East is a major defect. Flaws in the South East can result in theft and robberies, debts, disgrace, and loss of friends. If the land is lower than South West, it augurs well. But if it is lower than the North West and North East it can cause fire accidents, or criminal bend of mind. If it is higher than the North East and North West, it attracts riches.

South

South is governed by Yama, the Lord of Death, the embodiment of the rule of law who imparts justice according to one's deeds. Yama carries a rope in one hand and a mace in another.

The planet for South is Mars. Mars represents clothes, fire, fierce independence, control over elements, aggressiveness, weapons, a daring nature. Mars also represents the inside hall of the house.

Yama is the son of Vivasvan the Sun. He was the first mortal to die and discover the way to the other world, and so he became the guide of the dead. He thus presides over Death and has the full distinction of a god. He is also the Lord of Dharma and Justice; he judges all actions of human beings after death and renders punishments accordingly. A stern disciplinarian, he is the expositor of truth.

परे॑ यि॒वांसम्॒ प्र॒वतो म॒हीर॒ अनु॑ ब॒हुभ्यः॒॑ पन्थाम्॒ अनुपस्पशा॒नम् ।
वै॒व॒स्व॒तं सं॑गम॒नं जनानां॒ य॒मं राजानं ह॒विषा दुवस्य ॥ १००१४०१

Honour the King with thine oblations, Yama, Vivasvan's Son, who gathers men together, Who travelled to the lofty heights above us, who searches out and shows the path to many.

The story of Yama-Nachiketa is a particularly good exposition of the hospitality of Yama, his sense of dharma and knowledge of it, his superb honesty and great integrity and other divine virtues. When Nachiketa was told by his father that he would give him to Death, the boy went on musing on the mystery of death and went to Yama to find the answer, He waited for Yama at his door for three days without food, and when Yama saw him he granted him three boons.

For first boon Nachiketa asked that his father's anxiety on his disappearance be quieted. As the second boon Yama taught Nachiketa about the secrets of the mysterious Fire. In his third boon, Nachiketa wanted to know the secret of immortality.

Nolini Kant Gupta writes, "Yama is Vaivasvata, born of Vivasvan, the Sun-god, Surya Savitri...Surya Savitri stands for the highest Knowledge, He is the Supreme Consciousness from which comes the creation of the universe. Yama is the Life-Force, the Ordainer of the worlds with their rhythms of life. He is here in this manifestation of the play of life the representative of Savitri, and Fire is his vehicle, instrument or symbol. Just as Surya is Vivasvan, the Supreme Effulgent One, Yama is likewise the Cosmic Being, all cosmic power and universal force are his…"

A depression in the land in the South can lead to disease and financial constraints. If the land is raised in the South it brings in prosperity and health.

South-West

The guardian deity of South-West is Nairruti who is one of the Rudras. Nairruti is sometimes considered a demon, and is associated with all types of calamities, vices like gambling and prostitution, all kinds of trouble, bad dreams, poverty and illness.

The planet for South-West is Rahu. Rahu too represents gambling, waste material, filthy things, pollution, and the Main door.

In order to keep out the negative influence of Nairruti, the South-West is elevated and loaded with heavy load. It is an ideal place for building staircases, master bedrooms, storerooms, machine shops, etc. The South-West is also a good direction for building toilets, storage of waste materials, etc.

Defects on South-West side of a building are slow in action, far reaching in their consequences, and do not react soon to remedial measures. An elevated South-West ensures prosperity and fame, and a depressed South-West can lead to premature death of the owner.

West

The planet for West is Saturn. Saturn represents workforce, human resources, insignificant and petty duties, living beings who consume food, old age, iron, armory, and black grains. Saturn also represents the storeroom of the house.

The Lord of West is Varuna. Varun in *RigVeda* is a Samrat, King of all dominions:

म॒हान्ता॑ मि॒त्रावरुणा॑ स॒म्राजा॑ दे॒वाव् असु॑रा ।ऋ॒तावा॑नाव् ऋ॒तम् आ घो॑षतो बृ॒हत्॥ ८०२५०४
अस्तभ्ना॒द् द्याम् असु॑रो वि॒श्ववे॑दा॒ अमि॑मीत व॒रिमा॑णम् पृथि॒व्याः ।
आसी॑द॒द् विश्वा॒ भुव॑नानि स॒म्राड् विश्वेत् तानि॒ वरु॑णस्य व्र॒तानि॥ ८०४२०१

Lord of all wealth, the Asura propped the heavens, and measured out the broad earth's wide expanses. He, King supreme, approached all living creatures. All these are Varuna's holy operations.

He is the lord of all infinities, master of all the oceans and ether. Varuna's dwelling is in the vast, *urukshaya*;

क॒वी नो॑ मि॒त्रावरुणा॑ तुविजा॒ता उ॒रुक्षया॑ ।दक्षं॑ दधाते अ॒पस॑म् ॥ १००२०९

Our Sages, Mitra-Varuna, wide dominion, strong by birth, Vouchsafe us strength that worketh well.

Varuna is the lord of *rita*, the force which keeps everything working, Keeper of the cosmic order, omnipotent and omniscient, his name means "he who covers all". He is often referred to as Uru, which means wide. He has wide vision—*uru chaksshasam*: 1.25.16:

परा मे॑ यन्ति धी॒तयो॒ गावो॒ न ग॒व्यूती॒र॒नु ।इ॒च्छन्ती॑रु॒रुच॑क्षसम् ॥ १०२५१६

He is also called *urushamsa*—one with wide expression: 1.24.11

तत्त्वा॑ यामि॒ ब्रह्म॑णा॒ वन्द॑मान॒स्तदा शा॑स्ते॒ यज॑मानो ह॒विर्भिः॑ ।
अहे॑ळमानो वरुणे॒ह बो॒ध्यु॒रुशं॑स॒ मा न॒ आयुः॒ प्र मो॑षीः ॥

In the *Vedas*, *Shamsa* means Perfect Speech, and the *Vedas* were an oral tradition where *vak* or speech was given the highest respect. Thus, Varuna is the remover of the constrictions of our attitudes to give us a broader vision in life so that we may express ourselves with Perfect Speech.

Hymn 41 of Book 8 of *Rig Veda* has verses to Varuna by the descendents of Sage Nabhak, and these verses show Varuna as Luminous, holder of Dawn, omnipresent.

The nights he hath encompassed, and established the morns with magic art visible over all is he. His dear Ones, following his Law, have prospered the Three Dawns for him.
स क्षपः॒ परि॑ षस्वजे॒ न्यु१॒॑स्रो मा॒यया॑ दधे॒ स विश्व॒म्परि॑ दर्श॒तः । ।
तस्य॒ वेनी॑र॒नु व्र॒तमु॒षस्ति॒स्रो अ॑वर्धय॒न् नभन्ताम॒न्य॑के समे॑ ॥ ८०४१०३

He who supports the worlds of life, he who well knows the hidden names mysterious of the morning beams, He cherishes much wisdom, Sage, as heaven brings forth each varied form.
यो ध॒र्ता भुव॑नानां॒ य उ॒स्राणा॑म॒पीच्या॒वेद॒ नामा॑नि॒ गुह्या॑ ।
स क॒विः काव्या॑ पु॒रु रूप॒न्द्यौरि॑व पुष्यति॒ नभन्ताम॒न्य॑के समे॑ ॥ ८०४१०५

He wraps these regions as a robe; he contemplates the tribes of Gods and all the works of mortal men, Before the home of Varuṇa all the Gods follow his decree.

य आस्व् अत्क आ॑शये॑ विश्वा जा॑तान्य् एषाम् ।परि॑ धामानि॑ मर्मृश॒द् वरुणस्य पु॑रो गये॑
विश्वे दे॑वा अनु व्र॑तं नभन्ताम् अन्य॑के समे॑ ॥ ८०४१०७

"He is the hidden ocean and he climbs passing beyond heaven; when he has placed the sacrificial word in these dawns, then with his luminous feet he tramples illusions and ascends to the Heavens." [Sri Aurobindo].

स समु॑द्रो अपी॑च्यस् तु॑रो द्याम् इव रोहति॑ नि यद् आसु॑ यजुर् द॒धे ।
स मा॑या अ॑र्चिना प॑दास्तृणा॒न् नाक॑म् आरुह॒न् नभन्ताम् अन्य॑के समे॑ ॥ ८०४१०८

Thus the West part of the house is the best area for working with anything that requires good speech, writing, elaboration, legalities, etc. Furthermore, Vāstu defects in the West can result in problems relating to all types of partnerships: business partnership, misunderstanding with the spouse and friends, legal matters, litigations, etc.

North-West

The planet for the North-Western direction is the Moon. Moon represents water, mind, heart, silver, vital energy, mother, daughter, good nourishment, good things of life, silver, pond. Moon also represents windows and the left side of the front of the house. If the left window is a *puja* (worship) room, the owner will be bestowed with divine perception and wisdom; but if is a dark room which is used as a dumping room, then the women will suffer from ill-health.

The guardian of the North-Western direction is Vayu, the king of the Gandharvas who dwells in the foothills of Mount Meru. In the *Veda*, Vayu is the Cosmic Breath. In man, Vayu is represented by the *Prana* which is responsible for all vital functions of the human body, including sustenance of Life. Vayu travels in a chariot which is pulled by several horses and the charioteer is none other than Indra, the king of the gods.

निꣳयुꣳवाꣳणो अशस्तीर् निꣳयुत्वाꣳइन्द्रसारथिः ।
वाय॑व् आ च॑न्द्रेण रथेन या॑हि सु॑तस्य पी॑तये ॥ ४०४८०२

Put away from thee all denials of expression and with thy steeds of the yoking, with Indra for thy charioteer come, O Vayu, in thy car of happy light to the drinking of the Soma-wine.

The North-Western direction is ideal for building garages, cattle sheds, rooms for daughters who are old enough to be married, guestrooms, *godowns* (storage rooms) for finished goods, and things which you would want to move soon.

If the North-West is lower than the North-East, then it results in rivalry and diseases. For best results it should be higher than the North-East but lower than South-West and South-East.

North

North is an important direction. The *Shivatharvashirsh* says "the head of Rudra is in North and his feet are in South. He who is in North is Omkara, He is Om, Omnipresent, Infinite…Parabrahma, One, Rudra, Ishan, Maheshwara.

The planet for this direction is Mercury. Mercury represents philosophy, education, writing, astrology, prayers, family affluence and its prosperity. Because Mercury represents communication, therefore in the house Mercury represents the hall (drawing room) where friends and relatives meet and discuss things. Mercury also represents the treasury where such things as jewels and important documents are kept.

Because Mercury represents communications, a dark drawing room or a central hall indicates immoral affairs and earning through shady means in the family.

The guarding deity of the North is Kubera, the divine protector of wealth, the king of Yakshas, and the treasurer of the demigods. He is the king of Yakshas, son of Muni Vishwavu and Idavidu, sage Bharadwaj's daughter. He underwent strong penance for a thousand years, and being pleased with his penance and austerities, Brahma, the creator of the universe, granted him the guardianship of the North. In the *Linga Purana*, Sutji describes to the sages how Lord Brahma assigned Lordships to all the deities and the demons, and Kuber figures there:

"The Sun was made the lord of all the planets. Soma was made the lord of all the constellations and medicinal herbs. Varuna was made the Lord of water, while Kubera was assigned the Lordship of wealth. Lord Vishnu attained the Lordship of Aadityas, Pawak of Vasus, Daksha of Prajapatis, Indra of deities, and Prahlada attained the Lordship of all the demons."

Brahma also granted him immortality and the guardianship of all the treasures of earth. He made Alkapuri his permanent abode. (There still exists an area called Alkapuri in Upper Himalayas, beyond the Temple of Badrinath and the village of Mana towards Indo-Tibet border.)

The *Manusmriti* also refers to Kuber as Lord of Wealth in Chapter 7:

पृथुस्तु विनयाद् राज्यं प्राप्तवान् मनुरेव च । कुबेरश्च धनैश्वर्यं ब्राह्मण्यं चैव गाधिजः ॥

But by humility Prithu and Manu gained sovereignty, Kubera the position of the Lord of wealth, and the son of Gadhi the rank of a Brahmana.

Amarkosh describes Kubera, his garden, his son, his capital, and his treasures in the following words:

कुबेरस्त्र्यम्बकसखो यक्षराड् गुह्यकेश्वरः । मनुष्यधर्मा धनदो राजराजो धनाधिपः ॥
किन्नरेशो वैश्रवणः पौलस्त्यो नरवाहनः । यक्षेकपिङ्गलैलविलश्रीदपुण्यजनेश्वराः ॥
अस्योद्यानं चैत्ररथं पुत्रस्तु नलकूबरः । कैलासः स्थानमलका पूर्विमानं तु पुष्पकम् ॥
स्यात् किन्नरः किम्पुरुषस्तुरङ्गवदनो मयुः । निधिनाशिवधिर्भेदाः पद्मशङ्खाऽउदयोनिधेः ॥
महापद्मश्च पद्मश्चशङ्खो मकरकच्छपौ । मुकुन्द कुन्दनीलाश्च खर्वश्च निधयो नव ॥

In the *Dharma Sutra* (*Âpastambha Prashna* 1.8.20 3) there is a ritual described for those who desire prosperity. The ritual involves offerings to Kubera, and this ritual clearly indicates that he has been accepted as a god of riches.

> He who desires prosperity shall fast in the half of the year when the sun goes to the north, under the constellation Tishya, in the first half of the month, for (a day and) a night at least, prepare a Sthâlipâka-offering, offer burnt-oblations to Kubera (the god of riches), feed a Brâhmana with that (food prepared for the Sthâlipâka) mixed with clarified butter, and make him wish prosperity with (a Mantra) implying prosperity. (*The Laws of Manu* tr. George Bühler)

Though Kuber is a Yaksha, he finds equal place among the gods. In the *Durga Saptashati* he is present with the other gods at the time of the genesis of Durga and gifts Her a bowl full of *madhu*. (D.S. 2.30)

ददावशून्यं सुरया पानपात्रं धनाधिपः ।

In this way, it is always desirable to have a depressed North as it allows wealth to flow in. The more open the area here, the more enriched is the family. It is desirable that money, cashbox, etc., should be kept in the north part of the house.

North-East

The planet for the North-Eastern direction is Jupiter. Jupiter represents mantras, *Vedas*, gods, religious duty, cows, finance, movements in heaven, nectar, etc.

Although Ketu does not govern any direction, by an opinion it is also said to represent the North-East. Ketu represents philosophy, Ganapati, occult sciences, and esoteric knowledge. In the house Ketu represents stagnant water, the rear door, the ventilation of the front door, and staircase.

Ishwara is the protector of the North-Eastern direction. He is the fifth manifestation of Shiva, and therefore is identified with him. In Kashmiri Shaivism, Shiva is very commonly referred to as Ishan—he who has no equal. He is Rudra of *Rigveda* and Shiva of *Puranas* and *Agamas*—the benevolent God of the Trinity (Brahma, Vishnu and Shiva) who forces the creation upwards and destroys all those elements that obstruct the course.

According to the *Shivtharvashirha Stotra*, Rudra is the Divine who has manifested as Brahma, Vishnu, Skanda, Indra, Surya, Soma, the Planets, Bhuh, Bhuvaha, Swaha, Mahah, Prithvi, Antariksha, Dhauh, Apa, Teja, Kaal, Yama, Mrityu, Akash, and Sthoolam: Macro, Sookshamam: Micro, the Fair, the Dark, and Truth.

In Vāstu it is mandatory to keep the North-East low. If there is a heavy construction in the North-East, or if the North-East is elevated, has a kennel, wash room, etc., then it will keep riches away and attract miseries and failures in life.

THE SYSTEM OF MEASUREMENT IN VĀSTU SHĀSTRA

Vāstu follows two systems of measurements:

1. Unit based on the size of a grain: Yavamāna
2. Unit based on the human body: Manushya Pramāna

Yavamāna
Yav (barley) and Til (sesame) are popular grains which are in use even today for Hindu religious rituals, and the sizes of their seeds were accepted as standard sizes for all small measurements.

I Til = 0.47 mm
8 Til = I Yav = 3.76mm

These measurements were used only for measuring fine work. Interestingly, the smallest measurement described in Vāstu texts is of a Paramanu, equal to

100030517th part of a Yava, or .000114438 mm. Compare this with the thickness of a human hair which is 100 microns, or .01 mm, or the size of a typical organic molecule: .000001 mm.

Manushyapramana

Manushyapramana consists of scales which are based on the length of the human body. The human body has a perfect ratio of its parts to each other. For example, the height of a person is equal to the span of his arms. In Vāstu terms, kaya = vyama, kaya being the height from the sole to the root of the hair.

When the vyama is divided into eight parts, each part equals one pada, equal to one foot, and also equal to the length of a vitasti. The pada is further divided into eight parts, each part equal to an angula, approximately equal to the central phalanx of the middle finger. So 64 angula = 8 pada = 1 vyama = 1 kaya. Also, 3 angulas make a parva, and 8 parvas make a hasta, which is the length of the arm from the tip of the left finger to the shoulder.

Leonardo da Vinci also used ideal measurements when he was working on the human figure. The drawing entitled Vitruvian Man is based on a model of ideal proportions established by the ancient Roman Vitruvius.

Vitruvius, the architect, says in his work on architecture that the measurements of the human body are as follows: 4 fingers make 1 palm; 4 palms make 1 foot; 6 palms make 1 cubit; 4 cubits make a man's height, 4 cubits make one pace and 24 palms make a man.

The length of a man's outspread arms is equal to his height. From the roots of his hair to the bottom of his chin is a tenth of a man's height; from the bottom of the chin to the top of the head is one eighth of his height; from the top of the breast to the roots of the hair will be the seventh part of the whole man. From the nipples to the top of the head will be the fourth part of a man. The greatest width of the shoulders contains in itself the fourth part of a man. From the elbow to the tip of the hand will be the fifth part of a man; and from the elbow to the angle of the armpit will be the eighth part of a man. The whole hand will be the tenth part of the man. And the distance from the bottom of the chin to the nose and from the roots of the hair to the eyebrows is, in each case the same, and like the ear, a third of the face.

The length of a human body equals eight times the length of his foot length or his outstretched palm. This is one pada.

The following are the different scales used for different measurements:

Large Measurements: Yojana 23 Km (or eight miles)
Measuring Land: Rajju 23.0 m
Building Plot or depth of a water body: Danda (2.88 m)
Building's perimeter: Vyama
Length of elements: Hasta (72 cm)
Size of components: Pada (24 cm)
Details of Sections: Angula (3 cm)
Fine Details: Yava.

THE CALCULATIONS IN VĀSTU

Ayadi Calculations for the Owner's Suitability to the Plot

There are several types of calculations that are done in Vāstu Shāstra for different purposes. Generally they are called the Ayadi calculations. These are done to check the energic suitability of the plot and its relationship with the owner. These calculations are based upon the site of the plot and the horoscope of the owner. Hindu astrology makes extensive use of 27 constellations, in addition to the 12 zodiac signs and the nine *Navagrahas*, and Vāstu has a system of calculating the zodiac sign and the ruling constellation of any shape, size or number. Interestingly, this system is also used by Vāstu astrology to the direction, city, or even the section of the city where an individual would prosper if he lives there.

The Nakshatra calculations fix the ruling star of the land. The Aaya calculations determine a factor between 1 to 9 of the income and prosperity of the occupant of that plot. Similarly, the Vyaya calculations determine a factor between 1 to 9 of the expenditure and reduction in the prosperity of the occupant. The Vaar calculations determine the further compatibility with the owner, and similarly the Amsam calculation further fixes the finer attributes of the land. Thus, such calculations will help determine the benefits or difficulties one will receive by occupying the property or house before one moves into it.

Yoni Calculation: Direction of Energy Flow

The Yoni calculation determines the direction of Energy Flow of the land. This is one of the most important and primary calculations, because the direction of the energy flow determines whether the attributes of the land are beneficial or harmful.

If a magnet breaks into several pieces, then each piece exhibits the property of an independent magnet. Similarly, whenever a piece of land is confined by a boundary, it exhibits all the attributes of an independent Vāstu energy, and its centre begins to radiate energy which begins to flow in one of the eight directions.

The Yoni calculation determines the direction of that energy flow. If it flows in East, West, North, or South, it enhances such things as financial fortunes, good health, victory and success in competition, and overall prosperity. But if it flows in the 'angles': North-East, North-West, South-East or South-West, it causes ill health, bad fortunes, loss of money, failure in career, shattered happiness, and fractured relationships in life. So understanding the energy flow of a piece of land or house would benefit a person before moving into it.

CONCLUSION

Vāstu Shāstra found its highest expression in the temple architecture of the Hindus, whose layout resembles a reclining deity, where the entrance represents the feet, the sanctum sanctorum represents the nucleus of creation or the head of the deity, while the circumambulatory and other paths around the sanctum sanctorum represent the different energic bodies (koshas), and the whole superstructure, walls, the mandapa, pillars, and the plinth are the manifestations of different worlds inhabited by celestial beings like devas, apsaras, kinnars, gandharvas, animals and birds. The elevation of a temple represents the standing deity, each component matching various parts of the human body such as the head, neck, shoulders, trunk, thighs and feet. The layout of the temple building also represents the five subtle bodies of the human being, the energy chakras within the body, five senses, five elements and seven higher levels of existence. In this way, the structure was built for providing the most advantageous environment for its purpose, which was for people to use to reach the highest possible achievement for spiritual realization and unity with the Deity.

The modern mind identifies Ecology with nature, but excludes its spiritual element. For Vāstu Shāstra, however, the spiritual aspect and the five primordial elements—earth, water, fire, air and ether (space)—are the starting points for a design. To a Vāstu practitioner, therefore, each building is a temple, an altar raised to the divine Self, a house of the Cosmic Spirit, an appeal and aspiration to the Infinite.

Vāstu Shāstra is the Universal Science of Universal Space which is aimed at bringing the Cosmic Peace into a dwelling. It is for the benefit of humanity, is applicable to all, and is therefore a code for Universal brotherhood. It echoes the Universal prayer of the *Vedas*:

सं गच्छध्वं सं वदध्वं सं वो मनांसि जानताम्। देवा भागं यथा पूर्वे संजाना ना उपासते ॥

Assemble, speak together: let your minds be all of one accord, as ancient Gods unanimous sit down to their appointed share.

समानो मन्त्रः समितिस्समानी समानम् मनः सह चित्तम् एषाम्। समानम् मन्त्रम् अभि मन्त्रये वः समानेन वो हविषा जुहोमि ॥

The place is common, common the assembly, common the mind, so be their thought united. A common purpose do I lay before you, and worship with your general oblation.

समानी व आकूतिः समाना हृदयानि वः। समानम् अस्तु वो मनो यथा वः सुसहासति ॥

One and the same be your resolve, and be your minds of one accord. United be the thoughts of all that all may happily agree.

ॐ सह नाववतु। सह नौ भुनक्तु। सह वीर्यं करवावहै।
तेजस्वि नावधीतमस्तु मा विद्विषावहै।
॥ ॐ शान्तिः शान्तिः शान्तिः ॥

References

1. **Sri Aurobindo**, *Hymns to the Mystic Fire*, Sri Aurobindo Ashram, Pondicherry.

2. **Sri Aurobindo**, *Essays on the Gita*, Sri Aurobindo Ashram, Pondicherry.

3. **Sri Aurobindo**, *The Renaissance in India*, Sri Aurobindo Ashram, Pondicherry.

4. **Sri Aurobindo**, *The Secret of the Veda*, Sri Aurobindo Ashram, Pondicherry.

5. **Alice Boner (Tr.)**, *Vāstu sutra Upanishad*, Motilal Banarsidass, New Delhi 1992

6. **Ralph T.H. Griffith (Tr.)**, *Rgveda*

7. **Bruno Dagens (Tr.)**, *Mayamatha*, Sitaram Bhartiya Institute of Scientific Research, New Delhi, 1985.

8. **Dr. Balagopal T.S.Prabhu, Dr. A Achyuthan**, *Vāstu Vidhanadipika*, Vāstu vidyapratishthanam, Calicut.

9. *Vāstu Pratishtha Sangraha* (Sanskrit), Khemraj Shrikrishnadas Prakashan, Mumbai.

10. **Dr. R.P.Kulkarni,** *Bharatiya Vāstu Shāstra,* I Sri Madhyabharat Hindi Sahitya Samiti, Indore, 1995

Acknowledgements

I am indebted to Sri Shankacharya of Kancheepuram and Sri Aurobindo whose help and inspiration has been my guide in looking at the divine aspect of Vāstu Shāstra.

I am also deeply grateful to all my Vāstu Shāstra Acharyas.

I am thankful to www.sanskrit.gde.to who have been immensely helpful through their online library of Sanskrit texts. I have used their ITRANS versions for this article. I am also thankful to Omkaranand Ashram who have made available the ITRANS Translator as a free download on the internet, and which I have used.

I am also grateful to Stephen Knapp who asked me to write this article, and patiently bore my delays.

Arun Naik

Divine Nature:
Practical Application of Vedic Ethical Principles in Resolving the Environmental Crisis

Michael A. Cremo

When I first became involved with Vedic ways of life in the early 1970s, I was also interested in environmental questions. Looking back, I can see that I was sympathetic to those who wanted to reverse the pollution of our natural resources, such as air, water, and land. I was sympathetic to those who wanted to stop the devastation of forests and the killing off of various species of plants and animals. But other than expressing my sympathy by attending Earth Day rallies, I really did not know what to do. However, as I became more deeply involved in the study of Vedic philosophy and the practice of one of the paths of Vedic spirituality, bhakti yoga, I began to develop a systematic understanding of the actual roots of the environmental crisis and the outlines of a practical solution.

From my studies in Vedic philosophy, I concluded that the world's environmental crisis is ultimately a spiritual crisis that demands a spiritual solution. Part of the problem lies with our modern scientific cosmology, which is mechanistic and reductionistic. There is little place in modern science for the soul and God. Modern science concentrates on matter and its transformations, leading to an ethic of extravagant material production and consumption. But Vedic philosophy concentrates on consciousness and its transformations. This leads to an ethic of frugality that emphasizes the cultivation of consciousness over the exploitation of matter. The Vedic teachings give people powerful tools for achieving high levels of nonmaterial satisfaction. This leads to a lessening of demands for consumption, and this can lead to a reduction in the ever-increasing global processes of industrialization, which fuels the environmental crisis. The Vedic ethic of *ahimsa* or nonviolence favors a meatless diet, which itself would improve many environmental problems, ranging from acid rain to ground water contamination. A world living according to Vedic ecological principles would be a world of villages, towns, and small cities, with most economic necessities produced and consumed locally in a sustainable fashion. It would be a world of simple living and high thinking. Organizations dedicated to Vedic spiritual understandings, including the International Society for Krishna Conscicusness, with which I am personally associated, have practically implemented various elements of these Vedic ecological concepts in experimental rural communities on five continents.

In 1995, I attended a conference on population, consumption, and the environment, sponsored by the American Association for the Advancement of Science and the Boston Theological Institute.[1] Coming together at the conference were scientists, politicians, environmental activists, and religionists. I was invited as author of the book *Divine Nature: A Spiritual Perspective on the Environmental Crisis*,[2] which had drawn favorable comment from many environmentalists, including two former environment ministers for the Indian government.[3] *Divine Nature* looks at the environmental crisis from the standpoint of the Vedic teachings of India.

One of the keynote speakers at the conference on population, consumption, and the environment was Bruce Babbitt, Secretary of the Interior for the United States government.[4] He told of growing up in the town of Flagstaff, Arizona, from which can be seen a large mountain. The mountain inspired in Babbitt a sense of something wonderful, something godlike, in nature. Raised in the Catholic faith, Babbitt asked a priest about the mountain, hoping to gain some clue as to its spiritual significance. But he received no satisfactory answer, perhaps because his priest was used to thinking of God as remote from nature. Later, Babbitt approached a friend his own age. This friend, who happened to be a native American of the Hopi tribe, took Babbitt up to the mountain and explained to him its sacred nature. And from this Babbitt said he developed a sense of God's presence in nature—to a degree that had not been possible for him previously.

Of course, when I heard this, I was reminded of the *Bhagavad-gita*, wherein Lord Krishna says, "Of immovable things I am the Himalayas,[5] of flowing rivers I am the Ganges,[6] of seasons I am the flower-bearing spring."[7] Such expressions of God's immanence in nature are found throughout the *Gita* and other Indian spiritual texts.

Babbitt went on to say that he understood overconsumption was the underlying cause of most environmental problems. There was a general consensus at the conference that the real issue was not overpopulation in the developing world, but overconsumption, particularly in the developed countries and increasingly in the developing countries. Babbitt said that as a politician he could not present to the people a program that would really solve the environmental problem. It would require too much sacrifice from the voters, so much that they would vote against anyone or any party that told them what would really be necessary.

Secretary Babbitt then turned to the religionists present and said only they could bring about the large-scale changes of values needed to reverse the process of environmental degradation.

Also speaking at the conference was Dr. Henry Kendall, professor of physics at MIT and president of the Union of Concerned Scientists. Dr. Kendall said that science can point out the dimensions of the environmental problem, but it cannot solve the problem. Science, he says, has no silver bullet, no technological fix for the environmental crisis. Like Secretary Babbitt, he recognized overconsumption as the cause of environmental degradation, and like Secretary Babbitt he appealed to religion as the only force in the world capable of generating the changes in values needed to restrain humanity's destructive urge to overproduce and overconsume.

This is not the first time such suggestions have been made. In 1990, at the Global Forum of Spiritual and Parliamentary Leaders, held in Moscow, 32 scientists signed a joint declaration appealing to the world's religions to use their immense influence to preserve the environment.[8] The scientists declared that humanity was committing "Crimes against Creation." They also said, "Efffforts to safeguard and cherish the environment need to be infused with a vision of the sacred."

These statements are somewhat ironic, for it is science itself, or, should I say, a particular brand of science, that is largely responsible for eliminating the sacred from our vision of the universe.

When I use the word science, I mean science as governed by a certain set of metaphysical assumptions. Today's science is governed by a set of metaphysical assumptions that eliminates the sacred from our vision of the universe, if by sacred we mean things connected with a personal God and distinct individual souls. It is quite possible, however, to have a science governed by a set of metaphysical assumptions that would incorporate a genuine vision of the sacred.

But let's return to our consideration of the Moscow statement on the environment, in which leading scientists such as Carl Sagan and Stephen J. Gould spoke of crimes against creation. This is rather surprising language. Today, science is generally quite hostile to the word "creation." It is interesting, however, how science and religion tend to adopt each other's terminology when it suits them, often redefining the terms in the process. One of the tasks before us is to find a common language for science and religion, and use it with integrity for constructive dialogue.

For science, governed by its present materialistic assumptions, nature is simply an object to be dominated, controlled, and exploited. And it is science itself that has provided us with not only the motive but the instruments for such domination, control, and exploitation. Of course, I am speaking of technology. Let's consider the automobile. It is certainly a convenience, but it has its downside. It is one of the main contributors to pollution of the atmosphere, and in the United States alone about 50,000 people a year are killed in automobile accidents. For comparison's sake, we can consider that in the entire 8 years of the American military involvement in Vietnam, 50,000 American soldiers were killed. The same number of Americans are killed each year on their own highways.

The connection between a materialistic conception of the universe and a materialistic way of life was noted thousands of years ago in the *Bhagavad-gita*. The *Gita* describes materialist philosophers thus: "They say that this world is unreal, with no foundation, no God in control."[2] And what is the practical outcome for people who live in societies that are dominated by this worldview, which denies the fundamental reality of God and the soul? The *Gita* says, "They believe that to gratify the senses is the prime necessity of human civilization. Thus until the end of life their anxiety is immeasurable."[10] Such people, says the *Gita,* are "bound by a network of hundreds of thousands of desires."[11] And is this not our situation today? Are we not bombarded daily with messages from radio, television, newspapers, magazines, films, and computers, all attempting to entangle us further in hundreds and thousands of desires that can only be satisfied by consuming various products manufactured by our burgeoning industries? The *Gita* warns us that people like ourselves will "engage in unbeneficial, horrible acts, meant to destroy the world." And are we not gradually destroying our world, polluting its air and water and land, and driving hundreds of species into extinction?

This presents humanity with an ethical dilemma. Put simply, ethics is a process for determining what is good, and how to make choices that will establish and preserve what is good. Given the assumptions of modern materialistic science, it is very difficult to construct an ethic for preserving the environment or saving endangered species. According to currently dominant views, our planet, indeed our very universe, is the result of a cosmic accident, a chance fluctuation of the quantum mechanical vacuum. Given this assumption it is very difficult to say that any particular state of our planet's environment is inherently good. Ultimately, there is no reason to say that our earth, with its teeming life forms, is any better than Jupiter or Uranus, which according to modern astronomy are frozen lifeless planets, with atmospheres composed of elements we would regard as poisonous. Or looking at the history of our own planet, there is no reason to say that our present state of the environment is any better than that of the early earth, which, according to modern geoscience, was a lifeless rock, with a thin reducing atmosphere hostile to today's life forms.

So if we cannot say, on the basis of modern scientific assumptions, that any particular state of the environment is intrinsically good, and thus worthy of preservation, then perhaps we can approach the matter in another way. We can look at nature, at the environment, as an instrumental good, or source of derivative good. In other words, nature is something that yields things of value to living things. Generally speaking we adopt an anthropocentric view, and consider nature to be instrumental to the happiness of our own human species. But according to the assumptions of modern evolutionary science, our human species is the accidental product of millions of random genetic mutations. So there is nothing special about the human species and its needs. Of course, we might take a larger view and appeal to nature as an instrumental good for an entire ecosystem, comprised of many species. But again, we have the same problem. Why is today's ecosystem any better than the ecosystem that existed during the Precambrian, when there was no life at all on land, and in the oceans only jellyfish and crustaceans.

Another way to proceed is to regard the environment as a constitutive good. An acquaintance of mine, Jack Weir, a professor of philosophy at Morehead State University in Kentucky, has presented an argument along these lines.[12] Put briefly, given the evolutionary assumptions of modern science, we are what we are largely because of our environment. According to this view, we are in a sense constituted by our environmental surroundings. If our environmental surroundings were different, we would not be able to stay as we are. But here again we run into a problem. Given the evolutionary assumptions of modern science, what is so special about our current status as humans? Why should it, and the environment that constitutes it, be considered worthy of preservation. Why shouldn't we continue on our present course of overconsumption and environmental destruction. Let natural selection continue to operate, as it has in the past. Let old species perish and let new one's come into existence. Or let them all perish. Given that life itself is an accident of chemical combination in the earth's early oceans, it is difficult to say why there is any particular preference for a planet with life or without life.

Jack Weir backed up his claim that nature was a constitutive good with appeals to "scientific holism and epistemic coherency." But he admitted that "other appeals could be made, such as to stories and myths, religious traditions, and metaphysical beliefs." Of course, one could also appeal to a different science, founded upon a different set of metaphysical assumptions and perhaps arriving at different conclusions about the origin of life and the universe.

If we look at this history of science, from the time of Newton until the present, we find that scientists have accumulated quite a large body of evidence suggesting there is a vital force operating in living things, a force operating beyond the laws of physics and chemistry as currently understood. All around the world, we find great interest in alternative systems of medicine, such as the *Ayurveda*, which are based on the understanding of this vital force, or forces. At the UCLA medical school there is an institute devoted to integrating the insights of traditional Eastern medical systems with Western medicine. There is also quite an accumulation of evidence suggesting that there is a conscious self that can exist apart from the physical organism. This evidence comes from studies of phenomena ranging from out of body experiences to past life memories. Much of this evidence does not easily fit into the materialistic assumptions of modern science, and is therefore regarded with considerable suspicion. But this body of evidence is increasing daily, and it could be incorporated into the framework of a new science operating with an expanded set of metaphysical assumptions. There already are a number of scientific societies attempting this, among them the Scientific and Medical Network in England (with about 1200 scientists and physicians in its membership), the Institute for Noetic Sciences in the United States, the Society for Scientific Exploration, the International Society for the Study of Subtle Energy and Energy Medicine, and others, among them the Bhaktivedanta Institute. Furthermore, as scientists carry their research into the bio-molecular machinery within the cell, they encounter structures and systems of irreducible complexity, which leads some of them to once more seriously entertain the idea of intelligent design rather than chance evolution as an explanation. In this regard, I can recommend biochemist Michael Behe's various papers or his recent book *Darwin's Black Box*.

This past November I spoke to a gathering of physicists at the department of nuclear physics at the ELTE science university in Budapest, Hungary. I shared the podium with Maurice Wilkins, a British Nobel Laureate in physics, whose discoveries helped in the construction of the atomic bomb during the Second World War. The topic was, as here, science and religion. I chose as my topic physics and the paranormal. I proposed that if there was to be any synthesis of science and religion it would have to be on the mysterious ground of reality that lies between them, and undoubtedly their understanding of this mysterious ground of reality would have to be renegotiated.

In terms of physics it might involve a return to an understanding of reality that had a nonmaterial, non-mechanistic component. I pointed out that Newton wrote just as much about alchemy and spiritual topics than he did about his mathematics, physics, and optics, and that for Newton, his physics, alchemy, and writings about mystical topics were all part of one system, from which modern science has abstracted only the part that suits it. The idea of serious investigation into nonmaterial or paranormal components of physical reality is today taboo, but it has not always been so. In the last century, we find Sir William Crookes, Nobel laureate in physics, discoverer of thallium, inventor of the cathode ray tube, and president of the Royal Society, conducting extensive research into the paranormal. Nobel laureate physiologist Charles Richet, of France, who himself conducted extensive research into paranormal phenomena, tells us in his book *Thirty Years of Psychical Research* that he was sometimes assisted by Pierre and Marie Curie, who shared the Nobel prize in physics for their discoveries in the field of radioactive elements. For example, we find Marie Curie controlling a famous medium, while Pierre Curie measured the movements of objects moving under apparent psychokinetic influence. I am not bringing up these incidents to prove the reality of these effects but to illustrate the open-mindedness of these famous experimental physicists, their willingness to investigate a difficult and troubling phenomenon. But isn't that what science, at its best, is supposed to be about?

After I finished my talk in Budapest, I wondered, of course, how it had been received. I was surprised when the head of the physics department of a major European university approached me and revealed that in his home he had been privately conducting some paranormal experiments. To his extreme surprise, he had achieved some interesting results, and he asked me if I could put him in touch with others in America who were conducting similar investigations.

Now what does all this have to do with the environment, with nature? It has everything to do with it, because if we are going to formulate an environmental ethic, we first should understand what our environment really is. And from the Vedic, and in particular Vaishnava, standpoint, we would have to say that it is a divine energy, an energy emanating from a transcendent God who is nevertheless immanent in nature, which is itself populated with conscious entities, and structured in a definite way for a definite purpose, namely providing an opportunity for conscious entities to return to their original pure state. And there is a body of scientific evidence that is consistent with several elements of this view. In other words, religion may be something more than a socially useful set of beliefs that can be harnessed by science to help solve certain problems, such as the environmental crisis. I regard that as a false synthesis of science and religion. It just may be the case that religion has crucial insights into the nature of reality that can be foundational for a true synthesis of science and religion for the benefit of humankind.

With these foundational assumptions it becomes easier to formulate an environmental ethic. Given that, according to Vaisnava teaching, this world is a reflection of a variegated, and essentially gardenlike, spiritual reality, we could say that there is some intrinsic value in attempting to maintain a state of the environment that most closely matches the original. When children learn to write, they are generally asked to copy letters, and if their attempt resembles the original it is said to be good, if it does not it is said to be bad. In the same way, we can propose that there is some intrinsic goodness to a particular state of environmental affairs.

Furthermore, there are certain Vedic principles that contribute in various ways to a viable environmental ethic. The first of these is *athato brahma jijnasa*. This is the opening mantra of the *Vedanta-sutras*. It means that the purpose of human life is cultivation of consciousness, including cultivation of the loving relationship between the individual consciousness and the supreme consciousness.

I want to interject here that it is not every religious teaching that leads to a viable environmental ethic. There are many manifestations of religion which, like modern materialistic science, encourage the destructive processes of domination, exploitation, and unending consumption. But the Vedic system emphasizes the study and development of consciousness over the study and development of matter. Matter is not ignored, but it is seen in its connection with the supreme consciousness. In any case the principle of *brahma jijnasa* encourages an ethic of moderation, which contributes to reasonable levels of economic development and consumption that would not place such a great burden on the ecosystem.

The *Vedanta-sutras* also says *anandamayo 'bhyasat*. We are meant for happiness, and by cultivating consciousness by proper means we can attain nonmaterial satisfaction. And this also sustains an ethic of moderation. The *Gita* says *param drstva nivartate*. When you get the higher taste of developed spiritual consciousness you automatically refrain from excessive material gratification. A proper balance is achieved.

The Vedic principle of *ahimsa*, or nonviolence, also has its application. Nonviolence can be understood in many ways. For example, to encourage people to devote their lives to unrestrained material production and consumption can be considered a kind of violence against the human spirit, and I think we just have to look around us to see the effects of this violence. If we look at Americans at Christmas time crowding into their shiny malls, and instead of heeding the Vedic teaching *athato brahma jijnasa* devoting themselves to the teaching of shop until you drop, or power shopping, or whatever, I think we see a kind of violence. When we see the young Chinese workers who are crowded into dormitories around the factories that provide most of the Christmas goods found in the American malls, we might also sense that violence to the human spirit.

The principle of *ahimsa* can also be applied to the earth itself. We have recently heard of the Gaia principle, the idea that the earth is in some sense an organism. This principle has long been recognized in Vedic philosophy, and we should try not to commit violence to our planet by unnecessarily poisoning her air, land, and water.

And nonviolence also applies to other living things. Accepting the Vedic teaching of *ahimsa*, we will not hunt species to extinction. I will also point out that the killing of animals for food, especially animals raised in factory farms and killed in huge mechanized slaughterhouses, is one of the most environmentally destructive practices in the world today. It is wasteful of precious natural resources. It poisons the land and water.

It can thus be seen that Vedic philosophy provides numerous supports for an ethic of environmental preservation. Similar support can be derived from the teachings of other great religious traditions of the world. But putting this wisdom into practice is difficult. In many areas of ethical concern, we can adopt an objective stance. If we are talking about child molestation, for example, we can feel secure that not many of us are guilty of such a thing, and we can quite comfortably discuss the ethical implications of such behavior and what steps might be taken to control it without seeming to be hypocrites. But when we speak of the environmental crisis we find that we are all directly implicated. And it is difficult to speak about environmental ethics without seeming to be hypocritical. And this must engender in us a sense of humility, and also a sense that even small steps toward the real solution, which must be a spiritual solution, are to be welcomed and appreciated.

Alan Durning, a senior researcher at the World Watch Institute, wrote, "It would be hopelessy naive to believe that entire populations will suddenly experience a moral awakening, renouncing greed, envy, and avarice. The best that can be hoped for is a gradual widening of the circle of those practicing voluntary simplicity."

In this regard, I want to briefly mention that my spiritual teacher, His Divine Grace A. C. Bhaktivedanta Swami Prabhupada, during his life established several intentional rural communities for the specific purpose of demonstrating a life of such voluntary simplicity. Since his departure from this world in 1977, the number of such communities has increased to 40 on five continents, in locations ranging from the Atlantic rain forest region of Brazil to steppes of Russia.

After I spoke to the physicists in Budapest, I had a chance to visit one of these communities. I have to confess I was rather astonished to discover such a rural community founded on Vedic principles in the plains of southwestern Hungary. The center of the community was a somewhat modernistic temple, but when I inquired I learned that it had been constructed using rammed earth walls and other traditional techniques. No electricity from the state power grid was used in the temple or anywhere else in the community. Along the temple walls I saw brass lamps, which burned oil pressed from locally grown rape seeds. It was a rather cold day in November, and I saw the building was heated with superefficient wood burning stoves, using wood sustainably harvested from a 50 acre plot of forest owned by the community. I was then offered a vegetarian meal, which featured locally grown vegetables, chapatis made from wheat grown and ground in the community, and cheese from the community's cows. I learned that oxen are being trained to do farm work and transport. The people I met did not seem in any way deprived.

I told some of them, "You're doing the right thing." And isn't that what environmental ethics is all about, not just talking about the right thing, but doing it.

To summarize, from the standpoint of Vedic ecological principles, I would say the following elements are necessary for a complete solution to the environmental crisis: (1) a science that recognizes distinct conscious selves, emanating from an original conscious self, as fundamental entities; (2) a religion that goes beyond dogma and ritual to provide actual sources of nonmaterial satisfaction by practice of meditation, yoga, etc.; (3) respect for all living things, seeing them as conscious selves like us; (4) an ecofriendly vegetarian diet; (5) an economic system founded on villages and small cities, emphasizing local production and self sufficiency. Anything short of this simply will not give the desired result.

NOTES

[1.] The conference Consumption, Population, and the Environment was held November 9-11 at the Campion Retreat Center outside Boston.

[2.] Michael A. Cremo and Mukunda Goswami (1995), "Divine Nature, A Spiritual Perspective on the Environmental Crisis." Los Angeles, Bhaktivedanta Book Trust.

[3.] On May 5, 1995, Kamal Nath, then Minister of Environment and Forests, wrote: "At a time when the world's developing countries are tending to let industrial progress take over their economies, oblivious to environmental destruction, Divine Nature comes as a welcome breath of relief. The authors have persuasively argued that a return to the original value of humanity's deep spiritual kinship with all living things is the key to achieving pervasive environmental consciousness." And on June 16, 1995, Maneka Gandhi, a former Minister of Environment and Forests, wrote: "This book should be read as a management plan for the economy, especially by politicians and business managers who, having gotten us into the mess we are in by promoting cultural and eating patterns that are destructive, in the mistaken belief that money can be made through devastation, could now truly understand how to repair the earth in a way that all of us can live, not merely exist."

[4.] The Interior department is in charge of the national park system, and oversees the environmental resource management of large areas of goverment-owned land. The account of his statements is taken from my notes on his speech.

5. Bhagavad-gita 10.25. The translations quoted in this paper are from His Divine Grace A. C. Bhaktivedanta Swami Prabhupada, Bhagavad-gita As It Is, complete edition, revised and enlarged, Bhaktivedanta Book Trust, Los Angeles, 1989.

6. Bhagavad-gita 10.31

7. Bhagavad-gita 10.35. After listing numerous manifestations of His presence in nature, Krishna goes on to say in Bhagavad-gita 10.41: "Know that all opulent, beautiful, and glorious creations spring from but a spark of My splendor." This indicates that God, although immanent in nature, also transcends nature.

8. The statement was titled "Preserving and Cherishing the Earth: An Appeal for Joint Commitment in Science and Religion." The quotations in this paper are from a machine copy of the original statement.

9. Bhagavad-gita 16.8

10. Bhagavad-gita 16.11

11. Bhagavad-gita 16.12

12. Jack Weir (1995) Bread, Labor: Tolstoy, Gandhi, and Deep Ecology. Presented at the Kentucky State University Institute for Liberal Studies Sixth Annual Interdisciplinary Conference on Science and Culture, Frankfort, Kentucky. Unpublished.

An earlier version of this paper was presented at the Second World Congress for Synthesis of Science and Religion. Calcutta, India, January 4-6, and was later published in the conference proceedings: Michael Cremo (2001) Vedic Ethical Principles and the Solution to the Environmental Crisis, in T. D. Singh and Samaresh Bandyopadhyay eds., Thoughts on Synthesis of Science and Religion, Calcutta, Bhaktivedanta Institute, pp. 209-221. Another version was presented at the International Consortium for Environment and Environmental Technology Management, held. January 29-31, 1998, in Long Beach, California.

Michael A. Cremo
Research Associate
Bhaktivedanta Institute, 9701 Venice Blvd. #5, Los Angeles, CA 90034, USA
phone (310) 837-5283 fax (310) 837-1056
e-mail: mcremo@cs.com

Conclusion

Stephen Knapp

Herein we have shown some of the ways, both spiritually and materially, that the insights and knowledge in Vedic culture can be used for improving and enhancing your life. This is how it has been used and developed over the course of many hundreds of years. And it can continue in this modern age to assist people in finding their spiritual identity and purpose in life in a variety of ways, such as to find one's best occupation, or to assist in uncovering where one best fits into society, as well as to avoid pitfalls of disease and increase one's personal potential. It can certainly help us understand how to make arrangements for social improvements by seeing the similarities that we all share, and to assist in our concern and awareness for preserving the Earth's resources and ecological balance.

Since Vedic culture is based on Sanatana-dharma, or the eternal and spiritual nature of the living being, it is a system which we all can use, regardless of our level of development, and implement its many tools and systems of knowledge to increase our progress, both socially and individually. In this way, it is meant for universal advancement.

So in this book we have heard the accounts of fifteen people and how they got started in looking into the various aspects of Vedic science, what it has done for them, and how they have gone on to use it in ways that made a real difference in their lives. And now they are teaching it and using it to enhance the lives of others. Most of them have also written their own books that give further insight and understanding of Vedic culture and its various avenues of Self-development. So we also invite you to look more deeply into this culture and way of life and find out what more it can do for you.

Glossary

Acarya—the spiritual master who sets the proper standard by his own example.

Acintya-bhedabheda-tattva—simultaneously one and different. The doctrine Lord Sri Caitanya taught referring to the Absolute as being both personal and impersonal.

Adi Keshava—name of Vishnu.

Adinatha—the first of the 24 Jain *Tirthankaras*.

Adi Varaha—name of Vishnu as the Primeval Boar.

Advaita—nondual, meaning that the Absolute Truth is one, and that there is no individuality between the Supreme Being and the individual souls which merge into oneness, the Brahman, when released from material existence. The philosophy taught by Sankaracharya.

Agastya Muni—a sage who was the knower of the *Vedas*.

Agni—fire, or Agni the demigod of fire.

Agnihotra—the Vedic sacrifice in which offerings were made to the fire, such as ghee, milk, sesame seeds, grains, etc. The demigod Agni would deliver the offerings to the demigods that are referred to in the ritual.

Ahankara—false ego, identification with matter.

Ahimsa—nonviolence.

Airavateshvara—Shiva as Lord of the heavenly elephant.

Akarma—actions which cause no *karmic* reactions.

Akasha—the ether, or etheric plane; a subtle material element in which sound travels.

Amba, Ambika—name of Mother Durga.

Amrita—the nectar of immortality derived from churning the ocean of milk.

Amriteshvara—Shiva as Lord of Ambrosia.

Ananda—spiritual bliss.

Ananta—unlimited.

Annapurna—Parvati, a name meaning Filled with Food.

Apara-prakrti—the material energy of the Lord.

Aranyaka—sacred writings that are supposed to frame the essence of the *Upanishads.*

Arati—the ceremony of worship when incense and ghee lamps are offered to the Deities.

Arca-vigraha—the worshipable Deity form of the Lord made of stone, wood, etc.

Ardhanarishvara—Shiva as half Shiva and half Parvati.

Aryan—a noble person, one who is on the Vedic path of spiritual advancement.

Asana—postures for meditation, or exercises for developing the body into a fit instrument for spiritual advancement.

Asat—that which is temporary.

Ashrama—one of the four orders of spiritual life, such as *brahmacari* (celibate student), *grihastha* (married householder), *vanaprastha* (retired stage), and *sannyasa* (renunciate); or the abode of a spiritual teacher or *sadhu*.

Astanga-yoga—the eightfold path of mystic yoga.

Asura—one who is ungodly or a demon.

Atma—the self or soul. Sometimes means the body, mind, and senses.

Atman—usually referred to as the Supreme Self.

Avatara—an incarnation of the Lord who descends from the spiritual world.

Avidya—ignorance or nescience.

Aum—*om* or *pranava*

Ayodhya—the birthplace of Lord Rama in East India.

Ayurveda—the original wholistic form of medicine as described in the Vedic literature.

Babaji—wandering mendicant holy man.

Badrinatha—one of the holy places of pilgrimage in the Himalayas, and home of the Deity Sri Badrinatha along with many sages and hermits.

Betel—a mildly intoxicating nut.

Bhagavan—one who possesses all opulences, God.

Bhagiratha—a king who brought the Ganges down from heaven by the austerities he performed.

Bhairava—Shiva as the terrifying destroyer.

Bhajan—song of worship.

Bhajan kutir—a small dwelling used for one's worship and meditation.

Bhakta—a devotee of the Lord who is engaged in *bhakti-yoga*.

Bhakti—love and devotion for God.

Bhakti-yoga—the path of offering pure devotional service to the Supreme.

Bhang—pronounced bong, a sweet mixed with hashish.

Bhava—preliminary stage of love of God.

Bhavani—name of Parvati.

Bhu, Bhumidevi—Earth, a goddess associated with Vishnu.

Bhutanatha—Shiva as Lord of the *bhutas*, ghosts.

Brahma—the demigod of creation who was born from Lord Vishnu, the first created living being and the engineer of the secondary stage of creation of the universe when all the living entities were manifested.

Brahmacari—a celebate student, usually five to twenty-five years of age, who is trained by the spiritual master. One of the four divisions or *ashramas* of spiritual life.

Brahmajjyoti—the great white light or effulgence which emanates from the body of the Lord.

Brahmaloka—the highest planet or plane of existence in the universe; the planet where Lord Brahma lives.

Brahman—the spiritual energy; the all-pervading impersonal aspect of the Lord; or the Supreme Lord Himself.

Brahmana or brahmin—one of the four orders of society; the intellectual class of men who have been trained in the knowledge of the *Vedas* and initiated by a spiritual master.

Brahmana—the supplemental books of the four primary *Vedas*. They usually contained instructions for performing Vedic *agnihotras*, chanting the *mantras*, the purpose of the rituals, etc. The *Aitareya* and *Kaushitaki Brahmanas* belong to the *Rig-veda*, the *Satapatha Brahmana* belongs to the *White Yajur-veda*, and the *Taittiriya Brahmana* belongs to the *Black Yajur-veda*. The *Praudha* and *Shadvinsa Brahmanas* are two of the eight *Brahmanas* belonging to the *Atharva-veda*.

Brahmastra—a nuclear weapon that is produced and controlled by *mantra*.

Brahminical—to be clean and upstanding, both outwardly and inwardly, like a *brahmana* should be.

Buddha—Lord Buddha or a learned man.

Caitanya-caritamrta—the scripture by Krishnadasa Kaviraja which explains the teachings and pastimes of Lord Caitanya Mahaprabhu.

Caitanya Mahaprabhu—the most recent incarnation of the Lord who appeared in the 15th century in Bengal and who originally started the *sankirtana* movement, based on congregational chanting of the holy names.

Causal Ocean or Karana Ocean—is the corner of the spiritual sky where Maha-Vishnu lies down to create the material manifestation.

Chakra—a wheel, disk, or psychic energy center situated along the spinal column in the subtle body of the physical shell.

Chandra—the moon.

Chitragupta—name of Surya, the demigod of the sun.

Chit—eternal knowledge.

Darshan—the devotional act of seeing and being seen by the Deity in the temple.

Dakshinamurti—Shiva as teacher of yoga and universal knowledge.

Dasara or Dussera—the ten-day festival in September-October when Durga is worshiped and the victory of Lord Rama over the demon Ravana is celebrated.

Dashavatara—the ten incarnations of Lord Vishnu: Matsya, Kurma, Varaha, Narasimha, Vamana, Parashurama, Rama, Krishna, Buddha, and Kalki.

Deity—the *arca-vigraha*, or worshipful form of the Supreme in the temple, or deity as the worshipful image of the demigod. A capital D is used in referring to Krishna or one of His expansions, while a small d is used when referring to a demigod or lesser personality.

Devaloka—the higher planets or planes of existence of the devas.

Devaki—the devotee who acted as Lord Krishna's mother.

Devas—demigods or heavenly beings from higher levels of material existence, or a godly person.

Dham—a holy place.

Dharma—the essential nature or duty of the living being as a spirit soul.

Dharmachakra—Buddhist wheel of law, the first sermon given by Buddha at Sarnath.

Dharmashala—a shelter or guesthouse for pilgrims at temples or holy towns.

Digambara—one of the two main Jain sects, sky-clad.

Diksha—spiritual initiation.

Diwali—festival of lights, marks the end of the rainy season.

Dualism—as related in this book, it refers to the Supreme as both an impersonal force (Brahman) as well as the Supreme Person.

Durga—the form of Parvati, Shiva's wife, as a warrior goddess known by many names according to her deeds, such as Simhavahini when riding her lion, Mahishasuramardini for killing the demon Mahishasura, Jagaddhatri as the mother of the universe, Kali when she killed the demon Raktavija, Tara when killing Shumba, etc. She assumes or incarnates in as many as 64 different forms, depending on her activities. Dvapara-yuga—the third age which lasts 864,000 years.

Dwaita—dualism, the principle that the Absolute Truth consists of the infinite Supreme Being along with the infinitesimal, individual souls.

Ekadasi—a fast day on the eleventh day of the waxing and waning moon.

Gana—Shiva's dwarf attendants.

Ganapati—Ganesh as Lord of the *ganas*.

Gandharvas—the celestial angel-like beings who have beautiful forms and voices, and are expert in dance and music, capable of becoming invisible and can help souls on the earthly plane.

Ganesh—a son of Shiva, said to destroy obstacles (as Vinayaka) and offer good luck to those who petition him. It is generally accepted that the way Ganesh got the head of an elephant is that one time Parvati asked him to guard her residence. When Shiva wanted to enter, Ganesh stopped him, which made Shiva very angry. Not recognizing Ganesh, Shiva chopped off his head, which was then destroyed by one of Shiva's goblin associates. Parvati was so upset when she learned what had happened, Shiva, not being able to find Ganesh's original head, took the   head of the first creature he saw, which was an elephant, and put it on the body of Ganesh and brought him back to life. The large mouse carrier of Ganesh symbolizes Ganesh's ability to destroy all obstacles, as rodents can gradually gnaw their way through most anything.

Gangadhara—Shiva's name when bearing the weight of the Ganges descent to earth.

Gangapuja—the *arati* ceremony for worshiping the Ganges.

Ganges—the sacred and spiritual river which, according to the *Vedas*, runs throughout the universe, a portion of which is seen in India. The reason the river is considered holy is that it is said to be a drop of the Karana Ocean outside of the universe that leaked in when Lord Vishnu, in His incarnation as Vamanadeva, kicked a small hole in the universal shell with His toe. Thus, the water is spiritual as well as being purified by the touch of Lord Vishnu.

Gangeshvara—Shiva as Lord of Ganga.

Gangotri—the source of the Ganges River in the Himalayas.

Garbhodakasayi Vishnu—the expansion of Lord Vishnu who enters into each universe.

Garuda—Lord Vishnu's bird carrier.

Gaudiya—a part of India sometimes called Aryavarta or land of the Aryans, located south of the Himalayas and north of the Vindhya Hills.

Gaudiya *sampradaya*—the school of Vaishnavism founded by Sri Caitanya.

Gauri—name of Parvati meaning Fair One.

Gaurishankara—Shiva and Parvati together.

Gayatri—the spiritual vibration or *mantra* from which the other *Vedas* were expanded and which is chanted by those who are initiated as *brahmanas* and given the spiritual understanding of Vedic philosophy.

Ghat—a bathing place along a river or lake with steps leading down to the water.

Godasa—one who serves the senses.

Goloka Vrindavana—the name of Lord Krishna's spiritual planet.

Gompa—Buddhist monastery.

Gopuram—the tall ornate towers that mark the gates to the temples, often found in south India.

Gosvami—one who is master (Svami) of the senses (go).

Govinda—a name of Krishna which means one who gives pleasure to the cows and senses.

Govindaraja—Krishna as Lord of the Cowherds.

Grihastha—the householder order of life. One of the four *ashramas* in spiritual life.

Gunas—the modes of material nature of which there is *sattva* (goodness), *rajas* (passion), and *tamas* (ignorance).

Guru—a spiritual master.

Hanuman—the popular monkey servant of Lord Rama.

Hare—the Lord's pleasure potency, Radharani, who is approached for accessibility to the Lord.

Hari—a name of Krishna as the one who takes away one's obstacles on the spiritual path.

Haribol—a word that means to chant the name of the Lord, Hari.

Harinam—refers to the name of the Lord, Hari.

Har Ki Pauri—the holy bathing *ghats* in Hardwar where the Ganges leaves the mountains and enters the plains. It is at this spot where the Kumbha Mela is held every twelve years.

Hatha-yoga—a part of the yoga system which stresses various sitting postures and exercises.

Hayagriva—Lord Vishnu as the giver of knowledge.

Hinayana—Lesser Vehicle, the Buddhist school that stresses achieving one's own enlightenment.

Hiranyagarbha—another name of Brahma who was born of Vishnu in the primordial waters within the egg of the universe.

Hiranyakashipu—the demon king who was killed by Lord Vishnu in His incarnation as Narasimha.

Hrishikesa—a name for Krishna which means the master of the senses.

Impersonalism—the view that God has no personality or form, but is only an impersonal force (Brahman) which the individual souls merge back into when released from material existence.

Impersonalist—those who believe God has no personality or form.

Incarnation—the taking on of a body or form.

Indra—the King of heaven and controller of rain, who by his great power conquers the forces of darkness.

ISKCON—International Society for Krishna Consciousness.

Jagadambi—Parvati as Mother of the World.

Jagannatha—Krishna as Lord of the Universe, especially as worshipped in Jagannatha Puri.

Jagat Kishora—name of Krishna.

Jai or *Jaya*—a term meaning victory, all glories.

Janardhana—name of Vishnu.

Japa—the chanting one performs, usually softly, for one's own meditation.

Japa-mala—the string of beads one uses for chanting.

Jiva—the individual soul or living being.

Jivanmukta—a liberated soul, though still in the material body and universe.

Jiva-shakti—the living force.

Jnana—knowledge which may be material or spiritual.

Jnana-kanda—the portion of the *Vedas* which stresses empirical speculation for understanding truth.

Jnana-yoga—the process of linking with the Supreme through empirical knowledge and mental speculation.

Jnani—one engaged in *jnana-yoga*, or the process of cultivating knowledge to understand the Absolute.

Jyestha—goddess Shakti.

Jyotirlinga—the luminous energy of Shiva manifested at 12 places, such as Kedarnatha, Patan, Ujjain, and Varanasi.

Kailash—Shiva's mountain home.

Kala—eternal time, Yama.

Kali—the demigoddess who is the fierce form of the wife of Lord Shiva. The word *kali* comes from *kala*, the Sanskrit word for time: the power that dissolves or destroys everything.

Kali-yuga—the fourth and present age, the age of quarrel and confusion, which lasts 432,000 years and began 5,000 years ago.

Kalki—future incarnation of Lord Vishnu who appears at the end of Kali-yuga.

Kalpa—a day in the life of Lord Brahma which lasts a thousand cycles of the four *yugas*.

Kama—lust or inordinate desire.

Kama sutra—a treatise on sex enjoyment.

Kanyakumari—Parvati as a virgin.

Kapila—an incarnation of Lord Krishna who propagated the Sankhya philosophy.

Karanodakasayi Vishnu (Maha-Vishnu)—the expansion of Lord Krishna who created all the material universes.

Karma—material actions performed in regard to developing one's position or for future results which produce *karmic* reactions. It is also the reactions one endures from such fruitive activities.

Karma-kanda—the portion of the *Vedas* which primarily deals with recommended fruitive activities for various results.

Karma-yoga—system of yoga for using one's activities for spiritual advancement.

Karmi—the fruitive worker, one who accumulates more *karma*.

Karttikeya—son of Shiva and Parvati, also known as Skanda, Subramanya, Kumara, or son of the Pleiades (Krittika constellation).

Keshava—Krishna with long hair.

Kirtana—chanting or singing the glories of the Lord.

Krishna—the name of the original Supreme Personality of Godhead which means the most attractive and greatest pleasure. He is the source of all other incarnations, such as Vishnu, Rama, Narasimha, Narayana, Buddha, Parashurama, Vamanadeva, Kalki at the end of Kali-yuga, etc.

Krishnaloka—the spiritual planet where Lord Krishna resides.

Kshatriya—the second class of *varna* of society, or occupation of administrative or protective service, such as warrior or military personel.

Ksirodakasayi Vishnu—the Supersoul expansion of the Lord who enters into each atom and the heart of each individual.

Kumbha Mela—the holy festival in which millions of pilgrims and sages gather to bathe in the holy and purifying rivers for liberation at particular auspicious times that are calculated astrologically. The Kumbha Mela festivals take place every three years alternating between Allahabad, Nasik, Ujjain, and Hardwar.

Kuruksetra—the place of battle 5,000 years ago between the Pandavas and the Kauravas ninety miles north of New Delhi, where Krishna spoke the *Bhagavad-gita*.

Kuvera—the pot bellied chief of the *yakshas*, and keeper of earth's treasures.

Kurma—incarnation of Vishnu as a tortoise.

Lakshmi—the goddess of fortune and wife of Lord Vishnu.

Lila—pastimes.

Lilavataras—the many incarnations of God who appear to display various spiritual pastimes to attract the conditioned souls in the material world.

Linga—the phallic symbol of Lord Shiva, often represents universal space.

Madana-mohana—name of Krishna as one who fills the mind with love.

Madhava—Krishna.

Mahabhagavata—a great devotee of the Lord.

Mahabharata—the great epic of the Pandavas, which includes the *Bhagavad-gita*, by Vyasadeva.

Maha-mantra—the best *mantra* for self-realization in this age, called the Hare Krishna *mantra*.

Mahatma—a great soul or devotee.

Mahat-tattva—the total material energy.

Mahavira—Great Hero, referring to the last of the great Jain teachers, or *tirthankaras*.

Maha-Vishnu or Karanodakasayi Vishnu—the Vishnu expansion of Lord Krishna from whom all the material universes emanate.

Mahayana—Great Vehicle, the Buddhist school that stresses giving aid to all living beings toward enlightenment.

Mahishamardini—Durga as the slayer of the buffalo demon.

Mandakini—another name of River Ganga.

Mandir—a temple.

Mantra—a sound vibration which prepares the mind for spiritual realization and delivers the mind from material inclinations. In some cases a *mantra* is chanted for specific material benefits.

Martya-loka—the earth planet, the place of death.

Matsya—Lord Vishnu as the fish incarnation.

Maya—illusion, or anything that appears to not be connected with the eternal Absolute Truth.

Mayavadi—the impersonalist or voidist who believes that the Supreme has no form.

Meenakshi—Parvati as Fish-Eyed.

Mitra—the deity controlling the sun, and who gives life to earth.

Mleccha—a derogatory name for an untouchable person, a meat-eater.

Mohini—Lord Vishnu's incarnation as the most beautiful woman.

Moksha—liberation from material existence.

Mukteshvara—Shiva as the giver of liberation.

Mukunda—Krishna as the giver of spiritual liberation.

Murti—a Deity of the Lord or an image of a demigod or spiritual master that is worshiped.

Murugan—means the divine child, the Tamil name for Subramaniya, one of the sons of Shiva and Parvati, especially worshiped in South India. It is said that he was born to destroy the demon Tarakasura. He was born in a forest of arrow-like grass and raised by the six divine mothers of the Krittika constellation (Pleiades). Thus, he is also called Kartikeya and Sanmatura, and he assumed six faces (and twelve arms) to suckle the milk of the six mothers. Being young and virile, he is also called Kumara or Sanatkumara. He is also called Skanda for being very forceful in war. His two consorts are Velli, the daughter of a humble chieftan of an agricultural tribe, and Devasena, the daughter of the demigod Indra.

Nanda—the foster father of Krishna.

Nandi—Shiva's bull carrier.

Narasimha—Lord Vishnu's incarnation as the half-man half-lion who killed the demon Hiranyakashipu.

Narayana—the four-handed form of the Supreme Lord.

Nataraja—King of Dance, usually referring to Shiva, but also Krishna.

Nilakantha—Blue Throated Shiva after swallowing the poison first produced when the ocean of milk was churned by the demons and demigods.

Nirguna—without material qualities.

Nirvana—the state of no material miseries, usually the goal of the Buddhists or voidists.

Om or *Omkara*—*pranava*, the transcendental *om mantra*, generally referring to the attributeless or impersonal aspects of the Absolute.

Padmanabha—Vishnu.

Pan—a concoction of ground betel nut and spices that acts as a mild stimulant or intoxicant. It is very popular and often leaves the teeth stained red.

Pandal—a large tent where religious gatherings are held.

Papanasana—Shiva as destroyer of sin.

Paramahamsa—the highest level of self-realized devotees of the Lord.

Paramatma—the Supersoul, or localized expansion of the Lord.

Parampara—the system of disciplic succession through which transcendental knowledge descends.

Parashurama—incarnation of Vishnu with an axe who cleansed the world of the deviant *kshatriya* warriors.

Parsvanatha—one of the prominent Jain *thirthankaras*.

Parthasarathi—Krishna as Arjuna's chariot driver.

Parvati—Lord Shiva's spouse, daughter of Parvata. Parvata is the personification of the Himalayas. She is also called Gauri for her golden complexion, Candi, Bhairavi (as the wife of Bhairava, Shiva), Durga, Ambika, and Shakti.

Pashupati—Shiva as Lord of the animals.

Patanjali—the authority on the *astanga-yoga* system.

Pradhana—the total material energy in its unmanifest state.

Prajapati—deity presiding over procreation.

Prakriti—matter in its primordial state, the material nature.

Prana—the life air or cosmic energy.

Pranayama—control of the breathing process as in *astanga* or *raja-yoga*.

Pranava—same as *omkara*.

Prasada—food or other articles that have been offered to the Deity in the temple and then distributed amongst people as the blessings or mercy of the Deity.

Prema—matured love for Krishna.

Puja—the worship offered to the Deity.

Pujari—the priest who performs worship, *puja*, to the Deity.

Purusha or *Purusham*—the supreme enjoyer.

Radha—Krishna's favorite devotee and the personification of His bliss potency.

Rahu—deity representation of the planetary node that causes solar eclipses.

Raja-yoga—the eightfold yoga system.

Rajo-guna—the material mode of passion.

Ramachandra—an incarnation of Krishna as He appeared as the greatest of kings.

Ramanuja—Vaishnava philosopher.

Ramayana—the great epic of the incarnation of Lord Ramachandra.

Rasa—an enjoyable taste or feeling, a relationship with God.

Ravana—demon king of the *Ramayana*.

Rishi—saintly person who knows the Vedic knowledge.

Sacrifice—in this book it in no way pertains to human sacrifice, as many people tend to think when this word is used. But it means to engage in an austerity of some kind for a higher, spiritual purpose.

Sati—Shiva's wife who killed herself by immolation in fire.

Shabda-brahma—the original spiritual vibration or energy of which the *Vedas* are composed.

Sac-cid-ananda-vigraha—the transcendental form of the Lord or of the living entity which is eternal, full of knowledge and bliss.

Sadhana—a specific practice or discipline for attaining God realization.

Sadhu—Indian holy man or devotee.

Saguna Brahman—the aspect of the Absolute with form and qualities.

Samadhi—trance, the perfection of being absorbed in the Absolute.

Samsara—rounds of life; cycles of birth and death; reincarnation.

Sanatana-dharma—the eternal nature of the living being, to love and render service to the supreme lovable object, the Lord.

Sangam—the confluence of two or more rivers.

Sankhya—analytical understanding of material nature, the body, and the soul.

Sankirtana-yajna—the prescribed sacrifice for this age: congregational chanting of the holy names of God.

Sannyasa—the renounced order of life, the highest of the four *ashramas* on the spiritual path.

Sarasvati—the goddess of knowledge and intelligence.

Sattva-guna—the material mode of goodness.

Satya-yuga—the first of the four ages which lasts 1,728,000 years.

Shaivites—worshipers of Lord Shiva.

Shakti—energy, potency or power, the active principle in creation. Also the active power or wife of a deity, such as Shiva/Shakti.

Shastra—the authentic revealed scripture.

Shiva—the benevolent one, the demigod who is in charge of the material mode of ignorance and the destruction of the universe. Part of the triad of Brahma, Vishnu, and Shiva who continually create, maintain, and destroy the universe. He is known as Rudra when displaying his destructive aspect.

Sikha—a tuft of hair on the back of the head signifying that one is a Vaishnava.

Skanda—son of Shiva and Parvati, leader of the army of the gods; also known as Karttikeya and Subramanya or Murugan.

Smaranam—remembering the Lord.

Smriti—the traditional Vedic knowledge "that is remembered" from what was directly heard by or revealed to the *rishis*.

Sravanam—hearing about the Lord.

Sri, Sridevi—Lakshmi, the goddess who embodies beauty and prosperity, wife of Lord Vishnu.

Sridhara—Lord Vishnu.

Srimad-Bhagavatam—the most ripened fruit of the tree of Vedic knowledge compiled by Vyasadeva.

Sruti—scriptures that were received directly from God and transmitted orally by *brahmanas* or *rishis* down through succeeding generations. Traditionally, it is considered the four primary *Vedas*.

Svetambara—one of the two main Jain sects, white robed.

Sudra—the working class of society, the fourth of the *varnas*.

Surya—Sun or solar deity.

Svami—one who can control his mind and senses.

Tamo-guna—the material mode of ignorance.

Tapasya—voluntary austerity for spiritual advancement.

Thanka—Tibetan cloth painting, usually based on Buddhist philosophy.

Tilok—the clay markings that signify a person's body as a temple, and the sect or school of thought of the person.

Tirtha—a holy place of pilgrimage.

Tirthankara—the person who is the spiritual guide or teacher in Jainism.

Treta-yuga—the second of the four ages which lasts 1,296,000 years.

Trilochana—Three-eyed Shiva.

Trilokanatha—Shiva as Lord of the Three Worlds.

Trimurti—triad of Vishnu, Brahma, and Shiva.

Trivikrama—Lord Vishnu as Vamadeva, the *brahmana* dwarf who covered the entire universe in three steps.

Tulasi—the small tree that grows where worship to Krishna is found. It is called the embodiment of devotion, and the incarnation of Vrinda-devi.

Uma—Parvati

Upanishads—the portions of the *Vedas* which primarily explain philosophically the Absolute Truth. It is knowledge of Brahman which releases one from the world and allows one to attain self-realization when received from a qualified teacher. Except for the *Isa Upanishad*, which is the 40th chapter of the *Vajasaneyi Samhita* of the *Sukla* (*White*) *Yajur-veda*, the *Upanishads* are connected to the four primary *Vedas*, generally found in the *Brahmanas*.

Vaikunthas—the planets located in the spiritual sky.

Vaishnava—a worshiper of the Supreme Lord Vishnu or Krishna and His expansions or incarnations.

Vaishnava-*aparadha*—an offense against a Vaisnava or devotee, which can negate all of one's spiritual progress.

Vaisya—the third class of society engaged in business or farming.

Vajra—thunderbolt.

Vamana—dwarf incarnation of Vishnu who covered the universe in three steps.

Vanaprastha—the third of the four *ashramas* of spiritual life in which one retires from family life in preparation for the renounced order.

Varaha—Lord Vishnu's boar incarnation.

Varna—sometimes referred to as caste, a division of society, such as *brahmana* (a priestly intellectual), a *kshatriya* (ruler or manager), *vaisya* (a merchant, banker, or farmer), and *sudra* (common laborer).

Varnashrama—the system of four divisions of society and four orders of spiritual life.

Varuna—demigod of the oceans, guardian of the west.

Vasudeva—Krishna.

Vayu—demigod of the air.

Vedanta-sutras—the philosophical conclusion of the four *Vedas*.

Vedas—generally means the four primary *samhitas; Rig, Yajur, Sama, Atharva*.

Venktateshvara—Vishnu as Lord of the Venkata Hills, worshiped in Tirumala.

Vidya—knowledge.

Vikarma—sinful activities performed without scriptural authority and which produce sinful reactions.

Virabhadra—vengeful form of Shiva.

Virajanadi or Viraja River—the space that separates the material creation from the spiritual sky.

Vishalakshi—Parvati, consort of Vishvanatha or Vishalaksha, Shiva.

Vishnu—the expansion of Lord Krishna who enters into the material energy to create and maintain the cosmic world.

Vishvakarma—demigod architect of the heavens.

Vishvanatha—Shiva as Lord of the universe, worshiped in Varanasi as a *linga*.

Vishvarupa—universal form of Lord Vishnu.

Vrindavana—the place where Lord Krishna displayed His village pastimes 5,000 years ago, and is considered to be part of the spiritual abode.

Vyasadeva—the incarnation of God who appeared as the greatest philosopher who compiled the main portions of the vedic literature into written form.

Yajna—a ritual or austerity that is done as a sacrifice for spiritual merit, or ritual worship of a demigod for good *karmic* reactions.

Yamaraja—the demigod and lord of death who directs the living entities to various punishments according to their activities.

Yamuna—goddess personification of the Yamuna River.

Yantra—a machine, instrument, or mystical diagram used in ritual worship.

Yashoda—foster mother of Krishna.

Yoga—linking up with the Absolute.

Yoga-*siddhi*—mystic perfection.

Yoni—sexual emblem of Devi or Durga or Shakti, the universal female energy, often represented as a pedestal for the *Linga*.

Yuga-avataras—the incarnations of God who appear in each of the four *yugas* to explain the authorized system of self-realization in that age.

Index

The Writers

The authors who have participated in this book are all members of the Vedic Friends Association. They have been working individually for years in various avenues of Vedic study and teaching and spreading the Vedic knowledge and spiritual understanding in their own way. Most all of them are authors of other noteworthy books that can help anyone better understand the intricacies of Vedic knowledge, especially within their own particular field of study. We encourage people to acquire the books and information they have published for your continued spiritual and personal development. Contact information and websites of the authors are provided where available.

Jeffrey Armstrong has degrees in psychology, literature, history and comparative religions. He also has been practicing Vedic astrology since 1973. He has received initiation into the Vedic traditions by renown masters. He has also been a corporate speaker for several years and now offers insightful and dynamic presentations into the ancient Vedic texts and traditions for all students of the East. His goal is to revive that lost knowledge and present it as tools of empowerment that can be used everyday to create balance in the midst of modern problems and pressures, and to open new venues of possibilities for personal development.

He has a private astrology practice and offers regular lectures and talks on Vedic knowledge to students. He has written various articles and is the author of the book "God the Astrologer" on the soul, karma, reincarnation, and how we continually create our own destiny. He is available for private consultation and for giving lectures and talks around the country. He is based in Vancouver, Canada and his web site is: www.jeffreyarmstrong.com.

Howard Beckman (Hamsavatar Das) was born in Philadelphia, Pennsylvania and became a student of eastern mysticism and Vedic philosophy in the 1960's. His love affair with India and her culture began in his childhood when he visited India with his grand uncle, a very prominent international gem importer. After attending university majoring in philosophy and religion and psychology, he also gained a degree as a Graduate Gemologist from the Gemological Institute of America and recognition as a senior appraiser from the prestigious National Association of Jewelry Appraisers. He is also one of only a handful of gemologists world-wide recognized and awarded the degree of Planetary Gemologist by the Planetary Gemologists Association in Thailand. A student of yoga, jyotish, ayurveda and Vedantic philosophy for over 30 years now, Howard was also initiated as a Vaishnava Brahmin priest by His Divine Grace A.C. Bhaktivedanta Swami in 1972. He has authored 3 very popular books entitled "An Introduction to Vedic Astrology", "Mantras, Yantras & Fabulous Gems…" and "Vibrational Healing with Gems" and is considered one of the world's top experts in both ayurvedic clinical gem therapy and planetary gemology as used in jyotish. He is currently director of the Vedic Cultural Fellowship in Pecos, New Mexico, as well as the Pecos Yoga and Ayurveda Center where he teaches and maintains a busy practice as a Vedic astrologer and ayurvedic gem therapist. More information is available on the web site www.vedicworld.org and he may be reached by e-mail at balaji@vedicworld.org or balaji@newmexico.com, telephone 505-757-6194.

Michael A. Cremo is a researcher in human origins for the Bhaktivedanta Institute, the science studies branch of the International Society for Krishna Consciousness. Since 1984 he has been involved in establishing Vedic conceptions of human origins in the world of science. He has presented papers at meetings of the World Archeological Congress, the European Association of Archeologists, the International Congress for History of Science, and the International Union of Prehistoric and Protohistoric Sciences. In addition to lecturing at universities, he has also given invited lectures for the Royal Institution of Great Britain, the Russian Academy of Sciences, and other scientific institutions worldwide.

He is an internationally known expert on the history of archaeology and anomalous archaeological evidence for extreme human antiquity, consistent with the Puranic literature of ancient India. He is research associate in history of science for the Bhaktivedanta Institute (the science studies branch of the International Society for Krishna Consciousness), and is a member of the History of Science Society, the Philosophy of Science Association, and the European Association of Archaeologists. His most recent scientific publication is "Puranic Time and the Archaeological Record," presented at the World Archaeological Congress 3, 1994, and now included in the proceedings volume Time and Archaeology, edited by archaeologist Tim Murray for Routledge (1999). On Amazon.com, world's largest internet bookseller, Cremo's book *Forbidden Archeology* (1993), coauthored with Richard Thompson, has been a bestseller in the archeology and evolution categories. Dr. K.N. Prasada, former president of the Archaeological Society of India, said about this book: "I find the entire gamut of human origins and prehistory has been brought out in one single comprehensive volume, a task few people can achieve. I congratulate you for writing this excellent reference book, which will act as a catalyst for further research on a subject of immense interest, not only to scholars and students but also laymen." Cremo is also investigating anthropological and archaeological evidence for Vedic cultural contacts and influences around the world. Ecology and the environment are also among his interests. He wrote with Mukunda Goswami the book Divine Nature: A Spiritual Perspective on the Environmental Crisis. Another book by Mr. Cremo is *The Hidden History of the Human Race*. He has done numerous lectures, and radio and television presentations. His main departments of activity in the VFA are Vedic Ecology and Environmentalism, Cultural Studies, Scientists and Academicians. He is located in Los Angeles. You can find out more about him at: http://www.mcremo.com, and his email is: mcremo@cs.com.

Andy Fraenkel is the founder of The Center For Sacred Storytelling, located near Wheeling, WV. He travels extensively offering multicultural and sacred storytelling programs at schools, colleges, churches, temples, conferences and other special events, including NYU's Center for Near Eastern Studies, The New School For Social Research, Religious Communications Congress 2000, Centennial Event for Parliament of World Religions, and Indianapolis' Spirit & Place Festival. He also conducts the Vedic Storytelling Institute. Fraenkel explains that "it would be impossible to consider the philosophy and spirituality of the Vedic tradition without entering into story. Actually, the epics such as the Ramayana and Mahabharata are a vital part of the sacred heritage of all humankind. These epics have endured for millennia because they reflect the longings of the human spirit. They are considered the 'fifth Veda' and expound the timeless teaching of Sanatana Dharma." Fraenkel is also a member of the National Storytelling Network and brings his dramatic storytelling from world cultures to over twenty thousand school children each year. He is the author of The Fish Who Wouldn't Stop Growing And Other Wisdom Stories From Ancient India. He has recently released a CD entitled Sacred Voices—a pilgrimage of storytelling into various sacred traditions. For more information contact him at: story108@juno.com or visit www.sacredvoices.com.

Dr. David Frawley (Pandit Vamadeva Shastri) is one of the foremost western experts on Vedic Science. His work in various Vedic fields is widely respected in India. His prolific writings for over twenty years includes books on the Vedas, ancient India, Hinduism, modern India, Ayurveda, Yoga, Vedanta and Vedic astrology. Currently he is the director of the American Institute of Vedic Studies in Santa Fe New Mexico, USA, which offers information, training and resources on a number of Vedic topics. More information about him and some of his articles can be found on his website at—http://www.vedanet.com/index.html. His email is: vedicinst@aol.com. Books by David Frawley (*available on line)

On Ayurveda and Yoga:

Yoga for Your Type: An Ayurvedic Approach to Your Asana Practice (Frawley and Kozak)

Vedantic Meditation: Lighting the Flame of Awareness

Ayurvedic Healing: A Comprehensive Guide

Yoga of Herbs (Frawley and Lad)

Ayurveda, Nature's Medicine (Frawley and Ranade)

Yoga and Ayurveda: Self-healing and Self-realization

Ayurveda and the Mind: The Healing of Consciousness

Tantric Yoga and the Wisdom Goddesses: Spiritual Secrets of Ayurveda

On Vedic Astrology:

Astrology of the Seers: A Guide to Vedic/Hindu Astrology

Oracle of Rama—Practical oracle based on the Ramayana

On Vedas and Ancient History:

Rig Veda and the History of India (Rig Veda Bharata Itihasa)

In Search of the Cradle of Civilization (Feuerstein, Kak and Frawley)

Vedic Aryans and Origins of Civilization (Frawley and Rajaram)

Myth of the Aryan Invasion

Gods, Sages and Kings: Vedic Secrets of Ancient Civilization

Wisdom of Ancient Seers:Selected Mantras from the Rig Veda

On Hindu Dharma and India Today:

Hinduism and the Clash of Civilizations

How I Became a Hindu: My Discovery of Vedic Dharma

From the River of Heaven: Hindu and Vedic Knowledge for the Modern Age

Hinduism, The Eternal Tradition: Sanatana Dharma

Arise Arjuna: Hinduism and the Modern World

Awaken Bharata: A Call for India's Rebirth

Yogi Harinam Baba Prem Tom Beal has almost 20 years of study in Yoga and Meditation. He also has study in Sanskrit and the Vedas; in addition to a diploma in Yoga studies focusing on Karma, Bhakti, Hatha, Raja, and Kundalini yoga systems. He primarily teaches Kundalini yoga, in addition he previously published a newsletter entitled "Living Conscious". "Living Conscious" enjoyed thousands of readers worldwide with its electronic edition. His Vedic study is directed by Pandit Vamadeva Shastry (Dr. David Frawley). Harinam has lived in Orlando, Florida for over a decade and has been a guest lecturer at Rollins College, and Seminole Community College. In addition, Harinam has 800 hours of credit combined in the study of Ayurveda and Jyotish (Vedic Astrology) and he has received the Hindu "sacred thread". Harinam has produced numerous CD's on mantra and meditation, and he has written several books on related systems. He is the founder and director of Universal Yoga. He currently offers private instruction in yoga and meditation. Private sessions in living Ayurvedic philosophy, and Vedic astrology consultations.

Books by Yogi Harinam Baba Prem Tom Beal: *Mantra: Inner Transformation through the power of Sound.*
How to Meditate.
Understanding the Kundalini.
Universal Yoga: A path to enlightenment
My Journey to Consciousness…so far.
The Guru/Disciple relationship.

In addition he has two home study programs:
Yoga Philosophy Level 1.
Yoga teacher training Level 1.

More information can be found at: www.floridavedicinstitute.com, or e-mail: universalyoga@netzero.net.

Subhash Kak is a professor of electrical and computer engineering at Louisiana State University, the New Orleans area. He is also a Sanskrit scholar and has also written numerous academic papers on Vedic science and culture, along with several books which include, *The Nature of Physical Reality*, *The Astronomical Code of the Rig-Veda*, *India at Century's End*, and *In Search of the Cradle of Civilization* with Georg Feuerstein, Ph.D., and David Frawley. He regularly gives lectures and attends conferences on varied Vedic topics. More information about him can be found on his website at—http://www.ee.lsu.edu/kak/home.html. Also see http://www.ee.lsu.edu/kak/books.html for the listing of his books. He can be reached through his email: kak@sol.ee.lsu.edu.

Parama Karuna Devi has been studying and practicing Vedic knowledge since 1970. She worked with the Bhaktivedanta Book Trust, Italy, translating almost all their books of classical Vedic literature and spirituality. Subsequently, she worked with several other publishing houses, writing and translating many books on Indian philosophy and culture, native cultures, religion and spirituality, vegetarianism, natural medicine, new age culture, etc. In 1994 she moved to India, Jagannatha Puri, Orissa, where she is conducting the Jagannatha Vallabha Vedic Research Center (www.dharmaseva.net). The Center offers courses and seminars on various subjects, lectures and inter-cultural meetings, vocational training, welfare programs for the local rural and tribal people. It is also developing a mobile charitable dispensary based on natural medicine, a library and a publication center, a school, and permaculture organic farm. She can be contacted at: paramakaruna@satyam.net.in, or paramakaruna@rediffmail.com.

Stephen Knapp (Sri Nandanandana) is the president of the VFA. He has been researching Vedic spirituality and comparative religious study for over 30 years in a variety of settings. He has directly engaged in those spiritual disciplines that have been recommended for hundreds of years. He continued his study of Vedic knowledge and practice under the guidance of a spiritual master to get the insights and realizations that are normally absent from the ordinary academic atmosphere. Through this process he has been initiated into the genuine and authorized spiritual line of the Brahma-Madhava-Gaudiya *sampradaya*, or disciplic succession, under the sanction of His Divine Grace A. C. Bhaktivedanta Swami. He has also extensively traveled throughout India to most of the major holy sights and more, and is known for his slide shows on his travels to the holy places and spiritual festivals of India (even nicknamed "the slide show acharya"), and for his lectures on the Vedic and Indian philosophy. He has written several books on the science and spiritual practice of Vedic culture and Eastern philosophy, which include:
The Secret Teachings of the Vedas,
The Universal Path to Enlightenment,
The Vedic Prophecies: A New Look into the Future,
How the Universe was Created and Our Purpose In It,
Toward World Peace: Seeing the Unity Between Us All,
Facing Death: Welcoming the Afterlife,
The Key to Real Happiness,
Proof of Vedic Culture's Global Existence,
Reincarnation and Karma: How they Really Affect Us,
The Heart of Hinduism, and
Destined for Infinity, a spiritual adventure.
Several additional free booklets are available on his website made for distribution through email. He has also worked in the field of home health care, and has experience in Hospice work. He can help assist in a person's transition into the next life, for which his book *Facing Death* was written. Much more information about Stephen, his books, along with over 70 of his articles, numerous photographs of India, controversy of the origins of the Taj Mahal, a large collection of prints of Krishna and the Vedic Deities, and many additional resources are supplied on his website, at—http://www.stephen-knapp.com. He can be reached through email at: Srinandan@aol.com.

Pratichi Mathur hails from a 900-year lineage of Vedic healers from India. Pratichi represents classical and tradition based Ayurvedic medicine. In 2002 Pratichi was prominently featured by the San Francisco Chronicle for her work in Ayurveda. In 1998 Pratichi was awarded the title of "Ayurveda Shiromani" by the Ayodhya Nath Ayurveda Samiti (India) and in 1999 Pratichi was awarded the "Vaidehi Puruskar" by the Ayurveda Prachar Sanstha (India). Pratichi was healer to many politicians and celebrities in India and also loved by the poorest of the poor. Since her arrival in America in 1998 Pratichi established the Ganesha Institute for Ayurveda and Vedic Studies in California to help promote the Vedic sciences in their purest form and practice.

Pratichi received her classical Ayurvedic training under Dr. P.H. Kulkarmi, India's top Ayurvedic doctor and an authority on Ayurveda (ex-Dean, Department of Ayurveda, Pune University). In addition, she completed post-graduate studies in Ayurveda and Pancha Karma in Pune, India. Pratichi has extensive experience in Ayurvedic medicine, acquired over several years of clinical practice.

Pratichi is an active member on several Ayurvedic research and advisory committees and boards, in both India and in the United States. Pratichi served as a Director on the Board of the California Association of Ayurvedic Medicine (CAAM). She is also a member of the Academic Council and the International Propagation Committee of the Ayurveda Academy Pune, India; the Research Advisory Committee of the Ayurveda Research Institute, India.

For Pratichi, Ayurveda is not just a passion sprung from her heritage, it is her very life. Having grown up sickly with Asthma and Ankylosing Spondylitis, a genetic, progressively disabling, painful condition…Ayurveda is her savior. Pratichi stands tall and dignified, spreading the message of healing, as Ayurveda heals and nurtures her. Therefore, Pratichi Mathur offers traditional Ayurvedic therapy and education. Her style of treatment remains classic, based upon Ayurvedic texts and ancient modalities. The Ganesha Institute was created to offer a full range of authentic services in Ayurveda. It is Pratichi's vision that her clients be able to access true and classic Ayurveda. Pratichi resides in Sunnyvale, California. More information about her and her practice can be found at her website at—http://www.healingmission.com.

Arun Naik was born in Varanasi on October 2, 1954 to an engineer father and a writer mother. He spent his early years amongst temples, ghats and streets of Varanasi.

At a very young age he was drawn to the esoteric sciences, and over the years he underwent strict training under the discipline and watchful eyes of learned Masters.

An alumnus of University of Delhi, he is a practitioner of Vāstu Shāstra and also delivers lectures on Vāstu Shāstra at several institutes of repute.

His respect for the tradition of Vāstu stems from a deep and intensive study of the subject, and a genuine desire to utilize the science for creating a better life for people. He deeply believes in a successful fusion of traditional knowledge with modern technology to derive the maximum benefit.

"The purpose of my work is to design buildings in accordance with the tenets of Vāstu Shāstra which are safe, promote prosperity and inner peace to their occupants," says Arun Naik

Besides Vāstu Shāstra, he practices Tantra yoga and holistic healing.

He lives in New Delhi. He can be reached at:

C-84 Greater Kailash I Basement, New Delhi 110049 India.

Website: www.Vāstu sindhu.com.

Email: akn@Vāstu sindhu.com.

Phone: 91-11-30968736, 9891422794

Dhan Roussé received an M.S. degree in Engineering from the Univ. of Florida in 1973, and has studied Vedic wisdom since that time. He currently occupies his time writing and teaching, spending his time in California and India. He is a Director of PAVAN, the Prabhupada Association of Vedic Awareness, an educational institution dedicated to modeling and applying Vedic wisdom to sustainable living in Puri. He can be reached at integr8ted@hotmail.com.

Robert Taylor (Bhoumadeva dasa) has been a student and teacher of Vedic philosophy for over thirty years. He has lived in an assortment of monasteries and ashrams in some of India's holiest places. He has been initiated as a Brahmin priest by A. C. Bhaktivedanta Swami, one of India's foremost Vedic authors and proponents of Bhakti-yoga. Robert is known internationally for his discourses and presentations on Vedic culture. He frequently teaches through lectures and includes such diverse topics as reincarnation, astrology, self-realization, etc., all from the Vedic perspective. He has also directed, produced and hosted metaphysical radio and television shows for over 20 years in the Detroit area. He is also an accomplished astrologer and palmist, and is initiated into an ancient Vedic predictive technique known as the Bhrigu Yantra. Robert is available for consultations in person or by phone. His greatest joy is to give presentations to groups on the vast wisdom of the Vedas, which he can be scheduled to do. Contact: Robert Taylor, 842 Neff St., Grosse Pointe, MI 48230. Phone: 313-640-5792.

Chakrapani Ullal is a world-renowned Vedic Astrologer from Kerala, South India. He was born into a family of illustrious astrologers and has had continuous contact with many of the most revered spiritual teachers of India. The Ullal family has been keepers of that knowledge for many generations, and, as was the custom, Chakrapani began to receive training from his father while still a young boy. Because the application of astrological principals is deeply embedded in the customs and rituals of village life, education in the subject was as much a way of life as a focus of study. He later came to take his degree in business studies and law and subsequently traveled extensively in his capacity as an advisor to the companies he represented.

In 1979 he was invited by Swami Muktananda to come to America as an astrological advisor and consultant. He now resides in the Los Angeles area and travels throughout the world to teach and consult with his diverse international clientele. Beyond his Astrology practice Chakrapani sits on the boards of several organizations; the "International Journal of Humanities and Peace," which publishes a Journal for scholars in the Humanities, the Ganesha Foundation which promotes Vedic Sciences and the American College of Vedic Astrology which teaches and sponsors conferences on Vedic Astrology.

He has been at the forefront of the cultural exchange between India and America for decades, which bears witness to a revival of knowledge from the Vedic Tradition including yoga, ayurveda and astrology. He has been awarded the titles of Jyotish Kovid, Jyotish Vachaspati, and Jyotish Sagan by the Indian Council of Astrological Sciences. You can contact him at: 12044 Kearsarge Street. Los Angeles, CA 90049—Phone: (310) 476-9942—Fax: (310) 471-3205. E-mail: info@vedicastrology.com, web site: www.chakrapani.com.

George Vutetakis (Gopati das). A prominent vegetarian chef in America, George began his culinary career as a student of A.C. Bhaktivedanta Swami Prabhupada. During this time he cooked for thousands, ran a restaurant in Manhattan, helped feed Bangladesh refugees and catered dinners for diplomats in Washington, D.C. He also studied with saddhus, temple cooks and in personal homes during his four stays in India. His culinary teaching credits include Northwestern University, Columbia University, Montgomery County, Maryland Adult Education, Barnes & Noble demonstrations and numerous TV programs.

In 1981 he became founding chef of the Inn Season Café. After taking over in 1985, he brought the café national recognition before selling the award winning restaurant in 2002. Chef George integrates spiritual focus with the practical functions of this world. He prepares world-class healthy vegetarian cuisine, beautifully presented and bursting with flavorful rich textures. The influence of the years spent in India learning his craft is evident in the exquisite flavors imparted to all of his dishes. Traditional methods of preparation from all parts of the globe are used in his cuisine. The relationship of food with the earth and the inhabitants upon it is the basis of George's culinary endeavors. With the Vedic approach, the appreciation and consumption of foodstuffs is a process for self realization. George's work also includes sustainable agriculture, candle making, soap making, organic body care, herbal remedies and other pre-industrial traditions. He is now focusing on sharing his experiences and expertise with the public through writing, teaching and consulting. George is in the Detroit, Michigan area, and can be reached at 248-613-3394. Email: gopatidas@aol.com.

The Vedic Friends Association

Sharing the Universal Dharma

The Vedic Friends Association is an expanding, global network of progressive people helping each other understand, practice and promote the Universal Truths found in Vedic Dharma, the ancient knowledge of India. In this way we explore its spiritual, social and scientific dimensions for the good of all, and become a powerful force for beneficial change in this troubled world.

We are a group of people who were individually working in various ways to spread a greater understanding of what the Vedic culture and philosophy is and what it has to offer. We had been doing this for years separately but have now joined together. We also invite everyone else to join us to do the same—to act in ways to preserve, protect and share the universal Dharma with all others.

Learn more about us at our web site

www.vedicfriends.org

978-0-595-37120-4
0-595-37120-5

Printed in the United States
45404LVS00004B/1-75

9 780595 371204